Cost Accounting Essentials

Cost Accounting Essentials

Edited by
Keith Hagar

Larsen & Keller
www.larsen-keller.com

Cost Accounting Essentials
Edited by Keith Hagar
ISBN: 978-1-63549-658-1 (Hardback)

Larsen & Keller
Published by Larsen and Keller Education,
5 Penn Plaza,
19th Floor,
New York, NY 10001, USA

Cataloging-in-Publication Data

Cost accounting essentials / edited by Keith Hagar.
p. cm.
Includes bibliographical references and index.
ISBN 978-1-63549-658-1
1. Cost accounting. 2. Accounting. I. Hagar, Keith.
HF5686.C8 C67 2018
657.42--dc23

Printed and bound in China.

Table of Contents

Preface

As a branch of accounting, cost accounting refers to the study and process of recording, analysing, classifying, summarizing, evaluating and collecting the ways of reducing and controlling the cost of business operations. Its main purpose is to provide better management solutions which can minimize the cost of executing the ideas with the same or better results. The various types of cost accounting are life cycle costing, standard cost accounting, target costing, throughput accounting, environmental accounting, etc. This book elucidates new techniques of cost accounting and their applications in a multidisciplinary approach. Some of the diverse topics covered in it address the varied branches that fall under this category. This textbook is an essential guide for both academicians and those who wish to pursue this discipline further.

Given below is the chapter wise description of the book:

Chapter 1- The process used for assessing and evaluating the costs of running a business or any non-profitable organization is known as cost accounting. Some of the types of cost accounting are activity-based costing, throughput accounting, target costing, life cycle costing and standard cost accounting. This is an introductory chapter which will introduce briefly all the significant aspects of cost accounting.

Chapter 2- Direct costs are prices which are directly accountable to objects which have costs assigned to them. Indirect costs are costs that are not directly accountable to the object concerned. Cost allocation, total absorption costing, balanced scorecard and activity based costing are some of the other topics discussed in the following section. Cost accounting is best understood in confluence with the major topics listed in the following chapter.

Chapter 3- Job costing calculates overhead costs of raw material, means of production and cost of labor, all of which are part of manufacturing cost. Process costing calculates costs incurred in the manufacture of one unit of a commodity. The aspects elucidated in this chapter are of vital importance, and provide a better understanding of cost accounting.

Chapter 4- A financial plan that is defined as expanding over a period of time is known as budgeting. Types of budgets include flexible budgets, fixed budgets, current budgets, short term budgets, long term budgets, etc. The topics discussed in the chapter are of great importance to broaden the existing knowledge on cost accounting.

Indeed, my job was extremely crucial and challenging as I had to ensure that every chapter is informative and structured in a student-friendly manner. I am thankful for the support provided by my family and colleagues during the completion of this book.

Editor

1

Basics of Cost Accounting

The process used for assessing and evaluating the costs of running a business or any non-profitable organization is known as cost accounting. Some of the types of cost accounting are activity-based costing, throughput accounting, target costing, life cycle costing and standard cost accounting. This is an introductory chapter which will introduce briefly all the significant aspects of cost accounting.

Cost Accounting

Cost accounting involves recording, controlling estimating and reporting for costs.

Cost accounting process begins with the recording of expenditure or the bases on which they are calculated and ends with the preparation of statements for ascertaining and controlling costs.

Cost accounting is a process of collecting, recording, classifying, analyzing, summarizing, allocating and evaluating various alternative courses of action & control of costs. Its goal is to advise the management on the most appropriate course of action based on the cost efficiency and capability. Cost accounting provides the detailed cost information that management needs to control current operations and plan for the future.

Since managers are making decisions only for their own organization, there is no need for the information to be comparable to similar information from other organizations. Instead, information must be relevant for a particular environment. Cost accounting information is commonly used in financial accounting information, but its primary function is for use by managers to facilitate making decisions.

All types of businesses, whether service, manufacturing or trading, require cost accounting to track their activities. Cost accounting has long been used to help managers understand the costs of running a business. Modern cost accounting originated during the industrial revolution, when the complexities of running a large scale business led to the development of systems for recording and tracking costs to help business owners and managers make decisions.

In the early industrial age, most of the costs incurred by a business were what modern accountants call "variable costs" because they varied directly with the amount of production. Money was spent on labor, raw materials, power to run a factory, etc. in direct proportion to production. Managers could simply total the variable costs for a product and use this as a rough guide for decision-making processes.

Some costs tend to remain the same even during busy periods, unlike variable costs, which rise and fall with volume of work. Over time, these "fixed costs" have become more important to managers.

Examples of fixed costs include the depreciation of plant and equipment, and the cost of departments such as maintenance, tooling, production control, purchasing, quality control, storage and handling, plant supervision and engineering. In the early nineteenth century, these costs were of little importance to most businesses. However, with the growth of railroads, steel and large scale manufacturing, by the late nineteenth century these costs were often more important than the variable cost of a product, and allocating them to a broad range of products led to bad decision making. Managers must understand fixed costs in order to make decisions about products and pricing.

For example: A company produced railway coaches and had only one product. To make each coach, the company needed to purchase $60 of raw materials and components, and pay 6 laborers $40 each. Therefore, total variable cost for each coach was $300. Knowing that making a coach required spending $300, managers knew they couldn't sell below that price without losing money on each coach. Any price above $300 became a contribution to the fixed costs of the company. If the fixed costs were, say, $1000 per month for rent, insurance and owner's salary, the company could therefore sell 5 coaches per month for a total of $3000 (priced at $600 each), or 10 coaches for a total of $4500 (priced at $450 each), and make a profit of $500 in both cases.

Cost Accounting vs Financial Accounting

- Financial accounting aims at finding out results of accounting year in the form of Profit and Loss Account and Balance Sheet. Cost Accounting aims at computing cost of production/service in a scientific manner and facilitate cost control and cost reduction.
- Financial accounting reports the results and position of business to government, creditors, investors, and external parties.
- Cost Accounting is an internal reporting system for an organization's own management for decision making.
- In financial accounting, cost classification is based on type of transactions, e.g. salaries, repairs, insurance, stores etc. In cost accounting, classification is basically on the basis of functions, activities, products, process and on internal planning and control and information needs of the organization.
- Financial accounting aims at presenting 'true and fair' view of transactions, profit and loss for a period and Statement of financial position (Balance Sheet) on a given date. It aims at computing 'true and fair' view of the cost of production/services offered by the firm.

Types of Cost Accounting

The following are different cost accounting approaches:

- Standard cost accounting
- Activity-based costing
- Resource consumption accounting

- Throughput accounting
- Life Cycle Costing
- Environmental accounting
- Target costing

Elements of Cost

Basic cost elements are:

1. Raw materials
2. Manual labour
3. expenses/overhead
    - Material (Material is a very important part of business)
        - Direct material/Indirect material
    - Labor
        - Direct labor/Indirect labor
    - Overhead (Variable/Fixed)
        - Production or works overheads Factory Staff
        - Administration overheads Office Staff
        - Selling overheads - Catalogues,Advertising,Exhibitions,Sales Staff Costs
        - Distribution overheads
        - Maintenance & Repair (Office equipment/Factory machinery)
        - Supplies
        - Utilities Gas Electricity Water Rates
        - Other Variable Expenses
        - Salaries (Payroll - Wages, NI PAYE Pensions)
        - Occupancy (Rent)
        - Depreciation (Machinery/Office Equipment)
        - Other Fixed Expenses

(In some companies, machine cost is segregated from overhead and reported as a separate element)

Classification of Costs

Classification of cost means, the grouping of costs according to their common characteristics. The important ways of classification of costs are:

1. By Nature or Traceability:Direct Costs and Indirect costs. Direct Costs are Directly attributable/traceable to Cost object. Direct costs are assigned to Cost Object. Indirect Costs are not directly attributable/traceable to Cost Object. Indirect costs are allocated or apportioned to cost objects.

2. By Functions: production,administration, selling and distribution, R&D.

3. By Behavior: fixed, variable, semi-variable. Costs are classified according to their behavior in relation to change in relation to production volume within given period of time. Fixed Costs remain fixed irrespective of changes in the production volume in given period of time. Variable costs change according to volume of production. Semi-variable costs are partly fixed and partly variable.

4. By control ability: controllable, uncontrollable costs. Controllable costs are those which can be controlled or influenced by a conscious management action. Uncontrollable costs cannot be controlled or influenced by a conscious management action.

5. By normality: normal costs and abnormal costs. Normal costs arise during routine day-to-day business operations. Abnormal costs arise because of any abnormal activity or event not part of routine business operations. E.g. costs arising of floods, riots, accidents etc.

6. By Time: Historical costs and predetermined costs. Historical costs are costs incurred in the past. Predetermined costs are computed in advance on basis of factors affecting cost elements. Example: Standard Costs.

7. By Decision making Costs: These costs are used for managerial decision making.And these are :-

   - Marginal costs: Marginal cost is the change in the aggregate costs due to change in the volume of output by one unit.

   - Differential costs: This cost is the difference in total cost that will arise from the selection of one alternative to the other.

   - Opportunity costs: It is the value of benefit sacrificed in favor of an alternative course of action.

   - Relevant cost: The relevant cost is a cost which is relevant in various decisions of management.

   - Replacement cost: This cost is the cost at which existing items of material or fixed assets can be replaced. Thus this is the cost of replacing existing assets at present or at a future date.

- Shutdown cost:These costs are the costs which are incurred if the operations are shut down and they will disappear if the operations are continued.
- Capacity cost: These costs are normally fixed costs. The cost incurred by a company for providing production, administration and selling and distribution capabilities in order to perform various functions.
- Sunken cost: cost already incurred
- Other costs

Standard Cost Accounting

In modern cost account of recording historical costs was taken further, by allocating the company's fixed costs over a given period of time to the items produced during that period, and recording the result as the total cost of production. This allowed the *full cost* of products that were not sold in the period they were produced to be recorded in inventory using a variety of complex accounting methods, which was consistent with the principles of GAAP (Generally Accepted Accounting Principles). It also essentially enabled managers to ignore the fixed costs, and look at the results of each period in relation to the "standard cost" for any given product.

> For example: if the railway coach company normally produced 40 coaches per month, and the fixed costs were still $1000/month, then each coach could be said to incur an Operating Cost/overhead of $25 =($1000 / 40). Adding this to the variable costs of $300 per coach produced a full cost of $325 per coach.

This method tended to slightly distort the resulting unit cost, but in mass-production industries that made one product line, and where the fixed costs were relatively low, the distortion was very minor.

> For example: if the railway coach company made 100 coaches one month, then the unit cost would become $310 per coach ($300 + ($1000 / 100)). If the next month the company made 50 coaches, then the unit cost = $320 per coach ($300 + ($1000 / 50)), a relatively minor difference.

An important part of standard cost accounting is a variance analysis, which breaks down the variation between actual cost and standard costs into various components (volume variation, material cost variation, labor cost variation, etc.) so managers can understand *why costs were different from what was planned* and take appropriate action to correct the situation.

The Development of Throughput Accounting

As business became more complex and began producing a greater variety of products, the use of cost accounting to make decisions to maximize profitability came into question. Management circles became increasingly aware of the Theory of Constraints in the 1980s, and began to understand that "every production process has a limiting factor" somewhere in the chain of production. As business management learned to identify the constraints, they increasingly adopted throughput accounting to manage them and "maximize the *throughput dollars*" (or other currency) from each unit of constrained resource. Throughput accounting aims to make the best use of scarce resources(bottle neck) in a (JIT) Just in time environment.

Mathematical Formula

$$\text{throughput accounting ratio} = \frac{\text{return}}{\text{factory hours}}$$

Activity-based Costing

Activity-based costing (ABC) is a system for assigning costs to products based on the activities they require. In this case, activities are those regular actions performed inside a company. "Talking with customer regarding invoice questions" is an example of an activity inside most companies.

Companies may be moved to adopt ABC by a need to improve costing accuracy, that is, understand better the true costs and profitability of individual products, services, or initiatives. ABC gets closer to true costs in these areas by turning many costs that standard cost accounting views as indirect costs essentially into direct costs. By contrast, standard cost accounting typically determines so-called indirect and overhead costs simply as a percentage of certain direct costs, which may or may not reflect actual resource usage for individual items.

Under ABC, accountants assign 100% of each employee's time to the different activities performed inside a company (many will use surveys to have the workers themselves assign their time to the different activities). The accountant then can determine the total cost spent on each activity by summing up the percentage of each worker's salary spent on that activity.

A company can use the resulting activity cost data to determine where to focus their operational improvements. For example, a job-based manufacturer may find that a high percentage of its workers are spending their time trying to figure out a hastily written customer order. Via (ABC) Activity based costing, the accountants now have a currency amount pegged to the activity of "Researching Customer Work Order Specifications". Senior management can now decide how much focus or money to budget for resolving this process deficiency. Activity-based management includes (but is not restricted to) the use of activity-based costing to manage a business.

While (ABC) Activity based costing may be able to pinpoint the cost of each activity and resources into the ultimate product, the process could be tedious, costly and subject to errors.

As it is a tool for a more accurate way of allocating fixed costs into product, these fixed costs do not vary according to each month's production volume. For example, an elimination of one product would not eliminate the overhead or even direct labor cost assigned to it.Activity based costing (ABC) better identifies product costing in the long run, but may not be too helpful in day-to-day decision-making.

Integrating EVA and Process Based Costing

Recently, Mocciaro Li Destri, Picone & Minà (2012). proposed a performance and cost measurement system that integrates the Economic Value Added criteria with Process Based Costing (PBC). The EVA-PBC methodology allows us to implement the EVA management logic not only at the firm level, but also at lower levels of the organization. EVA-PBC methodology plays an interesting role in bringing strategy back into financial performance measures.

Lean Accounting

Lean accounting has developed in recent years to provide the accounting, control, and measurement methods supporting lean manufacturing and other applications of lean thinking such as healthcare, construction, insurance, banking, education, government, and other industries.

There are two main thrusts for Lean Accounting. The first is the application of lean methods to the company's accounting, control, and measurement processes. This is not different from applying lean methods to any other processes. The objective is to eliminate waste, free up capacity, speed up the process, eliminate errors & defects, and make the process clear and understandable. The second (and more important) thrust of Lean Accounting is to fundamentally change the accounting, control, and measurement processes so they motivate lean change & improvement, provide information that is suitable for control and decision-making, provide an understanding of customer value, correctly assess the financial impact of lean improvement, and are themselves simple, visual, and low-waste. Lean Accounting does not require the traditional management accounting methods like standard costing, activity-based costing, variance reporting, cost-plus pricing, complex transactional control systems, and untimely & confusing financial reports. These are replaced by:

- lean-focused performance measurements
- simple summary direct costing of the value streams
- decision-making and reporting using a *box score*
- financial reports that are timely and presented in "plain English" that everyone can understand
- radical simplification and elimination of transactional control systems by eliminating the need for them
- driving lean changes from a deep understanding of the value created for the customers
- eliminating traditional budgeting through monthly sales, operations, and financial planning processes (SOFP)
- value-based pricing
- correct understanding of the financial impact of lean change

As an organization becomes more mature with lean thinking and methods, they recognize that the combined methods of lean accounting in fact creates a lean management system (LMS) designed to provide the planning, the operational and financial reporting, and the motivation for change required to prosper the company's on-going lean transformation.

Marginal Costing

The cost-volume-profit analysis is the systematic examination of the relationship between selling prices, sales, production volumes, costs, expenses and profits. This analysis provides very useful information for decision-making in the management of a company. For example, the analysis can be used in establishing sales prices, in the product mix selection to sell, in the decision to choose marketing strategies, and in the analysis of the impact on profits by changes in costs. In the current environment of business, a business administration must act and take decisions in a fast and accurate manner. As a result, the importance of cost-volume-profit is still increasing as time passes.

Contribution Margin

A relationship between the cost, volume and profit is the contribution margin. The contribution margin is the revenue excess from sales over variable costs. The concept of contribution margin is particularly useful in the planning of business because it gives an insight into the potential profits that a business can generate. The following chart shows the income statement of a company X, which has been prepared to show its contribution margin:

Sales	$1,000,000
(-) Variable Costs	$600,000
Contribution Margin	$400,000
(-) Fixed Costs	$300,000
Income from Operations	$100,000

Contribution Margin Ratio

The contribution margin can also be expressed as a percentage. The contribution margin ratio, which is sometimes called the profit-volume ratio, indicates the percentage of each sales dollar available to cover fixed costs and to provide operating revenue. For the company Fusion, Inc. the contribution margin ratio is 40%, which is computed as follows:

$$\text{Contribution Margin Ratio} = (\text{Sales} - \text{Variable Costs}) / \text{Sales}$$

The contribution margin ratio measures the effect on operating income of an increase or a decrease in sales volume. For example, assume that the management of Fusion, Inc. is studying the effect of adding $80,000 in sales orders. Multiplying the contribution margin ratio (40%) by the change in sales volume ($80,000) indicates that operating income will increase $32,000 if additional orders are obtained. To validate this analysis the table below shows the income statement of the company including additional orders:

Sales	$1,080,000
(-) Variable Costs	$648,000 (1,080,000 x 60%)
Contribution Margin	$432,000 (1,080,000 x 40%)
(-) Fixed Costs	$300,000
Income from Operations	$132,000

Variable costs as a percentage of sales are equal to 100% minus the contribution margin ratio. Thus, in the above income statement, the variable costs are 60% (100% - 40%) of sales, or $648,000

($1,080,000 X 60%). The total contribution margin $432,000, can also be computed directly by multiplying the sales by the contribution margin ratio ($1,080,000 X 40%).

Accounting Information System

An accounting information system (AIS) is a system of collecting, storing and processing financial and accounting data that are used by decision makers. An accounting information system is generally a computer-based method for tracking accounting activity in conjunction with information technology resources. The resulting financial reports can be used internally by management or externally by other interested parties including investors, creditors and tax authorities. Accounting information systems are designed to support all accounting functions and activities including auditing, financial accounting & reporting, managerial/ management accounting and tax. The most widely adopted accounting information systems are auditing and financial reporting modules.

History

Traditionally, accounting is purely based on manual approach. Experience and skilfulness of an individual accountant are critical in accounting processes. Even using the manual approach can be ineffective and inefficient. Accounting information systems resolve many of above issues. AISs can support an automation of processing large amount of data and produce timely and accuracy of information.

Early accounting information systems were designed for payroll functions in 1970s. Initially, accounting information systems were predominantly developed "in-house" as legacy systems. Such solutions were expensive to develop and difficult to maintain. Therefore, many accounting practitioners preferred the manual approach rather than computer-based. Today, accounting information systems are more commonly sold as prebuilt software packages from large vendors such as Microsoft, Sage Group, SAP AG|SAP and Oracle Corporation|Oracle where it is configured and customized to match the organization's business processes. Small businesses often use accounting lower costs software packages such as MYOB and Quickbooks. Large organisations would often choose ERP systems. As the need for connectivity and consolidation between other business systems increased, accounting information systems were merged with larger, more centralized systems known as enterprise resource planning (ERP). Before, with separate applications to manage different business functions, organizations had to develop complex interfaces for the systems to communicate with each other. In ERP, a system such as accounting information system is built as a module integrated into a suite of applications that can include manufacturing, supply chain, human resources. These modules are integrated together and are able to access the same data and execute complex business processes. Today, Cloud-based accounting information systems are increasingly popular for both SMEs and large organisations for lower costs. With adoption of accounting information systems, many businesses have removed low skills, transactional and operational accounting roles.

An Example of Architecture

An AIS typically follows a multitier architecture separating the presentation to the user, application processing and data management in distinct layers. The presentation layer manages how the information is displayed to and viewed by functional users of the system (through mobile devices, web browsers or client application). The entire system is backed by a centralized database that stores all of the data. This can include transactional data generated from the core business processes (purchasing, inventory, accounting) or static, master data that is referenced when processing data (employee and customer account records and configuration settings). As transactions occur, the data is collected from the business events and stored into the system's database where it can be retrieved and processed into information that is useful for is a making decisions. The application layer retrieves the raw data held in the log database layer, processes it based on the configured business logic and passes it onto the presentation layer to display to the users. For example, consider the accounts payable department when processing an invoice. With an accounting information system, an accounts payable clerk enters the invoice, provided by a vendor, into the system where it is then stored in the database. When goods from the vendor are received, a receipt is created and also entered into the AIS. Before the accounts payable department pays the vendor, the system's application processing tier performs a three-way matching where it automatically matches the amounts on the invoice against the amounts on the receipt and the initial purchase order. Once the match is complete, an email is sent to an accounts payable manager for approval. From here a voucher can be created and the vendor can ultimately be paid.

Advantages and Implications

A big advantage of computer-based accounting information systems is that they automate and streamline reporting, develop advanced modelling and support data mining. Reporting is major tool for organizations to accurately see summarized, timely information used for decision-making and financial reporting. The accounting information system pulls data from the centralized database, processes and transforms it and ultimately generates a summary of that data as information that can now be easily consumed and analyzed by business analysts, managers or other decision makers. These systems must ensure that the reports are timely so that decision-makers are not acting on old, irrelevant information and, rather, able to act quickly and effectively based on report results. Consolidation is one of the hallmarks of reporting as people do not have to look through an enormous number of transactions. For instance, at the end of the month, a financial accountant consolidates all the paid vouchers by running a report on the system. The system's application layer provides a report with the total amount paid to its vendors for that particular month. With large corporations that generate large volumes of transactional data, running reports with even an AIS can take days or even weeks.

After the wave of corporate scandals from large companies such as Tyco International, Enron and WorldCom, major emphasis was put on enforcing public companies to implement strong internal controls into their transaction-based systems. This was made into law with the passage of the Sarbanes–Oxley Act of 2002 which stipulated that companies must generate an internal control report stating who is responsible for an organization's internal control structure and outlines the overall effectiveness of these controls. Since most of these scandals were rooted in the companies' accounting practices, much of the emphasis of Sarbanes Oxley was put on computer-based accounting information systems. Today, AIS vendors tout their governance, risk management, and compliance features to ensure business processes are robust and protected and the organization's assets (including data) are secured.

Implementation

Many large and SMEs are now adopting cost effective cloud-based accounting information system in recent years.

Looking back years ago, most organizations, even larger ones, hire outside consultants, either from the software publisher or consultants who understand the organization and who work to help select and implement the ideal configuration, taking all components into consideration.

The steps to implement an accounting information system are as follows:

Detailed Requirements Analysis

> where all individuals involved in the system are interviewed. The current system is thoroughly understood, including problems, and complete documentation of the system—transactions, reports, and questions that need to be answered—are gathered. User needs that are not in the current system are outlined and documented. Users include everyone, from top management to data entry. The requirements analysis not only provides the developer with the specific needs, it also helps users accept the change. Users who have the opportunity to ask questions and provide input are much more confident and receptive of the change, than those who sit back and don't express their concerns.

Systems Design (synthesis)

> The analysis is thoroughly reviewed and a new system is created. The system that surrounds the system is often the most important. What data needs to go into the system and how is this going to be handled? What information needs to come out of the system how is it going to be formatted? If we know what needs to come out, we know what we need to put into the system. The program we select will need to appropriately handle the process. The system is built with control files, sample master records, and the ability to perform processes on a test basis. The system is designed to include appropriate internal controls and to provide management with the information needed to make decisions. It is a goal of an accounting information system to provide information that is relevant, meaningful, reliable, useful, and current. To achieve this, the system is designed so that transactions are entered as they occur (either manually or electronically) and information is immediately available online for management.

> Once the system is designed, an RFP is created detailing the requirements and fundamental design. Vendors are asked to respond to the proposal, to provide demonstrations of the product, and to specifically respond to the needs of the organization. Ideally, the vendor will input control files, sample master records, and be able to show how transactions are processed that result in the information that management needs to make decisions. An RFP for the information technology infrastructure follows the selection of the software product because the software product generally has specific requirements for infrastructure. Sometimes, the software and the infrastructure is selected from the same vendor. If not, the organization must ensure that vendors will work together without "pointing fingers" when there is an issue with either the software or the infrastructure.

Documentation

As the system is being designed, it is documented. The documentation includes vendor documentation of the system and, more importantly, the procedures or detailed instructions that help users handle each process specific to the organization. Most documentation and procedures are online and it is helpful if organizations can add to the help instructions provided by the software vendor. Documentation and procedures tend to be an afterthought but is the insurance policy and the tool used during testing and training—before launch. The documentation is tested during the training so that when the system is launched, there is no question that it works and that the users are confident with the change.

Testing

Before launch, all processes are tested from input through output, using the documentation as a tool to ensure that all processes are thoroughly documented and that users can easily follow the procedures: They know it works and that the procedures will be followed consistently. The reports are reviewed and verified, so that there's no garbage in-garbage out. This is done in a test system not yet fully populated with live data. Unfortunately, most organizations launch systems before thorough testing, adding to end-user frustration when processes don't work. The documentation and procedures may be modified during this process. All identified transactions must be tested during this step. All reports and online information must be verified and traced through the audit trail so that management is ensured that transactions will be handled consistently and that the information can be relied upon to make decisions.

Training

Before launch, all users need to be trained, with procedures. This means a trainer using the procedures to show each end user how to handle a procedures. The procedures often need to be updated during training as users describe their unique circumstances and the "design" is modified with this additional information. The end user then performs the procedure with the trainer and the documentation. The end user then performs the procedure with the documentation alone. The end user is then on his or her own with the support, either in person or by phone, of the trainer or other support person. This is before data conversion.

Data Conversion

Tools are developed to convert the data from the current system (which was documented in the requirements analysis) to the new system. The data is mapped from one system to the other and data files are created that will work with the tools that are developed. The conversion is thoroughly tested and verified before final conversion. There's a backup so it can be restarted, if necessary.

Launch

The system is implemented only after all of the above is completed. The entire organization is aware of the launch date. Ideally, the current system is retained and often run in "parallel" until the new system is in full operation and working properly. With the current mass-market software used by thousands of companies and fundamentally proven to work, the "parallel" run that is mandatory with software tailor-made to a company is generally not done. This is only true, however, when the above process is followed, the system is thoroughly documented and tested, and users are trained before launch.

Tools

Online resources are available to assist with strategic planning of accounting information systems. Information systems and financial forms aid in determining the specific needs of each organization, as well as assigning responsibility to principles involved.

Support

The end users and managers have ongoing support available at all times. System upgrades follow a similar process and all users are thoroughly apprised of changes, upgraded in an efficient manner, and trained.

Many organizations chose to limit the time and money spent on the analysis, design, documentation, and training, and move right into software selection and implementation. If a detailed requirements analysis is performed with adequate time being spent on the analysis, the implementation and ongoing support will be minimal. Organizations that skip the steps to ensure the system meets their needs are often left with frustrated end users, costly support, and information that is not current or correct. Worse yet, these organizations build the system three times instead of once.

Career

Many AIS professionals work for consulting firms, large corporations, insurance companies, financial firms, government agencies and public accounting firms, among other types of companies. With technological advancement, traditional accounting practice will shift to accounting information systems practice. Both accounting and information technology professional bodies are working on the new directions of accounting programs and industry practices. System Auditors is one of the top choices in the past two decades, they look at the controls, data processing, data integrity, general operation, maintenance, security and other aspects of all types of information systems used by businesses. A lot of the companies will deal with software and finding a software that is right for the company, or maintaining a software for a company. If you are interested in the career, you might have the choice of working in the financial department of any type of business, or of working with a financially oriented company or a programming-oriented company that specializes in AIS. Some job titles in this field of work include financial manager, financial examiner and chief financial officer. You could also become a computer systems analyst, a computer information systems manager or a computer software engineer or programmer specializing in financial software.

If you are working with a financially oriented company, your job duties could range from analyzing an AIS for data integrity to managing the entire AIS. In a programming-oriented company, your focus may be directed towards developing new software in AIS or fixing bugs in an AIS. In both cases, you may also have the option of consulting, which requires travelling to different companies to provide analysis and advice concerning the company's AIS.

There are industry associations offer certificates that related to AIS area include CISA, AIS, CISSP, CIA, AFE, CFE, and CITP.

Accounting Period

An accounting period, in bookkeeping, is the period with reference to which accounting books of any entity are prepared.

It is the period for which books are balanced and the financial statements are prepared. Generally, the accounting period consists of 12 months. However the beginning of the accounting period differs according to the jurisdiction. For example, one entity may follow the regular calendar year, i.e. January to December as the accounting year, while another entity may follow April to March as the accounting period.

The International Financial Reporting Standards allow a period of 52 weeks as an accounting period instead of a proper year. This method is known as the 4-4-5 calendar in British and Commonwealth usage and the 52-week fiscal year in the United States. In the United States the method is permitted by generally accepted accounting principles, as well as by US Internal Revenue Code Regulation 1.441-2 (IRS Publication 538).

In some of the ERP tools there are more than 12 accounting periods in a financial year. They put one accounting period as "Year Open" period where all the carried over balances from last financial year are cleared and one period as "Year Close" where all the transactions for closed for the same financial year. Accounting is an art of recording classifying and summarising the financial positions of the company. It is done by the accountant.

52-week Fiscal Year

The 52-week fiscal year (or 4 calendar) is used by companies that desire that their fiscal year always end on the same day of the week. Any day of the week may be used, and Saturday and Sunday are common because the business may more easily be closed for counting inventory and other end-of-year accounting activities. There are two methods in use:

Last Saturday of the Month at Fiscal Year End

Under this method the company's fiscal year is defined as the final Saturday (or other day selected) in the fiscal year end month. For example, if the fiscal year end month is August, the company's year end could fall on any date from August 25 to August 31. Currently it would end on the following days:

2006-08-26 2006 August 26

2007-08-25 2007 August 25

2008-08-30 2008 August 30 (leap year)

2009-08-29 2009 August 29

2010-08-28 2010 August 28

2011-08-27 2011 August 27

2012-08-25 2012 August 25 (leap year)

2013-08-31 2013 August 31

2014-08-30 2014 August 30

2015-08-29 2015 August 29

2016-08-27 2016 August 27 (leap year)

2017-08-26 2017 August 26

2018-08-25 2018 August 25

2019-08-31 2019 August 31

The end of the fiscal year would move one day earlier on the calendar each year (two days in leap years) until it would otherwise reach the date seven days before the end of the month (August 24 in this case). At that point it resets to the end of the month (August 31) and the fiscal year has 53 weeks instead of 52. In this example the fiscal years ending in 2008, 2013, and 2019 have 53 weeks.

Saturday Nearest the End of Month

Under this method the company's fiscal year is defined as the Saturday (or other day selected) that falls closest to the last day of the fiscal year end month. For example, if the fiscal year end month is August, the company's year end could fall on any date from August 28 to September 3. Currently it would end on the following days:

2006-09-02 2006 September 2

2007-09-01 2007 September 1

2008-08-30 2008 August 30 (leap year)

2009-08-29 2009 August 29

2010-08-28 2010 August 28

2011-09-03 2011 September 3

2012-09-01 2012 September 1 (leap year)

2013-08-31 2013 August 31

2014-08-30 2014 August 30

2015-08-29 2015 August 29

2016-09-03 2016 September 3 (leap year)

2017-09-02 2017 September 2

2018-09-01 2018 September 1

2019-08-31 2019 August 31

The end of the fiscal year would move one day earlier on the calendar each year (two days in leap years) until it would otherwise reach the date four days before the end of the month (August 27 in this case). At that point the first Saturday in the following month (September 3 in this case) becomes the date closest to the end of August and it resets to that date and the fiscal year has 53 weeks instead of 52. In this example the fiscal years ending in 2011 and 2016 have 53 weeks.

The 52 week method is permitted by generally accepted accounting principles in the United States, by US Internal Revenue Code Regulation 1.441-2 (IRS Publication 538)., as well as the International Financial Reporting Standards.

Resource Consumption Accounting

Resource Consumption Accounting (RCA) is a management theory describing a dynamic, integrated, and comprehensive management accounting approach that provides managers with decision support information for enterprise optimization. RCA is a relatively new management accounting approach based largely on the German management accounting approach Grenzplankostenrechnung (GPK) and also allows for the use of activity-based drivers.

Background

RCA emerged as a management accounting approach beginning around 2000, and was subsequently developed at CAM-I (The Consortium of Advanced Management, International) in a Cost Management Section RCA interest group commencing in December 2001. Over the next seven years RCA was refined and validated through practical case studies, industry journal publications, and other research papers.

In 2008, a group of interested academics and practitioners established the RCA Institute to introduce Resource Consumption Accounting to the marketplace and raise the standard of management accounting knowledge by encouraging disciplined practices.

By July 2009, Professional Accountants in Business (PAIB) Committee of International Federation of Accountants (IFAC), recognized Resource Consumption Accounting in the International Good Practice Guidance (IGPG) publication called Evaluating and Improving Costing in Organizations and its companion document, Evaluating the Costing Journey: A Costing Levels Continuum Maturity Model. The guide focuses on universal costing principles and with the Costing Levels Maturity Model acknowledges RCA attains a higher level of accuracy and visibility compared to activity based costing for managerial accounting information when the incremental benefits of RCA's better information exceed the incremental administrative effort and cost to collect, calculate and report its information.

As stated in the International Good Practice Guidance,

"A sophisticated approach at the upper levels of the continuum of costing techniques provides the ability to derive costs directly from operational resource data, or to isolate and measure unused capacity costs. For example, in the resource consumption accounting approach, resources and their costs are considered as foundational to robust cost modeling and managerial decision support, because an organization's costs and revenues are all a function of the resources and the individual capacities that produce them."

—International Federation of Accountants, 2009

Resource Consumption Accounting was also recognized in a Sustainability Framework Report issued by the International Federation of Accountants (IFAC), for having the capability of helping organizations *"improve their understanding of environmental (and social) costs through their costing systems and models"*. This Sustainability Framework highlights RCA under the sub-heading *Improving Information Flows to Support Decision* and informs readers that proper cost allocation can be built 'directly into the cost accounting system', thereby enhancing an organization's performance for *"identifying, defining and classifying costs in a useful way"*.

Concepts of Resource Consumption Accounting

RCA concepts that distinguish it from other management accounting approaches include the following:

1. Germany's GPK method of quantity-based operational modeling using fixed and proportional costs established at the resource level in a company (i.e., cost center/resource pools or value streams");
2. Gordon Shillinglaw's concept of attributable cost;
3. Flexible use of activity-based drivers (only where needed) based on specific, and restrictive rules;
4. Value chain integration of management accounting into operational systems;
5. Use of fundamental operations transactions as the primary source for financial and quantitative data (rather than the general ledger);
6. Replacing the *principle of variability* with the *principle of responsiveness* for operational modeling;
7. Support for a multi-level, contribution margin-based *profit & loss statement* that supports managerial decision making without the cost distortions and complexity of inappropriate (not based on the *principle of causality*) allocations of cost.

The Core Elements of RCA

There are three core elements that enable RCA to lay a very different foundation for its cost model.

- The view of resources – resources and their costs are considered foundational to proper cost modeling and decision support. An organization's cost and revenues are all a function of the resources that produce them.
- Quantity-based modeling – the entire model is constructed using operational quantities. Operational data is the foundation of value creation and the leading indicator of economic outcomes.
- Cost behavior – value is added as a veneer to the quantity-based model and costs/dollars behavior is determined by the behavior of resource quantities as they are applied to value creating operations within an organization.

Additional Information

The goals of the RCA Institute, in promoting the acquisition of knowledge and skills to apply RCA, include the following:

- Improve management accounting knowledge and practice by clarifying and embracing sound principles that will enhance enterprise decision making and the public welfare through optimum resource usage.
- Advance the knowledge and practice of Resource Consumption Accounting (RCA) through:
  - A community of active, high quality practitioners and academics.
  - Consistent and disciplined practice centered on a core body of RCA knowledge that is not diluted by wide variations in use or form.
  - Education of adopters, practitioners and vendors and the certification of vendors' products and services.
  - Increased adoption of RCA, over the long-term, as the dominant management accounting approach in business, government, and non-profit organizations.

  The RCA Institute library contains an annotated bibliography that is currently divided into four sections:

1. RCA theory,
2. management accounting landscape and management accounting philosophy,
3. RCA related research and
4. other materials.

This annotated bibliography provides more information for recommended reading and some guidance on how to get the most out of the information that is there.

Throughput Accounting

Throughput Accounting (TA) is a principle-based and simplified management accounting approach that provides managers with decision support information for enterprise profitability improvement. TA is relatively new in management accounting. It is an approach that identifies factors that limit an organization from reaching its goal, and then focuses on simple measures that drive behavior in key areas towards reaching organizational goals. TA was proposed by Eliyahu M. Goldratt as an alternative to traditional cost accounting. As such, Throughput Accounting is neither cost accounting nor costing because it is cash focused and does not allocate all costs (variable and fixed expenses, including overheads) to products and services sold or provided by an enterprise. Considering the laws of variation, only costs that vary totally with units of output e.g. raw materials, are allocated to products and services which are deducted from sales to determine Throughput. Throughput Accounting is a management accounting technique used as the performance measure in the Theory of Constraints (TOC). It is the business intelligence used for maximizing profits, however, unlike cost accounting that primarily focuses on 'cutting costs' and reducing expenses to make a profit, Throughput Accounting primarily focuses on generating more throughput. Conceptually, Throughput Accounting seeks to increase the speed or rate at which throughput is generated by products and services with respect to an organization's constraint, whether the constraint is internal or external to the organization. Throughput Accounting is the only management accounting methodology that considers constraints as factors limiting the performance of organizations.

Management accounting is an organization's internal set of techniques and methods used to maximize shareholder wealth. Throughput Accounting is thus part of the management accountants' toolkit, ensuring efficiency where it matters as well as the overall effectiveness of the organization. It is an internal reporting tool. Outside or external parties to a business depend on accounting reports prepared by financial (public) accountants who apply Generally Accepted Accounting Principles (GAAP) issued by the Financial Accounting Standards Board (FASB) and enforced by the U.S. Securities and Exchange Commission (SEC) and other local and international regulatory agencies and bodies such as International Financial Reporting Standards (IFRS).

Throughput Accounting improves profit performance with better management decisions by using measurements that more closely reflect the effect of decisions on three critical monetary variables (throughput, investment (AKA inventory), and operating expense).

History

When cost accounting was developed in the 1890s, labor was the largest fraction of product cost and could be considered a variable cost. Workers often did not know how many hours they would work in a week when they reported on Monday morning because time-keeping systems were rudimentary. Cost accountants, therefore, concentrated on how efficiently managers used labor since it was their most important variable resource. Now however, workers who come to work on Monday morning almost always work 40 hours or more; their cost is fixed rather than variable. However, today, many managers are still evaluated on their labor efficiencies, and many "downsizing," "rightsizing," and other labor reduction campaigns are based on them.

Goldratt argues that, under current conditions, labor efficiencies lead to decisions that harm rather than help organizations. Throughput Accounting, therefore, removes standard cost accounting's reliance on efficiencies in general, and labor efficiency in particular, from management practice. Many cost and financial accountants agree with Goldratt's critique, but they have not agreed on a replacement of their own and there is enormous inertia in the installed base of people trained to work with existing practices.

Constraints accounting, which is a development in the Throughput Accounting field, emphasizes the role of the constraint, (referred to as the Archemedian constraint) in decision making.

The Concepts of Throughput Accounting

Goldratt's alternative begins with the idea that each organization has a goal and that better decisions increase its value. The goal for a profit maximizing firm is easily stated, to increase profit now and in the future. Throughput Accounting applies to not-for-profit organizations too, but they have to develop a goal that makes sense in their individual cases.

Throughput Accounting also pays particular attention to the concept of 'bottleneck' (referred to as *constraint* in the Theory of Constraints) in the manufacturing or servicing processes.

Throughput Accounting uses three measures of income and expense:

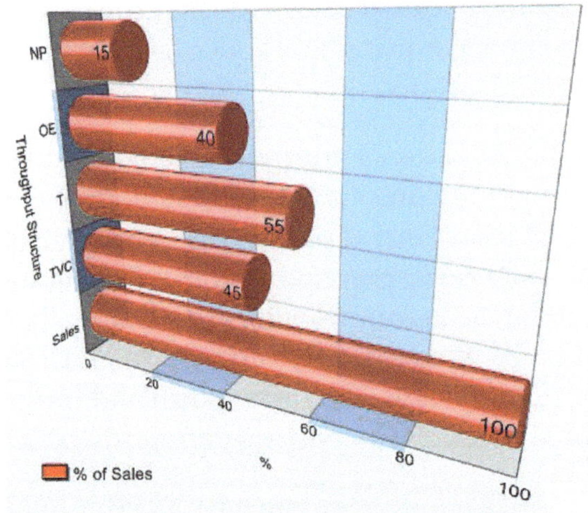

The chart illustrates a typical throughput structure of income (sales) and expenses (TVC and OE).
T=Sales less TVC and NP=T less OE.

- Throughput (T) is the rate at which the system produces "goal units." When the goal units are money (in for-profit businesses), throughput is net sales (S) less totally variable cost (TVC), generally the cost of the raw materials (T = S – TVC). Note that T only exists when there is a sale of the product or service. Producing materials that sit in a warehouse does not form part of throughput but rather investment. ("Throughput" is sometimes referred to as "throughput contribution" and has similarities to the concept of "contribution" in marginal costing which is sales revenues less "variable" costs – "variable" being defined according to the marginal costing philosophy.)
- Investment (I) is the money tied up in the system. This is money associated with inventory, machinery, buildings, and other assets and liabilities. In earlier Theory of Constraints (TOC) documentation, the "I" was interchanged between "inventory" and "investment." The preferred term is now only "investment." Note that TOC recommends inventory be valued strictly on totally variable cost associated with creating the inventory, not with additional cost allocations from overhead.
- Operating expense (OE) is the money the system spends in generating "goal units." For physical products, OE is all expenses except the cost of the raw materials. OE includes maintenance, utilities, rent, taxes and payroll.

Organizations that wish to increase their attainment of *The Goal* should therefore require managers to test proposed decisions against three questions. Will the proposed change:

1. Increase throughput? How?
2. Reduce investment (inventory) (money that cannot be used)? How?
3. Reduce operating expense? How?

The answers to these questions determine the effect of proposed changes on system wide measurements:

1. Net profit (NP) = throughput – operating expense = T – OE
2. Return on investment (ROI) = net profit / investment = NP/I
3. TA Productivity = throughput / operating expense = T/OE
4. Investment turns (IT) = throughput / investment = T/I

These relationships between financial ratios as illustrated by Goldratt are very similar to a set of relationships defined by DuPont and General Motors financial executive Donaldson Brown about 1920. Brown did not advocate changes in management accounting methods, but instead used the ratios to evaluate traditional financial accounting data.

Throughput Accounting is an important development in modern accounting that allows managers to understand the contribution of constrained resources to the overall profitability of the enterprise.

Explanation

Throughput = Sales revenue Total Variable Costs

Throughput accounting Ratio = Return per factory hour / Cost per factory hour

For example: The railway coach company was offered a contract to make 15 open-topped streetcars each month, using a design that included ornate brass foundry work, but very little of the metalwork needed to produce a covered rail coach. The buyer offered to pay $280 per streetcar. The company had a firm order for 40 rail coaches each month for $350 per unit.

The cost accountant determined that the cost of operating the foundry vs. the metalwork shop each month was as follows:

Overhead Cost by Department	Total Cost ($)	Hours Available per month	Cost per hour ($)
Foundry	7,300.00	160	45.63
Metal shop	3,300.00	160	20.63
Total	10,600.00	320	33.13

The company was at full capacity making 40 rail coaches each month. And since the foundry was expensive to operate, and purchasing brass as a raw material for the streetcars was expensive, the accountant determined that the company would lose money on any streetcars it built. He showed an analysis of the estimated product costs based on standard cost accounting and recommended that the company decline to build any streetcars.

Standard Cost Accounting Analysis	Streetcars	Rail coach
Monthly Demand	15	40
Price	$280	$350
Foundry Time (hrs)	3.0	2.0

Metalwork Time (hrs)	1.5	4.0
Total Time	4.5	6.0
Foundry Cost	$136.88	$91.25
Metalwork Cost	$30.94	$82.50
Raw Material Cost	$120.00	$60.00
Total Cost	$287.81	$233.75
Profit per Unit	$ (7.81)	$116.25

However, the company's operations manager knew that recent investment in automated foundry equipment had created idle time for workers in that department. The constraint on production of the railcoaches was the metalwork shop. She made an analysis of profit and loss if the company took the contract using throughput accounting to determine the profitability of products by calculating "throughput" (revenue less variable cost) in the metal shop.

Throughput Cost Accounting Analysis	Decline Contract	Take Contract
Coaches Produced	40	34
Streetcars Produced	0	15
Foundry Hours	80	113
Metal shop Hours	160	159
Coach Revenue	$14,000	$11,900
Streetcar Revenue	$0	$4,200
Coach Raw Material Cost	$(2,400)	$(2,040)
Streetcar Raw Material Cost	$0	$(1,800)
Throughput Value	$11,600	$12,260
Overhead Expense	$(10,600)	$(10,600)
Profit	$1,000	$1,660

After the presentations from the company accountant and the operations manager, the president understood that the metal shop capacity was limiting the company's profitability. The company could make only 40 rail coaches per month. But by taking the contract for the streetcars, the company could make nearly all the railway coaches ordered, and also meet all the demand for streetcars. The result would increase throughput in the metal shop from $6.25 to $10.38 per hour of available time, and increase profitability by 66 percent.

Relevance

One of the most important aspects of Throughput Accounting is the relevance of the information it produces. Throughput Accounting reports what currently happens in business functions such as operations, distribution and marketing. It does not rely solely on GAAP's financial accounting reports (that still need to be verified by external auditors) and is thus relevant to current decisions made by management that affect the business now and in the future. Throughput Accounting is used in Critical Chain Project Management (CCPM), Drum Buffer Rope (DBR)—in businesses that are internally constrained, in Simplified Drum Buffer Rope (S-DBR) —in businesses that are externally constrained (particularly where the lack of customer orders denotes a market constraint), as well as in strategy, planning and tactics, etc.

Whole-life Cost

Whole-life cost, or Life-cycle cost (LCC), refers to the total cost of ownership over the life of an asset. Also commonly referred to as "cradle to grave" or "womb to tomb" costs. Costs considered include the financial cost which is relatively simple to calculate and also the environmental and social costs which are more difficult to quantify and assign numerical values. Typical areas of expenditure which are included in calculating the whole-life cost include, planning, design, construction and acquisition, operations, maintenance, renewal and rehabilitation, depreciation and cost of finance and replacement or disposal.

Financial

Whole-life cost analysis is often used for option evaluation when procuring new assets and for decision-making to minimize whole-life costs throughout the life of an asset. It is also applied to comparisons of actual costs for similar asset types and as feedback into future design and acquisition decisions.

The primary benefit is that costs which occur after an asset has been constructed or acquired, such as maintenance, operation, disposal, become an important consideration in decision-making. Previously, the focus has been on the up-front capital costs of creation or acquisition, and organisations may have failed to take account of the longer-term costs of an asset. It also allows an analysis of business function interrelationships. Low development costs may lead to high maintenance or customer service costs in the future. When making this calculation, the depreciation cost on the capital expense should not be included.

Environmental and Social

The use of environmental costs in a whole-life analysis allows a true comparison options, especially where both are quoted as "good" for the environment. For a major project such as the construction of a nuclear power station it is possible to calculate the environmental impact of making the concrete containment, the water required for refining the copper for the power plants and all the other components. Only by undertaking such an analysis is it possible to determine whether one solution carries a lower or higher environmental cost than another.

Almost all major projects have some social impact. This may be the compulsory re-location of people living on land about to be submerged under a reservoir or a threat to the livelihood of small traders from the development of a hypermarket nearby.

Whole-life Cost Topics

Project Appraisal

Whole-life costing is a key component in the economic appraisal associated with evaluating asset acquisition proposals. An economic appraisal is generally a broader based assessment, considering benefits and indirect or intangible costs as well as direct costs.

In this way, the whole-life costs and benefits of each option are considered and usually converted using discount rates into net present value costs and benefits. This results in a benefit cost ratio for each option, usually compared to the "do-nothing" counterfactual. Typically the highest benefit-cost ratio option is chosen as the preferred option.

Historically, asset investments have been based on expedient design and lowest cost construction. If such investment has been made without proper analysis of the standard of service required and the maintenance and intervention options available, the initial saving may result in increased expenditure throughout the asset's life.

By using whole-life costs, this avoids issues with decisions being made based on the short-term costs of design and construction. Often the longer-term maintenance and operation costs can be a significant proportion of the whole-life cost.

Asset Management

During the life of the asset, decisions about how to maintain and operate the asset need to be taken in context with the effect these activities might have on the residual life of the asset. If by investing 10% more per annum in maintenance costs the asset life can be doubled, this might be a worthwhile investment.

Other issues which influence the lifecycle costs of an asset include:

- site conditions,
- historic performance of assets or materials,
- effective monitoring techniques,
- appropriate intervention strategies.

Although the general approach to determining whole-life costs is common to most types of asset, each asset will have specific issues to be considered and the detail of the assessment needs to be tailored to the importance and value of the asset. High cost assets (and asset systems) will likely have more detail, as will critical assets and asset systems.

Maintenance expenditure can account for many times the initial cost of the asset. Although an asset may be constructed with a design life of 30 years, in reality it will possibly perform well beyond this design life. For assets like these a balanced view between maintenance strategies and renewal/rehabilitation is required. The appropriateness of the maintenance strategy must be questioned, the point of intervention for renewal must be challenged. The process requires proactive assessment which must be based on the performance expected of the asset, the consequences and probabilities of failures occurring, and the level of expenditure in maintenance to keep the service available and to avert disaster.

IT Industry Usage

Whole-life cost is often referred to as "total cost of ownership (TCO)" when applied to IT hardware and software acquisitions. Use of the term "TCO" appears to have been popularised by Gartner Group in 1987 but its roots are considerably older, dating at least to the first quarter of the twentieth century.

It has since been developed as a concept with a number of different methodologies and software tools. A TCO assessment ideally offers a final statement reflecting not only the cost of purchase but all aspects in the further use and maintenance of the equipment, device, or system considered.

This includes the costs of training support personnel and the users of the system, costs associated with failure or outage (planned and unplanned), diminished performance incidents (i.e. if users are kept waiting), costs of security breaches (in loss of reputation and recovery costs), costs of disaster preparedness and recovery, floor space, electricity, development expenses, testing infrastructure and expenses, quality assurance, boot image control, marginal incremental growth, decommissioning, e-waste handling, and more. When incorporated in any financial benefit analysis (e.g., ROI, IRR, EVA, ROIT, RJE) TCO provides a cost basis for determining the economic value of that investment.

Understanding and familiarity with the term TCO has been somewhat facilitated as a result of various comparisons between the TCO of open source and proprietary software. Because the software cost of open source software is often zero, TCO has been used as a means to justify the up-front licensing costs of proprietary software. Studies which attempt to establish the TCO and provide comparisons have as a result been the subject of many discussions regarding the accuracy or perceived bias in the comparison.

Automobile Industry, Finances

Total cost of ownership is also common in the automobile industry. In this context, the TCO denotes the cost of owning a vehicle from the purchase, through its maintenance, and finally its sale as a used car. Comparative TCO studies between various models help consumers choose a car to fit their needs and budget.

TCO can and often does vary dramatically against TCA (total cost of acquisition), although TCO is far more relevant in determining the viability of any capital investment, especially with modern credit markets and financing. TCO also directly relates to a business's total costs across all projects and processes and, thus, its profitability. Some instances of "TCO" appear to refer to "total cost of operation", but this may be a subset of the total cost of ownership if it excludes maintenance and support costs.

Environmental Accounting

Environmental accounting is a subset of accounting proper, its target being to incorporate both economic and environmental information. It can be conducted at the corporate level or at the level of a national economy through the System of Integrated Environmental and Economic Accounting, a satellite system to the National Accounts of Countries (among other things, the National Accounts produce the estimates of Gross Domestic Product otherwise known as GDP).

Environmental accounting is a field that identifies resource use, measures and communicates costs of a company's or national economic impact on the environment. Costs include costs to clean up or remediate contaminated sites, environmental fines, penalties and taxes, purchase of pollution prevention technologies and waste management costs.

An environmental accounting system consists of environmentally differentiated conventional accounting and ecological accounting. Environmentally differentiated accounting measures effects of the natural environment on a company in monetary terms. Ecological accounting measures the influence a company has on the environment, but in physical measurements.

Why Environmental Accounting?

There are several advantages environmental accounting brings to business; notably, the complete costs, including environmental remediation and long term environmental consequences and externalities can be quantified and addressed.

More information about the statistical system of environmental accounts are available here: System of Integrated Environmental and Economic Accounting.

Subfields

Environmental accounting is organized in three sub-disciplines: global, national, and corporate environmental accounting, respectively. Corporate environmental accounting can be further sub-divided into environmental management accounting and environmental financial accounting.

- Global environmental accounting is an accounting methodology that deals areas includes energetics, ecology and economics at a worldwide level.
- National environmental accounting is an accounting approach that deals with economics on a country's level.

  Internationally, environmental accounting has been formalised into the System of Integrated Environmental and Economic Accounting, known as SEEA. SEEA grows out of the System of National Accounts. The SEEA records the flows of raw materials (water, energy, minerals, wood, etc.) from the environment to the economy, the exchanges of these materials within the economy and the returns of wastes and pollutants to the environment. Also recorded are the prices or shadow prices for these materials as are environment protection expenditures. SEEA is used by 49 countries around the world.
- Corporate environmental accounting focuses on the cost structure and environmental performance of a company.
- Environmental management accounting focuses on making internal business strategy decisions. It can be defined as:

  "...*the identification, collection, analysis, and use of two types of information for internal decision making:*

  1) Physical information on the use, flows and fates of energy, water and materials (including wastes) and

  2) Monetary information on environmentally related costs, earnings and savings."

  As part of an environmental management accounting project in the State of Victoria, Australia, four case studies were undertaken in 2002 involving a school (Methodist Ladies College, Perth), plastics manufacturing company (Cormack Manufacturing Pty Ltd, Sydney), provider of office services (a service division of AMP, Australia wide) and wool processing (GH Michell & Sons Pty Ltd, Adelaide). Four major accounting professionals and firms were involved in the project; KPMG (Melbourne), Price Waterhouse Coopers (Sydney), Professor Craig Deegan, RMIT University (Melbourne) and BDO Consultants Pty Ltd (Perth). In February 2003, John Thwaites, The Victorian Minister for the Environment launched the report which summarised the results of the studies.

These studies were supported by the Department of Environment and Heritage of the Australian Federal Government, and appear to have applied some of the principles outlined in the United Nations Division for Sustainable Development publication, *Environmental Management Accounting Procedures and Principles* (2001).

- Environmental financial accounting is used to provide information needed by external stakeholders on a company's financial performance. This type of accounting allows companies to prepare financial reports for investors, lenders and other interested parties.

Examples of Environmental Accounting Software

- EHS Data's Environmental and Sustainability Accounting and Management System
- Emisoft's Total Environmental Accounting and Management System (TEAMS)
- add energy's NEMS Accounter

Target Costing

Target costing is an approach to determine a product's life-cycle cost which should be sufficient to develop specified functionality and quality, while ensuring its desired profit. It involves setting a target cost by subtracting a desired profit margin from a competitive market price. A target cost is the maximum amount of cost that can be incurred on a product, however, the firm can still earn the required profit margin from that product at a particular selling price. Target costing decomposes the target cost from product level to component level. Through this decomposition, target costing spread the competitive pressure faced by the company to product's designers and suppliers. Target costing consists of cost planning in the design phase of production as well as cost control throughout the resulting product life cycle. The cardinal rule of target costing is to never exceed the target cost. However, the focus of target costing is not to minimize costs, but to achieve a desired level of cost reduction determined by target costing process.

Definition

Target costing is defined as "a disciplined process for determining and achieving a full-stream cost at which a proposed product with specified functionality, performance, and quality must be produced in order to generate the desired profitability at the product's anticipated selling price over a specified period of time in the future." This definition encompasses the principal concepts: products should be based on an accurate assessment of the wants and needs of customers in different market segments, and cost targets should be what result after a sustainable profit margin is subtracted from what customers are willing to pay at the time of product introduction and afterwards.

The fundamental objective of target costing is to manage the business to be profitable in a highly competitive marketplace. In effect, target costing is a proactive cost planning, cost management, and cost reduction practice whereby costs are planned and managed out of a product and business early in the design and development cycle, rather than during the later stages of product development and production.

History

Target costing was developed independently in both USA and Japan in different time periods. Target costing was adopted earlier by American companies to reduce cost and improve productivity, such as Ford Motor from 1900s, American Motors from 1950s-1960s. Although the ideas of target costing were also applied by a number of other American companies including Boeing, Caterpillar, Northern Telecom, few of them apply target costing as comprehensively and intensively as top Japanese companies such as Nissan, Toyota, Nippondenso. Target costing emerged from Japan from 1960s to early 1970s with the particular effort of Japanese automobile industry, including Toyota and Nissan. It did not receive global attention until late 1980s to 1990s when some authors such as Monden (1992), Sakurai (1989), Tanaka (1993), and Cooper (1992) described the way that Japanese companies applied target costing to thrive in their business (IMA 1994). With superior implementation system, Japanese manufacturers is more successful than the American companies in developing target costing. Traditional cost-plus pricing strategy has been impeding the productivity and profitability for a long time. As a new strategy, target costing is replacing traditional cost-plus pricing strategy by maximizing customer satisfaction by accepted level of quality and functionality while minimizing costs.

Process of Target Costing

The process of target costing can be divided into three sections: the first section involves in market-driven target costing, which focuses on studying market condition to identifying product's allowable cost in order to meet company's long-term profit at expected selling price; the second section involves in performing cost reduction strategies with the product designer's effort and creativity to identify the product-level target cost; the third section is component-level target cost which decomposes the production cost to functional and component levels to transmit cost responsibility to suppliers.

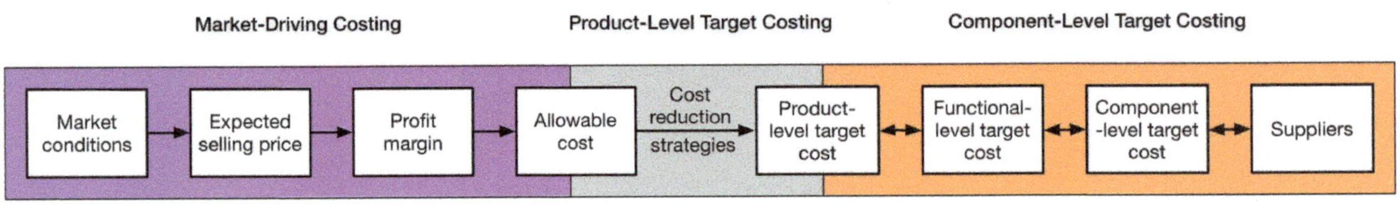

Target costing process

Market-driven Target Costing

Market driven target costing is the first section in target costing process which focuses on studying market condition and determining company's profit margin in order to identify allowable cost of a product. Market driven costing can go through 5 steps including: establish company's long-term sales and profit objective; develop the mix of products; identify target selling price for each product; identify profit margin for each product; and calculate allowable cost of each product.

Company's long-term sales and profit objective are developed from extensive analysis of relevant information relating to customers, market and products. Only realistic plan is accepted to process the next step. Product mix is designed carefully to ensure that it satisfies many customers, but also does not contain too many products to confuse customers. Company may use simulation to explore the impact of overall profit objective to different product mixes and determine the most feasible product mix. Target selling price, target profit margin and allowable cost are identified for each product. Target selling price need to consider to the expected market condition at the time launching the product. Internal factors such as product's functionality and profit objective, and external factors such as company's image or expected price of competitive products will influence target selling price. Company's long-term profit plan and life-cycle cost are considered when determining target profit margin. Firms might set up target profit margin based on either actual profit margin of previous products or target profit margin of product line. Simulation for overall group profitability can help to make sure achieving group target. Subtracting target profit margin from target selling price results in allowable cost for each product. Allowable cost is the cost that can spend on the product to ensure meeting profit target if selling it at target price. It is the signal about the magnitude of cost saving that team need to achieve.

Product-level Target Costing

Following the completion of market-driven costing, the next task of the target costing process is product-level target costing. Product-level target costing concentrates on designing products that satisfy the company's customers at the allowable cost. To achieve this goal, product-level target costing is typically divided into three steps as shown below.

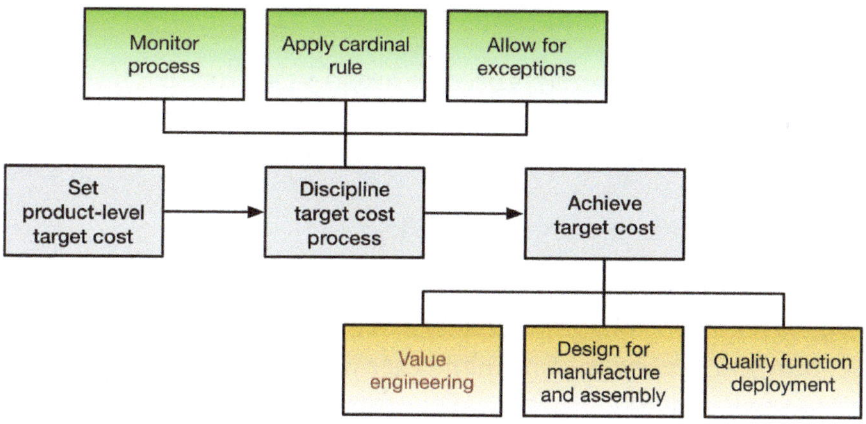

Product-level target costing

The first step is to set a product-level target cost. Since the allowable cost is simply obtained from external conditions without considering the design capabilities of the company as well as the realistic cost for manufacturing, it may not be always achievable in practice. Thus, it is necessary to adjust the unachievable allowable cost to an achievable target cost that the cost increase should be reduced with great effort. The second step is to discipline this target cost process, including monitoring the relationship between the target cost and the estimated product cost at any point during the design process, applying the cardinal rule so that the total target costs at the component-level does not exceed the target cost of the product, and allowing exceptions for products violating the cardinal rule. For a product exception to the cardinal rule, two analyses are often performed after the launch of the product. One involves reviewing the design process to find out why the target cost was unachieved. The other is an immediate effort to reduce the excessive cost to ensure that the period of violation is as short as possible. Once the target cost-reduction objective is identified, the product-level target costing comes to the final step, finding ways to achieve it. Engineering methods such as value engineering (VE), design for manufacture and assembly (DFMA), and quality function deployment (QFD) are commonly adopted in this step.

Target Costing and Value Engineering

Value engineering (VE), also known as value analysis (VA), plays a crucial role in the target costing process, particularly at the product level and the component level. Among the three aforementioned methods in achieving the target cost, VE is the most critical one because not only does it attempt to reduce costs, but also aim to improve the functionality and quality of products. There are a variety of practical VE strategies, including zero-look, first-look and second-look VE approaches, as well as teardown approaches.

Regarding the complexity of problems in the real world, implementing the target costing process often relies on the computer simulation to reproduce stochastic elements. For example, many firms use simulation to study the complex relationship between selling prices and profit margins, the impact of individual product decisions on overall group profitability, the right mix of products to enhance overall profit, or other economic modeling to overcome organizational inertia by getting the most productive reasoning. In addition, simulation helps estimate results rapidly for dynamic process changes.

Factors Affecting Target Costing

The factors influencing the target costing process is broadly categorized based on how a company's strategy for a product's quality, functionality and price change over time. However, some factors play a specific role based on what drives a company's approach to target costing.

Factors Influencing Market-driven Costing

Intensity of competition and nature of the customer affect market-driven costing. Competitors introducing similar products has been shown to drive rival companies to expend energy on implementing target costing systems such as in the case of Toyota and Nissan or Apple and Google. The costing process is also affected by the level of customer sophistication, changing requirements and the degree to which their future requirements are known. The automotive and camera industry are prime examples for how customers affect target costing based on their exact requirements.

Factors Influencing Product-level Costing

Product strategy and product characteristics affect product-level target costing. Characteristics of product strategy such as number of products in line, rate of redesign operations and level of innovation are shown to have an effect. Higher number of products has a direct correlation with the benefits of target costing. Frequent redesigns lead to the introduction of new products that have created better benefits to target costing. It has to be noted that the value of historical information reduces with greater innovation, thereby, reducing the benefits of product level target costing.

The degree of complexity of the product, level of investments required and the duration of product development process make up the factors that affect the target costing process based on product characteristics. Product viability is determined by the aforementioned factors. In turn, the target costing process is also modified to suit the different degrees of complexity required.

Factors Influencing Component-level Costing

Supplier-Base strategy is the main factor that determines component-level target costing because it is known to play a key role in the details a firm has about its supplier capabilities. There are three characteristics that make up the supplier-base strategy, including the degree of horizontal integration, power over suppliers and nature of supplier relations. Horizontal integration captures the fraction of product costs sourced externally. Cost pressures on suppliers can drive target costing if the buying power of firms is high enough. In turn, this may lead to better benefits. More cooperative supplier relations have been shown to increase mutual benefits in terms of target costs particularly at a component level.

Applications

Aside from the application of target costing in the field of manufacturing, target costing are also widely used in the following areas.

Energy

An Energy Retrofit Loan Analysis Model has been developed using a Monte Carlo (MC) method for target costing in Energy Efficient buildings and construction. MC method has been shown to be effective in determining the impact of financial uncertainties in project performance.

Target Value Design Decision Making Process (TVD-DMP) groups a set of energy efficiency methods at different optimization levels to evaluate costs and uncertainties involved in the energy efficiency process. Some major design parameters are specified using this methods including Facility Operation Schedule, Orientation, Plug load, HVAC and lighting systems.

The entire process consists of three phases: initiation, definition and alignment. Initiation stage involves developing a business case for energy efficiency using target value design (TVD) training, organization and compensation. The definition process involves defining and validating the case by tools such as values analysis and bench marking processes to determine the allowable costs. By setting targets and designing the design process to align with those targets, TVD-DMP has been shown to achieve a high level of collaboration needed for energy efficiency investments. This is done by using risk analysis tools, pull planning and rapid estimating processes.

Healthcare

Target costing and target value design have applications in building healthcare facilities including critical components such as Neonatal Intensive Care Units (NICUs). The process is influenced by unit locations, degree of comfort, number of patients per room, type of supply location and access to nature. According to National Vital Statistics Reports, 12.18% of 2009 births were premature and the cost per infant was $51,600. This led to opportunities for NICUs to implement target value design for deciding whether to build a single-family room or more open-bay NICUs. This was achieved using set-based design analysis which challenges the designer to generate multiple alternatives for the same functionality. Designs are evaluated keeping in mind the requirements of the various stakeholders in the NICU including nurses, doctors, family members and administrators. Unlike linear point-based design, set-based design narrows options to the optimal one by eliminating alternatives simultaneously defined by user constraints.

Construction

About 15% construction project in Japan adopted target costing for their cost planning and management as recognized by Jacomit (2008). In the U.S., target costing research has been carried out within the framework of lean construction as target value design (TVD) method and have been disseminated widely over construction industry in recent years. Research has proven that if being applied systematically, TVD can deliver a significant improvement in project performance with average reduction of 15% in comparison with market cost. TVD in construction project considers the final cost of project as a design parameter, similar to the capacity and aesthetics requirements for the project. TVD requires the project team to develop a target cost from the beginning. The project team is expected not to design exceeding the target cost without the owner's approval, and must use different skills to maintain this target cost. In some cases, the cost can increase but the project team must commit to decrease and must try their best to decrease without impacting on other functions of the project.

Financial Accounting

Financial accounting (or financial accountancy) is the field of accounting concerned with the summary, analysis and reporting of financial transactions pertaining to a business. This involves the preparation of financial statements available for public consumption. Stockholders, suppliers, banks, employees, government agencies, business owners, and other stakeholders are examples of people interested in receiving such information for decision making purposes.

Financial accountancy is governed by both local and international accounting standards. Generally Accepted Accounting Principles (GAAP) is the standard framework of guidelines for financial accounting used in any given jurisdiction. It includes the standards, conventions and rules that accountants follow in recording and summarizing and in the preparation of financial statements. On the other hand, International Financial Reporting Standards (IFRS) is a set of passionable accounting standards stating how particular types of transactions and other events should be reported in financial statements. IFRS are issued by the International Accounting Standards Board (IASB). With IFRS becoming more widespread on the international scene, *consistency* in financial reporting has become more prevalent between global organizations.

While financial accounting is used to prepare accounting information for people outside the organization or not involved in the day-to-day running of the company, managerial accounting provides accounting information to help managers make decisions to manage the business.

Objectives

Financial accounting and financial reporting are often used as synonyms.

1. According to International Financial Reporting Standards, the objective of financial reporting is:

To provide financial information about the reporting entity that is useful to existing and potential investors, lenders and other creditors in making decisions about providing resources to the entity.

2. According to the European Accounting Association:

Capital maintenance is a competing objective of financial reporting.

Qualities

Financial accounting is the preparation of financial statements that can be consumed by the public and the relevant stakeholders using either Historical Cost Accounting (HCA) or Constant Purchasing Power Accounting (CPPA). When producing financial statements, they must comply to the following:

- Relevance: Financial accounting which is decision-specific. It must be possible for accounting information to influence decisions. Unless this characteristic is present, there is no point in cluttering statements.
- Materiality: information is material if its omission or misstatement could influence the economic decisions of users taken on the basis of the financial statements.
- Reliability: accounting must be free from significant error or bias. It should be easily relied upon by managers. Often information that is highly relevant isn't very reliable, and vice versa.
- Understandability: accounting reports should be expressed as clearly as possible and should be understood by those to whom the information is relevant.
- Comparability: financial reports from different periods should be comparable with one another in order to derive meaningful conclusions about the trends in an entity's financial performance and position over time. Comparability can be ensured by applying the same accounting policies over time.

Three Components of Financial Statements

Statement of Cash Flows

The statement of cash flows considers the inputs and outputs in concrete cash within a stated period. The general template of a cash flow statement is as follows: *Cash Inflow - Cash Outflow + Opening Balance = Closing Balance.*

Example 1: in the beginning of September, Ellen started out with $5 in her bank account. During that same month, Ellen borrowed $20 from Tom. At the end of the month, Ellen bought a pair of shoes for $7. Ellen's cash flow statement for the month of September looks like this:

- Cash inflow: $20
- Cash outflow:$7

- Opening balance: $5
- Closing balance: $20 – $7 + $5 = $18

Example 2: in the beginning of June, WikiTables, a company that buys and resells tables, sold 2 tables. They'd originally bought the tables for $25 each, and sold them at a price of $50 per table. The first table was paid out in cash however the second one was bought in credit terms. WikiTables' cash flow statement for the month of June looks like this:

- Cash inflow: $50 - *How much WikiTables received in cash for the first table. They didn't receive cash for the second table (sold in credit terms).*
- Cash outflow: $50 - *How much they'd originally bought the 2 tables for.*
- Opening balance: $0
- Closing balance: $50 – $25 + $0 = $25=$0 - *Indeed, the cash flow for the month of June for WikiTables amounts to $0 and not $50.*

Important: the cash flow statement only considers the exchange of actual cash, and ignores what the person in question owes or is owed.

Statement of Profit or Loss (Income Statement or Statement of Operations)

The statement of profit or income statement reports the changes in value of a company's accounts over a set period (most commonly one fiscal year), and may compare the changes to changes in the same accounts over the previous period. All changes are summarized on the "bottom line" as net income, often reported as "net loss" when income is less than zero.

The net profit or loss is determined by:

Sales (revenue) – cost of goods sold – total expenses + total income – tax paid = profit/loss

Statement of Financial Position (Balance Sheet)

The balance sheet is the financial statement showing a firm's assets, liabilities and equity at a set point in time, usually the end of the fiscal year reported on the accompanying income statement. The total assets always equal the total combined liabilities and equity in dollar amount. The statement can be used to help show the status of a company.

Accounting standards often set out a general format that companies are expected to follow when presenting their balance sheets. International Financial Reporting Standards normally require that companies report current assets and liabilities separately from non-current amounts.

Current assets include:

- cash - physical money
- accounts receivable - revenues earned but not yet collected
- Merchandise inventory - consists of goods and services a firm currently owns until it ends up getting sold

- marketable securities - Stocks and bonds a firm has invested in other firms
- prepaid expenses - expenses paid for in advance for use during that year

Non-current assets include fixed or long-term assets and intangible assets:

- *fixed (long term) assets*
    - property
    - building
    - equipment (such as factory machinery)
- *intangible assets*
    - copyrights
    - trademarks
    - patents
    - goodwill

Liabilities include:

- *current liabilities*
    - trade accounts payable
    - dividends payable
    - employee salaries payable
    - interest (e.g. on debt) payable
- *long term liabilities*
    - mortgage notes payable
    - bonds payable

Owner's equity, sometimes referred to as net assets, is represented differently depending on the type of business ownership. Business ownership can be in the form of a sole proprietorship, partnership, or a corporation. For a corporation, the owner's equity portion usually shows common stock, and retained earnings (earnings kept in the company). Retained earnings come from the retained earnings statement, prepared prior to the balance sheet.

Basic Concepts

The Stable Measuring Unit Assumption One of the basic principles in accounting is "The Measuring Unit principle:

The unit of measure in accounting shall be the base money unit of the most relevant currency. This principle also assumes the unit of measure is stable; that is, changes in its general purchasing power are not considered sufficiently important to require adjustments to the basic financial statements."

Historical Cost Accounting, i.e., financial capital maintenance in nominal monetary units, is based on the stable measuring unit assumption under which accountants simply assume that money, the monetary unit of measure, is perfectly stable in real value for the purpose of measuring (1) monetary items not inflation-indexed daily in terms of the Daily CPI and (2) constant real value non-monetary items not updated daily in terms of the Daily CPI during low and high inflation and deflation.

Units of Constant Purchasing Power The stable monetary unit assumption is not applied during hyperinflation. IFRS requires entities to implement capital maintenance in units of constant purchasing power in terms of IAS 29 Financial Reporting in Hyperinflationary Economies.

Financial accountants produce financial statements based on the accounting standards in a given jurisdiction. These standards may be the Generally Accepted Accounting Principles of a respective country, which are typically issued by a national standard setter, or International Financial Reporting Standards (IFRS), which are issued by the International Accounting Standards Board (IASB).

Financial accounting serves the following purposes:

- producing general purpose financial statements
- producing information used by the management of a business entity for decision making, planning and performance evaluation
- producing financial statements for meeting regulatory requirements.

Objectives of Financial Accounting

- Systematic recording of transactions: basic objective of accounting is to systematically record the financial aspects of business transactions (i.e. book-keeping). These recorded transactions are later on classified and summarized logically for the preparation of financial statements and for their analysis and interpretation.
- Ascertainment of result of above recorded transactions: accountant prepares profit and loss account to know the result of business operations for a particular period of time. If expenses exceed revenue then it is said that business running under loss. The profit and loss account helps the management and different stakeholders in taking rational decisions. For example, if business is not proved to be remunerative or profitable, the cause of such a state of affair can be investigated by the management for taking remedial steps.
- Ascertainment of the financial position of business: businessman is not only interested in knowing the result of the business in terms of profits or loss for a particular period but is also anxious to know that what he owes (liability) to the outsiders and what he owns (assets) on a certain date. To know this, accountant prepares a financial position statement of assets and liabilities of the business at a particular point of time and helps in ascertaining the financial health of the business.
- Providing information to the users for rational decision-making: accounting as a 'language

of business' communicates the financial result of an enterprise to various stakeholders by means of financial statements. Accounting aims to meet the financial information needs of the decision-makers and helps them in rational decision-making.

- To know the solvency position: by preparing the balance sheet, management not only reveals what is owned and owed by the enterprise, but also it gives the information regarding concern's ability to meet its liabilities in the short run (liquidity position) and also in the long-run (solvency position) as and when they fall due.

Graphic Definition

The accounting equation (Assets = Liabilities + Owners' Equity) and financial statements are the main topics of financial accounting.

The trial balance, which is usually prepared using the double-entry accounting system, forms the basis for preparing the financial statements. All the figures in the trial balance are rearranged to prepare a profit & loss statement and balance sheet. Accounting standards determine the format for these accounts (SSAP, FRS, IFRS). Financial statements display the income and expenditure for the company and a summary of the assets, liabilities, and shareholders' or owners' equity of the company on the date to which the accounts were prepared.

Assets and expenses have normal debit balances, i.e., debiting these types of accounts increases them.

Liabilities, revenues, and capital have normal credit balances, i.e., crediting these increases them.

```
0 = Dr Assets                Cr Owners' Equity     Cr Liabilities
       .          _________________________/\_________________________.
       .    /     Cr Retained Earnings (profit)    Cr Common Stock \ .
       .    _________________/\______________________________        .
  .
       .    /     Dr Expenses      Cr Beginning Retained Earnings \ .  .
       .          Dr Dividends     Cr Revenue                        .
  .
       \_________________________/
\_______________________________________________________/
       increased by debits         increased by credits

           Crediting a credit
Thus ------------------------> account increases its absolute value
(balance)
           Debiting a debit

           Debiting a credit
Thus ------------------------> account decreases its absolute value
(balance)
           Crediting a debit
```

When the same thing is done to an account as its normal balance it increases; when the opposite is done, it will decrease. Much like signs in math: two positive numbers are added and two negative numbers are also added. It is only when there is one positive and one negative (opposites) that you will subtract.

Versus Cost Accounting

1. Financial accounting aims at finding out results of accounting year in the form of Profit and Loss Account and Balance Sheet. Cost Accounting aims at computing cost of production/ service in a scientific manner and facilitate cost control and cost reduction.
2. Financial accounting reports the results and position of business to government, creditors, investors, and external parties.
3. Cost Accounting is an internal reporting system for an organisation's own management for decision making.
4. In financial accounting, cost classification based on type of transactions, e.g. salaries, repairs, insurance, stores etc. In cost accounting, classification is basically on the basis of functions, activities, products, process and on internal planning and control and information needs of the organization.
5. Financial accounting aims at presenting 'true and fair' view of transactions, profit and loss for a period and Statement of financial position (Balance Sheet) on a given date. It aims at computing 'true and fair' view of the cost of production/services offered by the firm.

Related Qualification

Many professional accountancy qualifications cover the field of financial accountancy, including Certified Public Accountant (CPA), Chartered Accountant (CA or other national designations) and Chartered Certified Accountant (ACCA).

Management Accounting

In management accounting or managerial accounting, managers use the provisions of accounting information in order to better inform themselves before they decide matters within their organizations, which aids their management and performance of control functions.

Definition

One simple definition of management accounting is the provision of financial and non-financial decision-making information to managers.

According to the Institute of Management Accountants (IMA): *"Management accounting is a profession that involves partnering in management decision making, devising planning and performance management systems,and providing expertise in financial reporting and control to assist management in the formulation and implementation of an organization's strategy"*.

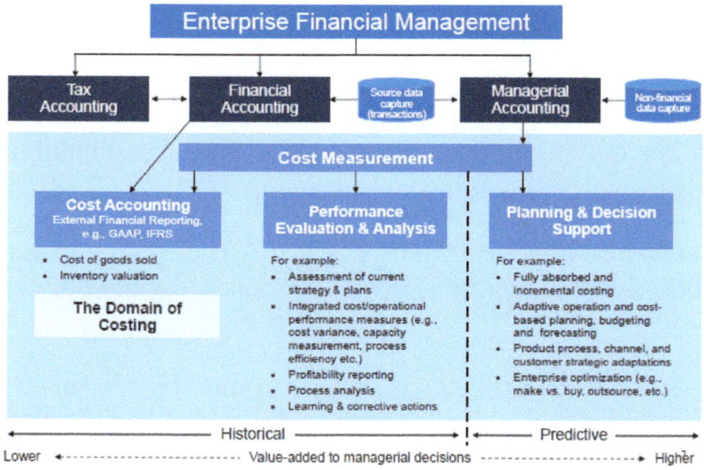

IFAC Definition of enterprise financial management concerning three broad areas: cost accounting; performance evaluation and analysis; planning and decision support. Managerial accounting is associated with higher value, more predictive information.

Scope, Practice, and Application

The American Institute of Certified Public Accountants (AICPA) states that management accounting as practice extends to the following three areas:

- Strategic management—advancing the role of the management accountant as a strategic partner in the organization.
- Performance management—developing the practice of business decision-making and managing the performance of the organization.
- Risk management—contributing to frameworks and practices for identifying, measuring, managing and reporting risks to the achievement of the objectives of the organization.

The Institute of Certified Management Accountants (CMA) states *"A management accountant applies his or her professional knowledge and skill in the preparation and presentation of financial and other decision oriented information in such a way as to assist management in the formulation of policies and in the planning and control of the operation of the undertaking"*. Management accountants therefore are seen as the "value-creators" amongst the accountants. They are more concerned with forward looking and taking decisions that will affect the future of the organization, than in the historical recording and compliance (score keeping) aspects of the profession. Management accounting knowledge and experience can therefore be obtained from varied fields and functions within an organization, such as information management, treasury, efficiency auditing, marketing, valuation, pricing and logistics. In 2014 CIMA created the Global Management Accounting Principles (GMAPs). The result of research from across 20 countries in five continents, the principles aim to guide best practice in the discipline.

Differences Between Financial Accountancy and Management Accounting

Management accounting information differs from financial accountancy information in several ways:

- while shareholders, creditors, and public regulators use publicly reported [financial accountancy] information, only managers within the organization use the normally confidential management accounting information;
- while financial accountancy information is historical, management accounting information is primarily forward-looking;
- while financial accountancy information is case-based, management accounting information is model-based with a degree of abstraction in order to support generic decision making;
- while financial accountancy information is computed by reference to general financial accounting standards, management accounting information is computed by reference to the needs of managers, often using management information systems.

Focus:

- Financial accounting focuses on the company as a whole.
- Management accounting provides detailed and disagregated information about products, individual activities, divisions, plants, operations and tasks.

Traditional Versus Innovative Practices

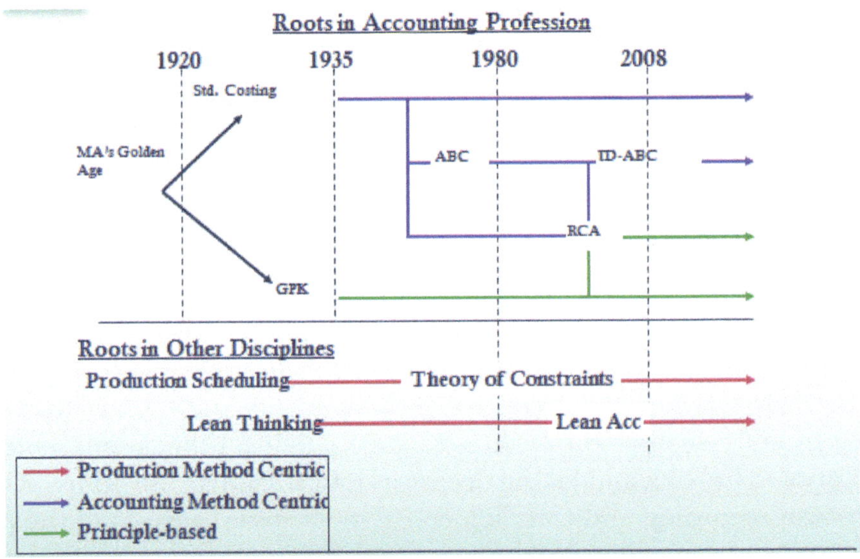

Managerial costing time line

The distinction between traditional and innovative accounting practices is perhaps best illustrated with the visual timeline of managerial costing approaches presented at the Institute of Management Accountants 2011 Annual Conference.

Traditional standard costing (TSC), used in cost accounting, dates back to the 1920s and is a central method in management accounting practiced today because it is used for financial statement reporting for the valuation of income statement and balance sheet line items such as cost of goods sold (COGS) and inventory valuation. Traditional standard costing must comply with generally accepted accounting principles (GAAP US) and actually aligns itself more with answering financial accounting requirements rather than providing solutions for management accountants. Traditional approaches limit themselves by defining cost behavior only in terms of production or sales volume.

In the late 1980s, accounting practitioners and educators were heavily criticized on the grounds that management accounting practices (and, even more so, the curriculum taught to accounting students) had changed little over the preceding 60 years, despite radical changes in the business environment. In 1993, the Accounting Education Change Commission Statement Number 4 calls for faculty members to expand their knowledge about the actual practice of accounting in the workplace. Professional accounting institutes, perhaps fearing that management accountants would increasingly be seen as superfluous in business organizations, subsequently devoted considerable resources to the development of a more innovative skills set for management accountants.

Variance analysis is a systematic approach to the comparison of the actual and budgeted costs of the raw materials and labour used during a production period. While some form of variance analysis is still used by most manufacturing firms, it nowadays tends to be used in conjunction with innovative techniques such as *life cycle cost analysis* and *activity-based costing*, which are designed with specific aspects of the modern business environment in mind. *Life-cycle costing* recognizes that managers' ability to influence the cost of manufacturing a product is at its greatest when the product is still at the design stage of its product life-cycle (i.e., before the design has been finalized and production commenced), since small changes to the product design may lead to significant savings in the cost of manufacturing the products.

Activity-based costing (ABC) recognizes that, in modern factories, most manufacturing costs are determined by the amount of 'activities' (e.g., the number of production runs per month, and the amount of production equipment idle time) and that the key to effective cost control is therefore optimizing the efficiency of these activities. Both lifecycle costing and activity-based costing recognize that, in the typical modern factory, the avoidance of disruptive events (such as machine breakdowns and quality control failures) is of far greater importance than (for example) reducing the costs of raw materials. Activity-based costing also de-emphasizes direct labor as a cost driver and concentrates instead on activities that drive costs, as the provision of a service or the production of a product component.

Other approach that can be viewed as innovative to the U.S. is the German approach, Grenzplankostenrechnung (GPK). Although it has been in practiced in Europe for more than 50 years, neither GPK nor the proper treatment of 'unused capacity' is widely practiced in the U.S. GPK and the concept of unused capacity is slowly becoming more recognized in America, and *"could easily be considered 'advanced' by U.S. standards"*.

One of the more innovative accounting practices available today is resource consumption accounting (RCA). RCA has been recognized by the International Federation of Accountants (IFAC) as a *"sophisticated approach at the upper levels of the continuum of costing techniques"* because it provides the ability to derive costs directly from operational resource data or to isolate and measure unused capacity costs. RCA was derived by taking the best costing characteristics of the German management accounting approach Grenzplankostenrechnung (GPK), and combining the use of activity-based drivers when needed, such as those used in activity-based costing. With the RCA approach, resources and their costs are considered as *"foundational to robust cost modeling and managerial decision support, because an organization's costs and revenues are all a function of the resources and the individual capacities that produce them"*.

A modern approach to close accounting is Continuous Accounting, which focuses on achieving a point-in-time close, where accounting processes typically performed at period-end are distributed evenly throughout the period.

Role Within a Corporation

Consistent with other roles in modern corporations, management accountants have a dual reporting relationship. As a strategic partner and provider of decision based financial and operational information, management accountants are responsible for managing the business team and at the same time having to report relationships and responsibilities to the corporation's finance organization and finance of an organization.

The activities management accountants provide inclusive of forecasting and planning, performing variance analysis, reviewing and monitoring costs inherent in the business are ones that have dual accountability to both finance and the business team. Examples of tasks where accountability may be more meaningful to the business management team vs. the corporate finance department are the development of new product costing, operations research, business driver metrics, sales management scorecarding, and client profitability analysis. Conversely, the preparation of certain financial reports, reconciliations of the financial data to source systems, risk and regulatory reporting will be more useful to the corporate finance team as they are charged with aggregating certain financial information from all segments of the corporation.

In corporations that derive much of their profits from the information economy, such as banks, publishing houses, telecommunications companies and defence contractors, IT costs are a significant source of uncontrollable spending, which in size is often the greatest corporate cost after total compensation costs and property related costs. A function of management accounting in such organizations is to work closely with the IT department to provide IT cost transparency.

Given the above, one view of the progression of the accounting and finance career path is that financial accounting is a stepping stone to management accounting. Consistent with the notion of value creation, management accountants help drive the success of the business while strict financial accounting is more of a compliance and historical endeavor.

Specific Methodologies

Activity-based Costing (ABC)

Activity-based costing was first clearly defined in 1987 by Robert S. Kaplan and W. Bruns as a chapter in their book Accounting and Management: A Field Study Perspective. They initially focused on the manufacturing industry, where increasing technology and productivity improvements have reduced the relative proportion of the direct costs of labor and materials, but have increased relative proportion of indirect costs. For example, increased automation has reduced labor, which is a direct cost, but has increased depreciation, which is an indirect cost.

Grenzplankostenrechnung (GPK)

Grenzplankostenrechnung is a German costing methodology, developed in the late 1940s and 1960s, designed to provide a consistent and accurate application of how managerial costs are calculated and assigned to a product or service. The term Grenzplankostenrechnung, often referred to as GPK, has best been translated as either *marginal planned cost accounting* or *flexible analytic cost planning and accounting*.

The origins of GPK are credited to Hans Georg Plaut, an automotive engineer, and Wolfgang Kilger, an academic, working towards the mutual goal of identifying and delivering a sustained methodology designed to correct and enhance cost accounting information. GPK is published in cost accounting textbooks, notably *Flexible Plankostenrechnung und Deckungsbeitragsrechnung* and taught at German-speaking universities.

Lean Accounting (Accounting for Lean Enterprise)

In the mid- to late-1990s several books were written about accounting in the lean enterprise (companies implementing elements of the Toyota Production System). The term *lean accounting* was coined during that period. These books contest that traditional accounting methods are better suited for mass production and do not support or measure good business practices in just-in-time manufacturing and services. The movement reached a tipping point during the 2005 Lean Accounting Summit in Dearborn, Michigan, United States. 320 individuals attended and discussed the advantages of a new approach to accounting in the lean enterprise. 520 individuals attended the 2nd annual conference in 2006 and it has varied between 250 and 600 attendees since that time.

Resource Consumption Accounting (RCA)

Resource consumption accounting (RCA) is formally defined as a dynamic, fully integrated, principle-based, and comprehensive management accounting approach that provides managers with decision support information for enterprise optimization. RCA emerged as a management accounting approach around 2000 and was subsequently developed at CAM-I the Consortium for Advanced Manufacturing–International, in a Cost Management Section *RCA interest group* in December 2001.

Throughput Accounting

The most significant recent direction in managerial accounting is throughput accounting; which recognizes the interdependencies of modern production processes. For any given product, customer or supplier, it is a tool to measure the contribution per unit of constrained resource.

Transfer Pricing

Management accounting is an applied discipline used in various industries. The specific functions and principles followed can vary based on the industry. Management accounting principles in banking are specialized but do have some common fundamental concepts used whether the industry is manufacturing-based or service-oriented. For example, transfer pricing is a concept used in manufacturing but is also applied in banking. It is a fundamental principle used in assigning value and revenue attribution to the various business units. Essentially, transfer pricing in banking is the method of assigning the interest rate risk of the bank to the various funding sources and uses of the enterprise. Thus, the bank's corporate treasury department will assign funding charges to the business units for their use of the bank's resources when they make loans to clients. The treasury department will also assign funding credit to business units who bring in deposits (resources) to the bank. Although the funds transfer pricing process is primarily applicable to the loans and deposits of the various banking units, this proactive is applied to all assets and liabilities of the business segment. Once transfer pricing is applied and any other management accounting entries or adjustments are posted to the ledger (which are usually memo accounts and are not included in the legal entity results), the business units are able to produce segment financial results which are used by both internal and external users to evaluate performance.

Resources and Continuous Learning

There are a variety of ways to keep current and continue to build one's knowledge base in the field of management accounting. Certified Management Accountants (CMAs) are required to achieve continuing education hours every year, similar to a Certified Public Accountant. A company may also have research and training materials available for use in a corporate owned library. This is more common in "Fortune 500" companies who have the resources to fund this type of training medium.

There are also journals, online articles and blogs available. The journal *Cost Management* (ISSN 1092-8057) and the Institute of Management Accounting (IMA) site are sources which includes Management Accounting Quarterly and *Strategic Finance* publications.

Tasks and Services Provided

Listed below are the primary tasks/services performed by management accountants. The degree of complexity relative to these activities are dependent on the experience level and abilities of any one individual.

- Rate and volume analysis
- Business metrics development
- Price modeling
- Product profitability
- Geographic vs. industry or client segment reporting
- Sales management scorecards
- Cost analysis
- Cost–benefit analysis
- Cost-volume-profit analysis

- Life cycle cost analysis
- Client profitability analysis
- IT cost transparency
- Capital budgeting
- Buy vs. lease analysis
- Strategic planning
- Strategic management advice
- Internal financial presentation and communication
- Sales forecasting
- Financial forecasting
- Annual budgeting
- Cost allocation

Related Qualifications

There are several related professional qualifications and certifications in the field of accountancy including:

- Management Accountancy Qualifications
    - CIMA
    - ICMA
    - ICAI
    - CMA
- Other Professional Accountancy Qualifications
    - Chartered Institute of Public Finance and Accountancy, CIPFA
    - Chartered Certified Accountant, (ACCA)
    - Chartered Accountant, (CA)
    - Certified Public Accountant, (CPA)
        - American Institute of Certified Public Accountants
    - Certified Practicing Accountant (CPA Australia)
    - Chartered Global Management Accountant

Methods

- Activity-based costing
- Grenzplankostenrechnung (GPK)
- Lean accounting
- Resource Consumption Accounting
- Standard cost accounting
- Throughput accounting
- Transfer pricing

Objectives and Advantages

Objectives

The main objectives of Cost Accounting are as follows:

1. Ascertainment of cost.
2. Cost control and cost reduction.
3. Assisting management in decision-making including pricing, profit planning, budgeting.

Advantages

1. Helps in identifying unprofitable activities, losses or inefficiencies in any form.
2. Application of cost reduction techniques, operation research techniques and value analysis technique.

Accounting Ethics

"Accountants and the accountancy profession exist as a means of public service; the distinction which separates a profession from a mere means of livelihood is that the profession is accountable to standards of the public interest, and beyond the compensation paid by clients."

—Robert H. Montgomery, describing ethics in accounting in 2009

Accounting ethics is primarily a field of applied ethics and is part of business ethics and human ethics, the study of moral values and judgments as they apply to accountancy. It is an example of professional ethics. Accounting introduced by Luca Pacioli, and later expanded by government groups, professional organizations, and independent companies. Ethics are taught in accounting courses at higher education institutions as well as by companies training accountants and auditors.

Due to the diverse range of accounting services and recent corporate collapses, attention has been drawn to ethical standards accepted within the accounting profession. These collapses have resulted in a widespread disregard for the reputation of the accounting profession. To combat the criticism and prevent fraudulent accounting, various accounting organizations and governments have developed regulations and remedies for improved ethics among the accounting profession.

Importance of Ethics

The nature of the work carried out by accountants and auditors requires a high level of ethics. Shareholders, potential shareholders, and other users of the financial statements rely heavily on the yearly financial statements of a company as they can use this information to make an informed decision about investment. They rely on the opinion of the accountants who prepared the statements, as well as the auditors that verified it, to present a true and fair view of the company. Knowledge of ethics can help accountants and auditors to overcome ethical dilemmas, allowing for the right choice that, although it may not benefit the company, will benefit the public who relies on the accountant/auditor's reporting.

Most countries have differing focuses on enforcing accounting laws. In Germany, accounting legislation is governed by "tax law"; in Sweden, by "accounting law"; and in the United Kingdom, by the "company law". In addition, countries have their own organizations which regulate accounting. For example, Sweden has the Bokföringsnämden (BFN - Accounting Standards Board), Spain the Instituto de Comtabilidad y Auditoria de Cuentas (ICAC), and the United States the Financial Accounting Standards Board (FASB).

History

Luca Pacioli, here in a 1495 portrait by an unknown Renaissance artist, wrote on accounting ethics in 1494.

Luca Pacioli, the "Father of Accounting", wrote on accounting ethics in his first book *Summa de arithmetica, geometria, proportioni, et proportionalita*, published in 1494. Ethical standards have since then been developed through government groups, professional organizations, and independent companies. These various groups have led accountants to follow several codes of ethics to perform their duties in a professional work environment. Accountants must follow the code of ethics set out by the professional body of which they are a member. United States accounting societies such as the Association of Government Accountants, Institute of Internal Auditors, and the National Association of Accountants all have codes of ethics, and many accountants are members of one or more of these societies.

In 1887, the American Association of Public Accountants (AAPA) was created; it was the first step in developing professionalism in the United States accounting industry. By 1905, the AAPA's first ethical codes were formulated to educate its members. During its twentieth anniversary meeting in October 1907, ethics was a major topic of the conference among its members. As a result of discussions, a list of professional ethics was incorporated into the organization's bylaws. However, because membership to the organization was voluntary, the association could not require individuals to conform to the suggested behaviors. Other accounting organizations, such as the Illinois Institute of Accountants, also pursued discussion on the importance of ethics for the field. The AAPA was renamed several times throughout its history, before becoming the American Institute of Certified Public Accountants (AICPA) as it's named today. The AICPA developed five divisions of ethical principles that its members should follow: "independence, integrity, and objectivity"; "competence and technical standards"; "responsibilities to clients"; "responsibilities to colleagues"; as well as "other responsibilities and practices". Each of these divisions provided guidelines on how a Certified Public Accountant (CPA) should act as a professional. Failure to comply with the guidelines could have caused an accountant to be barred from practicing. When developing the ethical principles, the AICPA also considered how the profession would be viewed by those outside of the accounting industry.

Teaching Ethics

Courses on this subject have grown significantly in the last couple of decades. Teaching accountants about ethics can involve role playing, lectures, case studies, guest lectures, as well as other mediums. Recent studies indicate that nearly all accounting textbooks touch on ethics in some way. In 1993, the first United States center that focused on the study of ethics in the accounting profession opened at Binghamton University. Starting in 1999, several U.S. states began requiring ethics classes prior to taking the CPA exam.

Seven Goals of Accounting Ethics Education

- Relate accounting education to moral issues.
- Recognize issues in accounting that have ethical implications.
- Develop "a sense of moral obligation" or responsibility.
- Develop the abilities needed to deal with ethical conflicts or dilemmas.
- Learn to deal with the uncertainties of the accounting profession.
- "Set the stage for" a change in ethical behavior.
- Appreciate and understand the history and composition of all aspects of accounting ethics and their relationship to the general field of ethics. —Stephen E. Loeb

In 1988, Stephen E. Loeb proposed that accounting ethics education should include seven goals (adapted from a list by Daniel Callahan). To implement these goals, he pointed out that accounting ethics could be taught throughout accounting curriculum or in an individual class tailored to the subject. Requiring it be taught throughout the curriculum would necessitate all accounting teachers to have knowledge on the subject (which may require training). A single course has issues as to where to include the course in a student's education (for example, before preliminary accounting classes or near the end of a student's degree requirements), whether there is enough material to cover in a semester class, and whether most universities have room in a four-year curriculum for a single class on the subject.

There has been debate on whether ethics should be taught in a university setting. Supporters point out that ethics are important to the profession, and should be taught to accountants entering the field. In addition, the education would help to reinforce students' ethical values and inspire them to prevent others from making unethical decisions. Critics argue that an individual is ethical or not, and that teaching an ethics course would serve no purpose. Despite opposition, instruction on accounting ethics by universities and conferences, has been encouraged by professional organizations and accounting firms. The Accounting Education Change Commission (AECC) has called for students to "know and understand the ethics of the profession and be able to make value-based judgments."

Phillip G. Cottel argued that in order to uphold strong ethics, an accountant "must have a strong sense of values, the ability to reflect on a situation to determine the ethical implications, and a commitment to the well-being of others." Iris Stuart recommends an ethics model consisting of four steps: the accountant must recognize that an ethical dilemma is occurring; identify the parties that would be interested in the outcome of the dilemma; determine alternatives and evaluate its effect on each alternative on the interested parties; and then select the best alternative.

Accounting Scandals

Accounting ethics has been deemed difficult to control as accountants and auditors must consider the interest of the public (which relies on the information gathered in audits) while ensuring that they remained employed by the company they are auditing. They must consider how to best apply accounting standards even when faced with issues that could cause a company to face a significant loss or even be discontinued. Due to several accounting scandals within the profession, critics of accountants have stated that when asked by a client "what does two plus two equal?" the accountant would be likely to respond "what would you like it to be?". This thought process along with other criticisms of the profession's issues with conflict of interest, have led to various increased standards of professionalism while stressing ethics in the work environment.

The role of accountants is critical to society. Accountants serve as financial reporters and intermediaries in the capital markets and owe their primary obligation to the public interest. The information they provide is crucial in aiding managers, investors and others in making critical economic decisions. Accordingly, ethical improprieties by accountants can be detrimental to society, resulting in distrust by the public and disruption of efficient capital market operations.

"Every company in the country is fiddling its profits. Every set of published accounts is based on books which have been gently cooked or completely roasted. The figures which are fed twice a year to the investing public have all been changed in order to protect the guilty. It is the biggest con trick since the Trojan horse. In fact this deception is all in perfectly good taste. It is totally legitimate. It is creative accounting."

—Ian Griffiths in 1986, describing creative accounting

From the 1980s to the present there have been multiple accounting scandals that were widely reported on by the media and resulted in fraud charges, bankruptcy protection requests, and the closure of companies and accounting firms. The scandals were the result of creative accounting, misleading financial analysis, as well as bribery. Various companies had issues with fraudulent accounting practices, including Nugan Hand Bank, Phar-Mor, WorldCom, and AIG. One of the most widely reported violation of accounting ethics involved Enron, a multinational company, that for several years had not shown a true or fair view of their financial statements. Their auditor Arthur Andersen, an accounting firm considered one of the "Big Five", signed off on the validity of the accounts despite the inaccuracies in the financial statements. When the unethical activities were reported, not only did Enron dissolve but Arthur Andersen also went out of business. Enron's shareholders lost $25 billion as a result of the company's bankruptcy. Although only a fraction of Arthur Anderson's employees were involved with the scandal, the closure of the firm resulted in the loss of 85,000 jobs.

Causes

Fraudulent accounting can arise from a variety of issues. These problems usually come to light eventually and could ruin not only the company but also the auditors for not discovering or revealing the misstatements. Several studies have proposed that a firm's corporate culture as well as the values it stresses may negatively alter an accountant's behavior. This environment could contribute to the degradation of ethical values that were learned from universities.

Until 1977, ethics rules prevented accounting and auditing firms from advertising to clients. When the rules were lifted, spending by the largest CPA firms on advertisements rose from US$4 million in the 1980s to more than $100 million in the 2000s. Critics claimed that, by allowing the firms to advertise, the business side overstepped the professional side of the profession, which led to a conflict of interest. This focus allowed for occurrences of fraud, and caused the firms, according to Arthur Bowman, "... to offer services that made them more consultants and business advisers than auditors." As accounting firms became less interested in the lower-paying audits due to more focus on higher earning services such as consulting, problems arose. This disregard for the lack of time spent on audits resulted in a lack of attention to catching creative and fraudulent accounting.

A 2007 article in *Managerial Auditing Journal* determined the top nine factors that contributed to ethical failures for accountants based on a survey of 66 members of the International Federation of Accountants. The factors include (in order of most significant): "self-interest, failure to maintain objectivity and independence, inappropriate professional judgment, lack of ethical sensitivity, improper leadership and ill-culture, failure to withstand advocacy threats, lack of competence, lack of organizational and peer support, and lack of professional body support." The main factor, self-interest, is the motivation by an accountant to act in his/her best interest or when facing a conflict of interest. For example, if an auditor has an issue with an account he/she is auditing, but is receiving financial incentives to ignore these issues, the auditor may act unethically.

Principles and Rules

"When people need a doctor, or a lawyer, or a certified public accountant, they seek someone whom they can trust to do a good job — not for himself, but for them. They have to trust him, since they cannot appraise the quality of his 'product'. To trust him they must believe that he is competent, and that his primary motive is to help them."

—John L. Carey, describing ethics in accounting

The International Financial Reporting Standards (IFRS) are standards and interpretations developed by the International Accounting Standards Board, which are principle-based. IFRS are used by over 115 countries or areas including the European Union, Australia, and Hong Kong. The United States Generally Accepted Accounting Principles (GAAP), the standard framework of guidelines for financial accounting, is largely rule-based. Critics have stated that the rules-based GAAP is partly responsible for the number of scandals that the United States has suffered. The principles-based approach to monitoring requires more professional judgment than the rules-based approach.

There are many stakeholders in many countries such as The United States who report several concerns in the usage of rules-based accounting. According to recent studies, many believe that the principles-based approach in financial reporting would not only improve but would also support an auditor upon dealing with client's pressure. As a result, financial reports could be viewed with fairness and transparency. When the U.S. switched to International accounting standards, they are composed that this would bring change. However, as a new chairperson of the SEC takes over the system, the transition brings a stronger review about the pros and cons of rules- based accounting. While the move towards international standards progresses, there are small amount of research that examines the effect of principle- based standards in an auditor's decision- making process. According to 114 auditing experts, most are willing to allow clients to manage their net income based on rules- based standards. These results offers insight to the SEC, IASB and FASB in weighing the arguments in the debate of principles- vs. rules based- accounting.

IFRS is based on "understandability, relevance, materiality, reliability, and comparability". Since IFRS has not been adopted by all countries, these practices do not make the international standards viable in the world domain. In particular, the United States has not yet conformed and still uses GAAP which makes comparing principles and rules difficult. In August 2008, the Securities and Exchange Commission (SEC) proposed that the United States switch from GAAP to IFRS, starting in 2014.

Responses to Scandals

Since the major accounting scandals, new reforms, regulations, and calls for increased higher education have been introduced to combat the dangers of unethical behavior. By educating accountants on ethics before entering the workforce, such as through higher education or initial training at companies, it is believed it will help to improve the credibility of the accounting profession. Companies and accounting organizations have expanded their assistance with educators by providing education materials to assist professors in educating students.

New regulations in response to the scandals include the Corporate Law Economic Reform Program Act 2004 in Australia as well as the Sarbanes-Oxley Act of 2002, developed by the United States. Sarbanes-Oxley limits the level of work which can be carried out by accounting firms. In addition, the Act put a limit on the fee which a firm can receive from one client as a percentage of their total fees. This ensures that companies are not wholly reliant on one firm for its income, in the hope that they do not need to act unethically to keep a steady income. The act also protects whistleblowers and requires senior management in public companies to sign off on the accuracy of its company's accounting records. In 2002, the five members of the Public Oversight Board (POB), which oversaw ethics within the accounting profession, resigned after critics deemed the board ineffective and the SEC proposed developing a new panel, the Public Company Accounting Oversight Board (PCAOB). The PCAOB was developed through the Act, and replaced the POB.

In 2003, the International Federation of Accountants (IFAC) released a report entitled *Rebuilding Public Confidence in Financial Reporting: An International Perspective*. By studying the international company collapses as a result of accounting issues, it determined areas for improvement within organizations as well as recommendations for companies to develop more effective ethics codes. The report also recommended that companies pursue options that would improve training and support so accountants could better handle ethical dilemmas. A collaborative effort by members of the international financial regulatory community led by Michel Prada, Chairman of the French Financial Markets Authority, resulting in establishment of the Public Interest Oversight Board (PIOB) on 1 March 2005. The PIOB provides oversight of the IFAC standards-setting boards: the International Auditing and Assurance Standards Board (IAASB), the International Accounting Education Standards Board (IAESB) and the International Ethics Standards Board for Accountants (IESBA).

The most recent reform came into effect in July 2010 when President Obama signed "The Dodd-Frank Wall Street Reform and Consumer Protection Act". The act covers a broad range of changes. The highlights of the legislation are consumer protections with authority and independence, ends too big to fail bail outs, advance warning system, transparency and accountability for exotic instruments, executive compensation and corporate governance, protects investors, and enforces regulations on the books. The legislation also resulted in the Office of the Whistleblower, which was established to administer the SEC's whistleblower program. Congress authorized the SEC to provide monetary awards to whistleblowers who come forward with information that results in a minimum of a $1,000,000 sanction. The rewards are between 10% and 30% of the dollar amount collected. Whistleblowers help identify fraud and other unethical behaviors early on. The result is less harm to investors, quickly holding offenders responsible, and to maintain the integrity of the U.S. markets.

Cost

In production, research, retail, and accounting, a cost is the value of money that has been used up to produce something, and hence is not available for use anymore. In business, the cost may be one of acquisition, in which case the amount of money expended to acquire it is counted as cost. In this case, money is the input that is gone in order to acquire the thing. This acquisition cost may be the sum of the cost of production as incurred by the original producer, and further costs of transaction as incurred by the acquirer over and above the price paid to the producer. Usually, the price also includes a mark-up for profit over the cost of production.

More generalized in the field of economics, cost is a metric that is totaling up as a result of a process or as a differential for the result of a decision. Hence cost is the metric used in the standard modeling paradigm applied to economic processes.

Costs (pl.) are often further described based on their timing or their applicability.

Types of Accounting Costs

In accounting, costs are the monetary value of expenditures for supplies, services, labor, products, equipment and other items purchased for use by a business or other accounting entity. It is the amount denoted on invoices as the price and recorded in bookkeeping records as an expense or asset cost basis.

Opportunity cost, also referred to as *economic cost* is the value of the best alternative that was not chosen in order to pursue the current endeavor—i.e., what could have been accomplished with the resources expended in the undertaking. It represents opportunities forgone.

In theoretical economics, cost used without qualification often means opportunity cost.

Comparing Private, External, and Social Costs

When a transaction takes place, it typically involves both private costs and external costs.

Private costs are the costs that the buyer of a good or service pays the seller. This can also be described as the costs internal to the firm's production function.

External costs (also called externalities), in contrast, are the costs that people other than the buyer are forced to pay as a result of the transaction. The bearers of such costs can be either particular individuals or society at large. Note that external costs are often both non-monetary and problematic to quantify for comparison with monetary values. They include things like pollution, things that society will likely have to pay for in some way or at some time in the future, but that are not included in transaction prices.

Social costs are the sum of private costs and external costs.

For example, the manufacturing cost of a car (i.e., the costs of buying inputs, land tax rates for the car plant, overhead costs of running the plant and labor costs) reflects the *private cost* for the manufacturer (in some ways, normal profit can also be seen as a cost of production; see, e.g., Ison and Wall, 2007, p. 181). The polluted waters or polluted air also created as part of the process of producing the car is an *external cost* borne by those who are affected by the pollution or who value unpolluted air or water. Because the manufacturer does not pay for this external cost (the cost of emitting undesirable waste into the commons), and does not include this cost in the price of the car (a Kaldor-Hicks compensation), they are said to be external to the market pricing mechanism. The air pollution from driving the car is also an externality produced by the car user in the process of using his good. The driver does not compensate for the environmental damage caused by using the car.

Cost Estimation

When developing a business plan for a new or existing company, product, or project, planners typically make cost estimates in order to assess whether revenues/benefits will cover costs. This is done in both business and government. Costs are often underestimated, resulting in cost overrun during execution.

Cost-plus pricing, is where the price equals cost plus a percentage of overhead or profit margin.

Manufacturing Costs vs. Non-manufacturing Costs

Manufacturing costs are those costs that are directly involved in manufacturing of products. Examples of manufacturing costs include raw materials costs and charges related to workers. Manufacturing cost is divided into three broad categories:

1. Direct materials cost.
2. Direct labor cost.
3. Manufacturing overhead cost.

Non-manufacturing costs are those costs that are not directly incurred in manufacturing a product. Examples of such costs are salary of sales personnel and advertising expenses. Generally non-manufacturing costs are further classified into two categories:

1. Selling and distribution costs.
2. Administrative costs.

Other Costs

A defensive cost is an environmental expenditure to eliminate or prevent environmental damage. Defensive costs form part of the genuine progress indicator (GPI) calculations.

Labour costs would include travel time, holiday pay, training costs, working clothes, social insurance, taxes on employment &c.

Path cost is a term in networking to define the worthiness of a path.

Cost Estimate

A cost estimate is the approximation of the cost of a program, project, or operation. The cost estimate is the product of the cost estimating process. The cost estimate has a single total value and may have identifiable component values. A problem with a cost overrun can be avoided with a credible, reliable, and accurate cost estimate. A cost estimator is the professional who prepares cost estimates. There are different types of cost estimators, whose title may be preceded by a modifier, such as building estimator, or electrical estimator, or chief estimator. Other professional titles may also prepare cost estimates or contribute to cost estimates, such as quantity surveyors, cost engineers, etc. In the US, there were 185,400 cost estimators in 2010. There are around 75,000 professional quantity surveyors working in the UK.

Overview

The U.S. Government Accountability Office (GAO) defines a cost estimate as, "the summation of individual cost elements, using established methods and valid data, to estimate the future costs of a program, based on what is known today." The GAO reports that "realistic cost estimating was imperative when making wise decisions in acquiring new systems." A cost estimate is often needed to support evaluations of project feasibility or funding requirements in support of planning. A cost estimate is often used to establish a budget as the cost constraint for a project or operation.

In project management, project cost management is a major functional division. Cost estimating is one of three activities performed in project cost management.

In cost engineering, cost estimation is a basic activity. A cost engineering reference book has chapters on capital investment cost estimation and operating cost estimation. The fixed capital investment provides the physical facilities. The working capital investment is a revolving fund to keep the facilities operating.

In system, product, or facility acquisition planning, a cost estimate is used to evaluate the required funding and to compare with bids or tenders.

In construction contracting, a cost estimate is usually prepared to submit a bid or tender to compete for a contract award.

In facility maintenance and operation, cost estimates are used to establish funding or budgets.

In an attempt to manage liability risk, some firms avoid the use of the word estimate and instead refer to the estimate as an "Opinion of Probable Cost."

Cost Estimate Types

Various projects and operations have distinct types of cost estimating, which vary in their composition and preparation methods. Some of the major areas include:

- Construction cost (i) detailed construction estimate (ii) abstract construction estimate
- Manufacturing cost
- Software development cost
- Aerospace mission cost
- Resource exploration cost
- Facility operation cost
- Facility maintenance and repair cost
- Facility rehabilitation and renewal cost
- Facility retirement cost

Cost Estimate Classifications

Common cost estimate classifications historically used are

- Order of magnitude
- Detailed estimate
- Preliminary
- Definitive

These correspond to modern published classes 5, 3, and 1, respectively. The U.S. Department of Energy and many others use a system of five classes of estimates:

Estimate class	Name	Purpose	Project definition level
Class 5	Order of magnitude	Screening or feasibility	0% to 2%
Class 4	Intermediate	Concept study or feasibility	1% to 15%
Class 3	Preliminary	Budget, authorization, or control	10% to 40%
Class 2	Substantive	Control or bid/tender	30% to 70%
Class 1	Definitive	Check estimate or bid/tender	50% to 100%

Methods used to prepare the estimates range from stochastic or judgment at early definition to deterministic at later definition. Some estimates use mixed methods.

Cost estimate classifications have been published by ASTM and AACE International. The American Society of Professional Estimators (ASPE) defines estimate levels in the reverse order as Level 1 – Order (Range) of Magnitude, Level 2 – Schematic/Conceptual Design, Level 3- Design Development, Level 4 – Construction Document, and Level 5 – Bid.>." ACostE defines a Class I Estimate as definitive, a Class II Estimate as semi-detailed, and a Class III Estimate as pre-budget.

Other names for estimates of different classes include:

Class 1	**Class 3**	**Class 5**
Detailed estimate	Semi-detailed estimate	Conceptual estimate
Final estimate	Scope estimate	Pre-design estimate
Control estimate	Sanction estimate	Preliminary estimate
As-bid estimate		Pre-budget estimate
As-sold estimate		Evaluation estimate
CD estimate	DD estimate	SD estimate
		Parametric estimate
		Rough order-of-magnitude (ROM) estimate
		Very rough order-of-magnitude (VROM) estimate
		SWAG (scientific, wild-ass guess) estimate
		PIDOOMA (pulled-it-directly-out-of-my-ass) estimate

Estimate Quality

Estimate quality refers to the delineation of quality requirements for the estimate. These requirements are set out in accordance with formal quality assurance standards. There may also be other expectations for the estimate which are not specific requirements, but may affect the perceived quality of the estimate. Published quality requirements generally have to do with credibility, accuracy, confidence level, precision, risk, reliability, and validity of the estimate, as well as thoroughness, uniformity, consistency, verification, and documentation.

"The result of bidding without good estimates is certain: jobs that end up with less profit, no profit, or a loss. The bidder ultimately will go out of business; the only question is how long will it take."

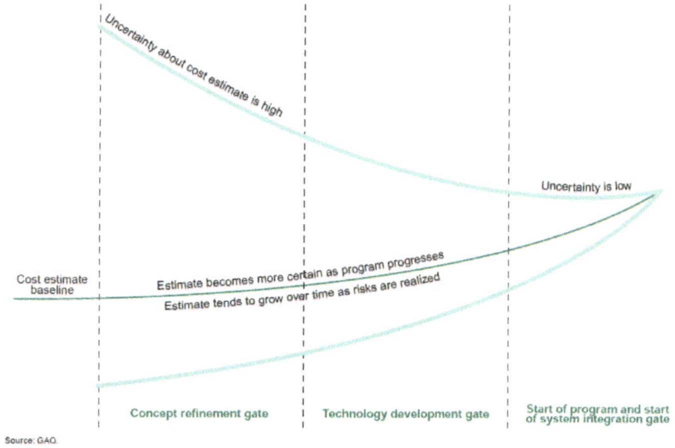

Since a cost estimate is the approximation of the cost of a project or operation, then estimate accuracy is a measure of how closely the estimate is able to predict the actual expenditures for the project or operation. This can only be known after the project is completed. If, for example, a project estimate was $1,252,000 for a specific scope and conditions, and at completion the records showed that $1,172,451.26 was expended, the estimate was 6.8% too high. If the project ended up having a different scope or conditions, an unadjusted computation does not fairly assess the estimate accuracy. Predictions of the estimate accuracy may accompany the estimate. Typically this is expressed as a range higher or lower as compared with the point estimate with an expected probability that the actual cost will fall in the range. An example for a definitive estimate might be that the estimate has a -5/+10% range of accuracy with a 90% confidence that the final value will fall in that range. The accuracy of an early estimate relates to the estimate quality. Factors affecting the quality of the estimate include the people who prepared the estimate, how the estimate was prepared, and what was known about the project. For the same project, the range of uncertainty about the total estimate decreases over time, as illustrated in the cone of uncertainty diagram.

High-quality cost estimates can be produced by following a rigor of 12 steps outlined by the U.S. GAO. Detailed documentation is recommended to accompany the estimate. "The documentation addresses the purpose of the estimate, the program background and system description, its schedule, the scope of the estimate (in terms of time and what is and is not included), the ground rules and assumptions, all data sources, estimating methodology and rationale, the results of the risk analysis, and a conclusion about whether the cost estimate is reasonable. Therefore, a good cost estimate—while taking the form of a single number—is supported by detailed documentation that describes how it was derived and how the expected funding will be spent in order to achieve a given objective." This documentation is often titled Basis of Estimate (or BOE). Additional documentation may accompany the estimate, including quantity takeoff documentation and supporting calculations, quotes, etc.

Although the pursuit of cost estimate accuracy should always be encouraged, a study in 2002 found that the estimates used to determine whether important infrastructure should be built were "highly and systematically misleading."

Contingency

A contingency may be included in an estimate to provide for unknown costs which are indicated as likely to occur by experience, but are not identifiable. When using an estimate which has no contingency to set a budget or to set aside funding, a contingency is often added to improve the probability that the budget or funding will be adequate to complete the project. Being unable to complete a project risks public ridicule. The estimate or budget contingency is not intended to compensate for poor estimate quality, and is not intended to fund design growth, owner changes, or anything else unrelated to delivering the scope as defined in the estimate documentation. Generally more contingency is needed for earlier estimates due to the higher uncertainty of estimate accuracy.

Cost Estimating Methods and Best Practices

Estimating methods may vary by type and class of estimate. The method used for most definitive estimates is to fully define and understand the scope, take off or quantify the scope, and apply costing to the scope, which can then be summed to a total cost. Proper documentation and review are also important. Pricing transforms the cost estimate into what the firm wishes to charge for the scope. Early estimates may employ various means of cost modeling. The basic characteristics of effective estimating include: clear identification of task, broad participation in preparing estimates, availability of valid data, standardized structure for the estimate, provision for program uncertainties, recognition of inflation, recognition of excluded costs, independent review of estimates, and revision of estimates for significant program changes. Application of best practices helps ensure a high-quality estimate. "Certain best practices should be followed if accurate and credible cost estimates are to be developed. These best practices represent an overall process of established, repeatable methods that result in high-quality cost estimates that are comprehensive and accurate and that can be easily and clearly traced, replicated, and updated."

Tools that may be part of costs estimation are cost indexes. These factors promote time adjustment of capital costs, following changes in technology, availability of materials and labor, and inflation. Due to the inherent unavailability of up-to-date cost literature, several inflation or cost indexes are available.

Construction Cost Estimates

Estimates for the cost of facility construction are a major part of the cost estimate domain. A construction general contractor or subcontractor must normally prepare definitive cost estimates to prepare bids in the construction bidding process to compete for award of the contract. Although many estimators participate in the bidding and procurement processes, those are not a necessary function of cost estimate preparation. Earlier estimates are prepared by differing methods by estimators and others to support the planning process and to compare with bids. One way to make those estimates is by determining the resources needed (e.g., the amount of construction material quantities that are required) and then multiplying the estimated construction material quantities by the corresponding unit cost. One advantage of making estimates in this way is that it allows for the segregation of quantities and costs. This way they can be updated separately as new information becomes available. They can also be tracked separately allowing decision makers to make better decisions about the project during its conceptual phase.

Definitive Estimates (Class 1)

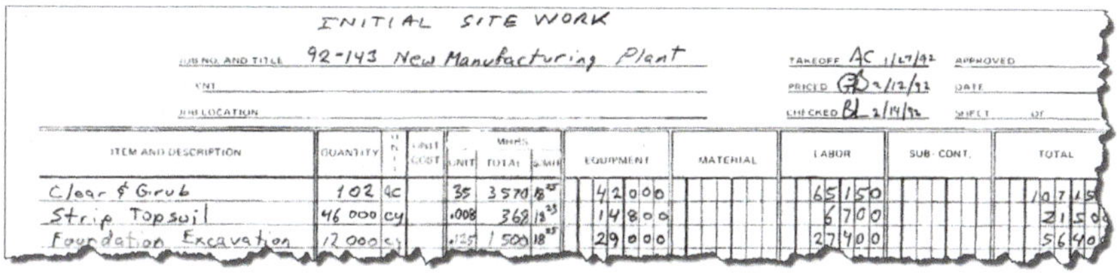

INITIAL SITE WORK

JOB NO. AND TITLE 92-143 New Manufacturing Plant

TAKEOFF AC 1/27/92 — APPROVED

PRICED 2/12/92 — DATE

CHECKED BL 2/14/92 — SHEET OF

ITEM AND DESCRIPTION	QUANTITY	UNIT	UNIT COST	MHRS UNIT	MHRS TOTAL	$/MH	EQUIPMENT	MATERIAL	LABOR	SUB-CONT.	TOTAL
Clear & Grub	102	ac		35	3570	18.25	42 000		65 150		107 15
Strip Topsoil	46 000	cy		.008	368	18.25	14 800		6 700		21 50
Foundation Excavation	12 000	cy		.125	1 500	18.25	29 000		27 400		56 40

A handwritten spreadsheet.

A definitive estimate is prepared from fully designed plans and specifications (or nearly so), preferably what are called contract documents (CD). The contract documents also establish the Scope of Work (SOW). The standard method is to review and understand the design package and take off (or perform a quantity survey of) the project scope by itemizing it into line items with measured quantities. RSMeans refers to this as, "Scope out the project," and, "Quantify." Some jurisdictions or areas of practice define the itemization and measuration in certain terms, such as RICS and may have specific rules for development of a Bill of quantities, or BOQ. The ASPE proposes a best practice standard method for the quantity survey. This includes using the Construction Specifications Institute Uniform Numbering System (MasterFormat) to ensure that all work is accounted for.

Then costs are applied to the quantified line items. This may be called costing or pricing. In estimating for contracting, the cost is what something costs you to build, and price is what you charge another party for building it. RSMeans refers to this as, "Price the quantities." ASPE recommends the "quantity times material and labor costs format" for the compilation of the estimate. This format is illustrated in the handwritten spreadsheet sample. For labor, the estimator should, "Determine basic production rates and multiply them by the units of work to determine total hours for the work." and then multiply the hours by the per hour average labor cost. Labor burdens, material costs, construction equipment costs, and, if applicable, subcontractor costs are also extended on the estimate detail form. Other costs and pricing are added, such as overhead, profit, sales or use taxes, payment and performance bonds, escalation, and contingency.

The costs which are applied to the line-item quantities may come from a cost book (either internal or external) or cost database. For construction contractors or construction managers it is important to track and compile past data of trends, completed projects, production factors, equipment changes, and various labor markets.

The labor requirements are often the most variable and are a primary focus of construction cost estimators. The labor hours required to construct each installation item are calculated by using a man-hour rate times the take-off quantity (a similar method is to divide the take-off quantity by the production rate). Many estimators use a man-hour norm reference for standard man-hours and apply an adjustment factor for project or task conditions, location, methods, equipment, labor skill, etc. to adjust for the anticipated effect on labor.

Direct costs are itemized for all necessary parts of the project. Direct costs are all of the costs which can be attributed directly to the project. Direct costs include costs for general requirements (Division 1 of MasterFormat), which includes such items as project management and coordination, quality control, temporary facilities and controls, cleaning and waste management. Direct costs may also include the costs of project planning, investigation, studies, and design; land or right of way acquisition, and other non-construction costs. Usually, a subtotal of total direct costs is provided in the estimate.

Description	Size	Unit	Man-hours Norm	Productivity Factor	Project Man-hours Rate
Rigid Steel Conduit	1/2"	lf	0.045	1.200	0.054
Rigid Steel Conduit	3/4"	lf	0.050	1.200	0.060
Rigid Steel Conduit	1"	lf	0.055	1.200	0.066
Rigid Steel Conduit	1-1/2"	lf	0.075	1.200	0.090
Rigid Steel Conduit	2"	lf	0.085	1.200	0.102

For normal installation conditions and projects, man-hours include:
receiving, unloading, unpacking, and moving to installation location
drawing review, layout, and marking locations
measure, cut, and thread
temporary supporting, climbing, etc.
standby time, cleanup time, etc.
Excludes:
box connections and fittings, but includes couplings
permanent hangers, supports or fastenings

Sample labor norms

Provisions are made for Indirect costs in addition to the direct costs. Indirect costs include overhead, profit, sales or use taxes, payment and performance bonds, escalation, and contingency. Profit is cost to the buyer, but is not a cost to the provider, rather a projection of anticipated income.

A well documented cost estimate includes a Basis of Estimate (BOE), which describes the scope basis, pricing basis, methods, assumptions, inclusions, and exclusions.

Order-of-Magnitude Estimates (Class 5)

An order-of-magnitude estimate is prepared when little or no design information is available for the project. It is called order of magnitude because that may be all that can be determined at an early stage. In other words, perhaps we can only determine that it is of a 10,000,000 magnitude as opposed to a 1,000,000 magnitude. Various techniques are employed for these estimates, including experience and judgment, historical values and charts, rules of thumb, and simple mathematical calculations. Factor estimating is one of the more popular methods. This involves taking the known cost of a similar facility and factoring the cost for size, place, and time. Cost modeling is another common technique. In cost modeling the estimator models the various parameters of the facility and applies costs to the derived scope.

Building estimators or architects may use the Uniformat system of breaking down the building into functional systems or assemblies during the schematic design (SD) phase of planning and design. The RSMeans Square Foot Costs book organizes building costs according to the 7 divisions of the UNIFORMAT II classification system. The 7 divisions are:

- A Substructure
- B Shell
- C Interiors
- D Services
- E Equipment & Furnishings
- F Special Construction
- G Building Site Work

Cost Curve

In economics, a cost curve is a graph of the costs of production as a function of total quantity produced. In a free market economy, productively efficient firms use these curves to find the optimal point of production (minimizing cost), and profit maximizing firms can use them to decide output quantities to achieve those aims. There are various types of cost curves, all related to each other, including total and average cost curves, and marginal ("for each additional unit") cost curves, which are equal to the differential of the total cost curves. Some are applicable to the short run, others to the long run.

Short-run Average Variable Cost Curve (SRAVC)

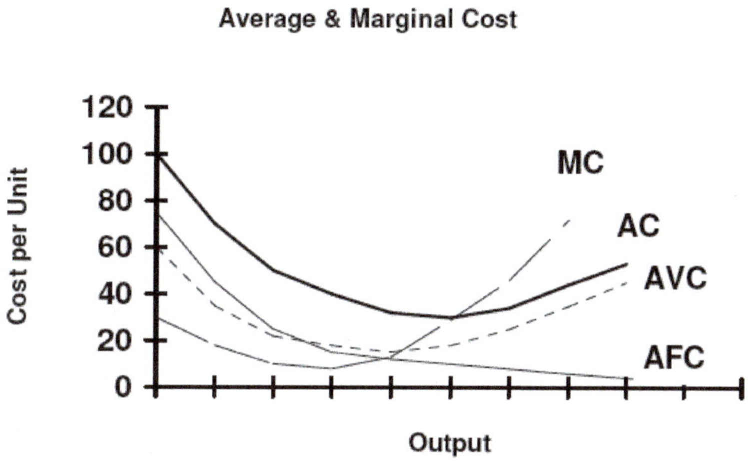

A U shaped short run Average Cost(AC) curve. AVC is the Average Variable Cost, AFC the Average Fixed Cost, MC the marginal cost crossing the minimum of the Average Cost curve.

Average variable cost (which is a short-run concept) is the variable cost (typically labor cost) per unit of output: SRAVC = wL / Q where w is the wage rate, L is the quantity of labor used, and Q is the quantity of output produced. The SRAVC curve plots the short-run average variable cost against the level of output and is typically drawn as U-shaped. However, whilst this is convenient for economic theory, it bears little relationship to the real world. Estimates show that, at least for manufacturing, the proportion of firms reporting a U-shaped cost curve is in the range of 5 to 11 percent.

Short-Run Average Total Cost Curve (SRATC or SRAC)

The average total cost curve is constructed to capture the relation between cost per unit of output and the level of output, *ceteris paribus*. A perfectly competitive and productively efficient firm organizes its factors of production in such a way that the factors of production is at the lowest point. In the short run, when at least one factor of production is fixed, this occurs at the output level where it has enjoyed all possible average cost gains from increasing production. This is at the minimum point in the diagram on the right.

Short-run total cost is given by

$$STC = P_K.K + P_L.L,$$

where P_K is the unit price of using physical capital per unit time, P_L is the unit price of labor per unit time (the wage rate), K is the quantity of physical capital used, and L is the quantity of labor used. From this we obtain short-run average cost, denoted either SATC or SAC, as STC / Q:

$$\text{SRATC or SRAC} = P_K K/Q + P_L L/Q = P_K / AP_K + P_L / AP_L,$$

where $AP_K = Q/K$ is the average product of capital and $AP_L = Q/L$ is the average product of labor.

Within the graph shown in the figure, The Marginal cost curve, Average Fixed Cost curve and Average Variable cost curve can not start with zero as at quantity zero, these values are not defined.

Short run average cost equals average fixed costs plus average variable costs. Average fixed cost continuously falls as production increases in the short run, because K is fixed in the short run. The shape of the average variable cost curve is directly determined by increasing and then diminishing marginal returns to the variable input (conventionally labor).

Short-Run Marginal Cost Curve (SRMC)

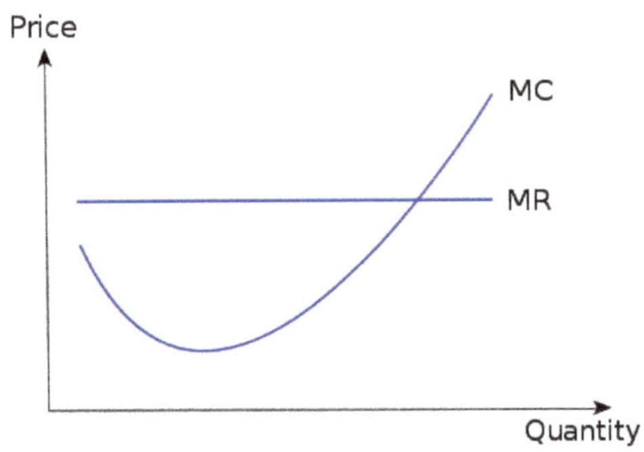

Typical marginal cost curve

A short-run marginal cost curve graphically represents the relation between marginal (i.e., incremental) cost incurred by a firm in the short-run production of a good or service and the quantity of output produced. This curve is constructed to capture the relation between marginal cost and the level of output, holding other variables, like technology and resource prices, constant. The marginal cost curve is usually U-shaped. Marginal cost is relatively high at small quantities of output; then as production increases, marginal cost declines, reaches a minimum value, then rises. The marginal cost is shown in relation to marginal revenue (MR), the incremental amount of sales revenue that an additional unit of the product or service will bring to the firm. This shape of the marginal cost curve is directly attributable to increasing, then decreasing marginal returns (and the law of diminishing marginal returns). Marginal cost equals w/MP_L. For most production processes the marginal product of labor initially rises, reaches a maximum value and then continuously falls as production increases. Thus marginal cost initially falls, reaches a minimum value and then increases. The marginal cost curve intersects both the average variable cost curve and (short-run) average total cost curve at their minimum points. When the marginal cost curve is above an average cost curve the average curve is rising. When the marginal costs curve is below an average curve the average curve is falling. This relation holds regardless of whether the marginal curve is rising or falling.

Long-Run Marginal Cost Curve (LRMC)

The long-run marginal cost curve shows for each unit of output the added total cost incurred in the long run, that is, the conceptual period when all factors of production are variable so as minimize long-run average total cost. Stated otherwise, LRMC is the minimum increase in total cost associated with an increase of one unit of output when all inputs are variable.

The long-run marginal cost curve is shaped by returns to scale, a long-run concept, rather than the law of diminishing marginal returns, which is a short-run concept. The long-run marginal cost curve tends to be flatter than its short-run counterpart due to increased input flexibility as to cost minimization. The long-run marginal cost curve intersects the long-run average cost curve at the minimum point of the latter. When long-run marginal costs are below long-run average costs, long-run average costs are falling (as to additional units of output). When long-run marginal costs are above long run average costs, average costs are rising. Long-run marginal cost equals short run marginal-cost at the least-long-run-average-cost level of production. LRMC is the slope of the LR total-cost function.

Graphing Cost Curves Together

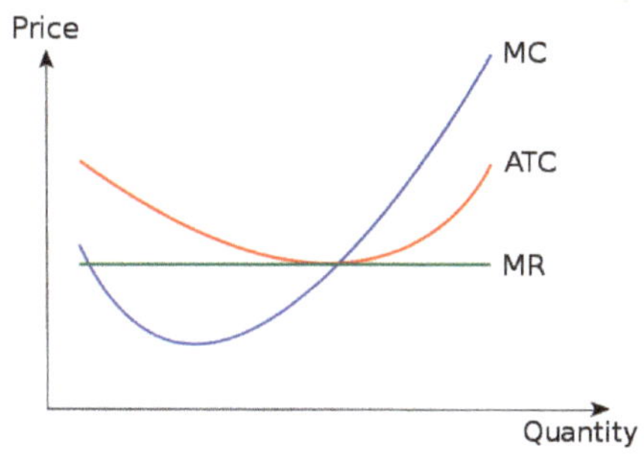

Cost curves in perfect competition compared to marginal revenue

Cost curves can be combined to provide information about firms. In this diagram for example, firms are assumed to be in a perfectly competitive market. In a perfectly competitive market the price that firms are faced with would be the price at which the marginal cost curve cuts the average cost curve.

Cost Curves and Production Functions

Assuming that factor prices are constant, the production function determines all cost functions. The variable cost curve is the inverted short-run production function or total product curve and its behavior and properties are determined by the production function. Because the production function determines the variable cost function it necessarily determines the shape and properties of marginal cost curve and the average cost curves.

If the firm is a perfect competitor in all input markets, and thus the per-unit prices of all its inputs are unaffected by how much of the inputs the firm purchases, then it can be shown that at a particular level of output, the firm has economies of scale (i.e., is operating in a downward sloping region of the long-run average cost curve) if and only if it has increasing returns to scale. Likewise, it has diseconomies of scale (is operating in an upward sloping region of the long-run average cost curve) if and only if it has decreasing returns to scale, and has neither economies nor diseconomies of scale if it has constant returns to scale. In this case, with perfect competition in the output market the long-run market equilibrium will involve all firms operating at the minimum point of their long-run average cost curves (i.e., at the borderline between economies and diseconomies of scale).

If, however, the firm is not a perfect competitor in the input markets, then the above conclusions are modified. For example, if there are increasing returns to scale in some range of output levels, but the firm is so big in one or more input markets that increasing its purchases of an input drives up the input's per-unit cost, then the firm could have diseconomies of scale in that range of output levels. Conversely, if the firm is able to get bulk discounts of an input, then it could have economies of scale in some range of output levels even if it has decreasing returns in production in that output range.

Relationship Between Different Curves

- Total Cost = Fixed Costs (FC) + Variable Costs (VC)
- Marginal Cost (MC) = dC/dQ; MC equals the slope of the total cost function and of the variable cost function
- Average Total Cost (ATC) = Total Cost/Q
- Average Fixed Cost (AFC) = FC/Q
- Average Variable Cost (AVC) = VC/Q.
- ATC = AFC + AVC
- The MC curve is related to the shape of the ATC and AVC curves:
    - At a level of Q at which the MC curve is above the average total cost or average variable cost curve, the latter curve is rising.
    - If MC is below average total cost or average variable cost, then the latter curve is falling.
    - If MC equals average total cost, then average total cost is at its minimum value.
    - If MC equals average variable cost, then average variable cost is at its minimum value.

Relationship Between Short Run and Long Run Cost Curves

Basic: For each quantity of output there is one cost minimizing level of capital and a unique short run average cost curve associated with producing the given quantity.

- Each STC curve can be tangent to the LRTC curve at only one point. The STC curve cannot cross (intersect) the LRTC curve. The STC curve can lie wholly "above" the LRTC curve with no tangency point.
- One STC curve is tangent to LRTC at the long-run cost minimizing level of production. At the point of tangency LRTC = STC. At all other levels of production STC will exceed LRTC.
- Average cost functions are the total cost function divided by the level of output. Therefore, the SATC curveis also tangent to the LRATC curve at the cost-minimizing level of output. At the point of tangency LRATC = SATC. At all other levels of production SATC > LRATC To the left of the point of tangency the firm is using too much capital and fixed costs are too high. To the right of the point of tangency the firm is using too little capital and diminishing returns to labor are causing costs to increase.
- The slope of the total cost curves equals marginal cost. Therefore, when STC is tangent to LTC, SMC = LRMC.
- At the long run cost minimizing level of output LRTC = STC; LRATC = SATC and LRMC = SMC,.
- The long run cost minimizing level of output may be different from minimum SATC,.
- With fixed unit costs of inputs, if the production function has constant returns to scale, then at the minimal level of the SATC curve we have SATC = LRATC = SMC = LRMC.
- With fixed unit costs of inputs, if the production function has increasing returns to scale, the minimum of the SATC curve is to the right of the point of tangency between the LRAC and the SATC curves. Where LRTC = STC, LRATC = SATC and LRMC = SMC.
- With fixed unit costs of inputs and decreasing returns the minimum of the SATC curve is to the left of the point of tangency between LRAC and SATC. Where LRTC = STC, LRATC = SATC and LRMC = SMC.
- With fixed unit input costs, a firm that is experiencing increasing (decreasing) returns to scale and is producing at its minimum SAC can always reduce average cost in the long run by expanding (reducing) the use of the fixed input.
- LRATC will always equal to or be less than SATC.
- If production process is exhibiting constant returns to scale then minimum SRAC equals minimum long run average cost. The LRAC and SRAC intersect at their common minimum values. Thus under constant returns to scale SRMC = LRMC = LRAC = SRAC .
- If the production process is experiencing decreasing or increasing, minimum short run average cost does not equal minimum long run average cost. If increasing returns to scale

exist long run minimum will occur at a lower level of output than SRAC. This is because there are economies of scale that have not been exploited so in the long run a firm could always produce a quantity at a price lower than minimum short run average cost simply by using a larger plant.

- With decreasing returns, minimum SRAC occurs at a lower production level than minimum LRAC because a firm could reduce average costs by simply decreasing the size or its operations.
- The minimum of a SRAC occurs when the slope is zero. Thus the points of tangency between the U-shaped LRAC curve and the minimum of the SRAC curve would coincide only with that portion of the LRAC curve exhibiting constant economies of scale. For increasing returns to scale the point of tangency between the LRAC and the SRAC would have to occur at a level of output below level associated with the minimum of the SRAC curve.

These statements assume that the firm is using the optimal level of capital for the quantity produced. If not, then the SRAC curve would lie "wholly above" the LRAC and would not be tangent at any point.

U-shaped Curves

Both the SRAC and LRAC curves are typically expressed as U-shaped. However, the shapes of the curves are not due to the same factors. For the short run curve the initial downward slope is largely due to declining average fixed costs. Increasing returns to the variable input at low levels of production also play a role, while the upward slope is due to diminishing marginal returns to the variable input. With the long run curve the shape by definition reflects economies and diseconomies of scale. At low levels of production long run production functions generally exhibit increasing returns to scale, which, for firms that are perfect competitors in input markets, means that the long run average cost is falling; the upward slope of the long run average cost function at higher levels of output is due to decreasing returns to scale at those output levels.

Cost Curves in Reality

Evidence shows that cost curves are not typically U-shaped. In a survey by Wilford J. Eiteman and Glenn E. Guthrie in 1952 managers of 334 companies were shown a number of different cost curves, and asked to specify which one best represented the company's cost curve. 95% of managers responding to the survey reported cost curves with constant or falling costs.

Alan Blinder, former vice president of the American Economics Association, conducted the same type of survey in 1998, which involved 200 US firms in a sample that should be representative of the US economy at large. He found that about 40% of firms reported falling variable or marginal cost, and 48.4% reported constant marginal/variable cost.

Capitalised Cost

The cost incurred on fixed assets are capitalised cost. E.g. cost incurred to purchase machineries. These cost are not covered here, except which is subsequently treated as expenses (depreciation).

Cost Classification

- By elements
- By function
- As direct and indirect
- By variability
- By controllability
- By normality
- By relevance

By Nature or Element

Under this classification the costs are divided into three categories i.e. material cost, labour cost and expenses.

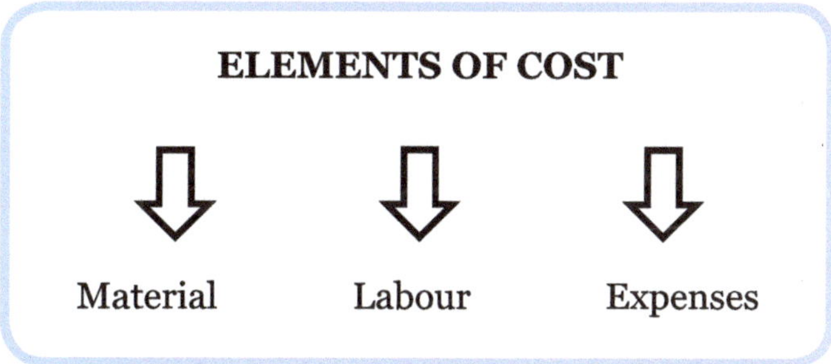

Material

The cost which is incurred on physical substance or thing.

e.g. Components or raw materials purchased.

Labour

The cost incurred on human efforts.

e.g. Salary, Wages, Bonus, Incentives, Retirement Benefits, Perquisites.

Expenses

The cost incurred for services.

Expenses are other than material and labour are covered here.

e.g. Electricity expenses, Rent, Telephone.

By Function

In this classification costs are divided according to the function for which they have been incurred. E.g. production cost, office & administration cost, selling & distribution costs.

Production cost: materials, direct labour, stores overheads etc.

Office & administration cost: cost of formulating policy, directing the organisation and controlling the operations.

E.g Rent of Office, Depreciation of Office equipments, Salary to Office staff, Director Fees, Remuneration to CEO.

Selling and distribution expenses or marketing cost: expenditure incurred generating demand, on moving articles to prospective customers etc.

Direct Cost

Direct costs are costs which can be easily attributed to a particular cost center/ product.

E.g.- the cost of hard disks while assembling an PC.

Indirect Cost

Cost that must be allocated in order to be assigned to a product or department. This cannot be assigned directly to any particular cost centre.

Eg. Costs incurred by the computer maintenance and support group, wages paid to security staff, storage cost of units produced.

By Controllability

Costs here may be classified as controllable and un- controllable cost. Controllable costs are the cost which can be influenced by an action of the specified member of the undertaking. Uncontrollable cost are those which are not controllable.

The distinction between controllable and uncontrollable costs is not very sharp.

Infact no cost is uncontrollable; it is only in relation to a particular individual that we may specify a particular to be either controllable or uncontrollable.

For example, expenditure incurred by tool room is controllable by foreman in- charge of that section but share which is apportioned to machine shop can not to be controlled by machine shop foreman.

By Normality

According to this basis cost may be categorized as normal Cost and abnormal cost. Normal cost is normally incurred at a given level of output under the conditions in which that level of output is normally attained.

And cost which is abnormally incurred is called as abnormal cost.

E.g. cost of material which is evaporated is normal loss where as goods lost by fire or theft is treated as abnormal loss.

By Relevance

Relevant costs are those future costs which differ between alternatives. Relevant costs may also be defined as the cost which are affected and changed by a decision.

Sunk costs are all costs incurred in the past that cannot be changed by any decision made now or in the future. Sunk costs should not be considered in decisions.

E.g. cost incurred on research of a product will be irrelevant while making decision whether to undertake production or not, in make or buy (the raw materials) decision cost of the material, wage rate will be relevant on the other hand factory rent will be irrelevant.

Variable Cost

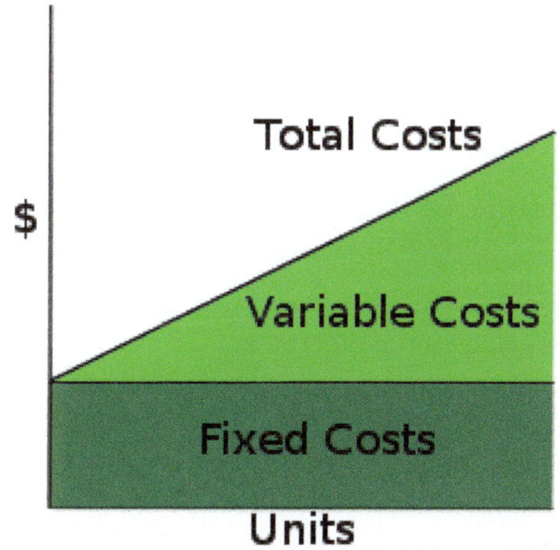

Decomposing Total Costs as Fixed Costs plus Variable Costs.

Variable costs are costs that change in proportion to the good or service that a business produces. Variable costs are also the sum of marginal costs over all units produced. They can also be considered normal costs. Fixed costs and variable costs make up the two components of total cost. Direct costs, however, are costs that can easily be associated with a particular cost object. However, not all variable costs are direct costs. For example, variable manufacturing overhead costs are variable costs that are indirect costs, not direct costs. Variable costs are sometimes called unit-level costs as they vary with the number of units produced.

Direct labor and overhead are often called conversion cost, while direct material and direct labor are often referred to as prime cost.

In marketing, it is necessary to know how costs divide between variable and fixed. This distinction is crucial in forecasting the earnings generated by various changes in unit sales and thus the financial impact of proposed marketing campaigns. In a survey of nearly 200 senior marketing managers, 60 percent responded that they found the "variable and fixed costs" metric very useful.

The level of variable cost is influenced by many factors, such as fixed cost, duration of project, uncertainty and discount rate. An analytical formula of variable cost as a function of these factors has been derived. It can be used to assess how different factors impact variable cost and total return in an investment.

Explanation

Example 1

Assume a business produces clothing. A variable cost of this product would be the direct material, i.e., cloth, and the direct labor. If it takes one laborer 6 yards of cloth and 8 hours to make a shirt, then the cost of labor and cloth increases if two shirts are produced.

	1 shirt	2 shirts	3 shirts
Cloth (Direct Materials)	6yds	12yds	18yds
Labor (Direct Labor)	8hrs	16hrs	24hrs

The amount of materials and labor that goes into each shirt increases in direct proportion to the number of shirts produced. In this sense, the cost "varies" as production varies.

Example 2

For example, a firm pays for raw materials. When activity is decreased, less raw material is used, and so the spending for raw materials falls. When activity is increased, more raw material is used, and spending therefore rises. Note that the changes in expenses happen with little or no need for managerial intervention. These costs are variable costs.

A company will pay for line rental and maintenance fees each period regardless of how much power gets used. And some electrical equipment (air conditioning or lighting) may be kept running even in periods of low activity. These expenses can be regarded as fixed. But beyond this, the company will use electricity to run plant and machinery as required. The busier the company, the more the plant will be run, and so the more electricity gets used. This extra spending can therefore be regarded as variable.

In retail the cost of goods is almost entirely a variable cost; this is not true of manufacturing where many fixed costs, such as depreciation, are included in the cost of goods.

Although taxation usually varies with profit, which in turn varies with sales volume, it is not normally considered a variable cost.

For some employees, salary is paid on monthly rates, independent of how many hours the employees work. This is a fixed cost. On the other hand, the hours of hourly employees can often be varied, so this type of labour cost is a variable cost. The cost of material is a variable cost.

Fixed Cost

In economics, fixed costs, indirect costs or overheads are business expenses that are not dependent on the level of goods or services produced by the business. They tend to be time-related, such as salaries or rents being paid per month, and are often referred to as overhead costs. This is in contrast to variable costs, which are volume-related (and are paid per quantity produced). For a simple example, such as a bakery, the monthly rent for the baking facilities, and the monthly payments for the security system and basic phone line are fixed costs, as they do not change according to how much bread the bakery produces and sells. On the other hands, the wage costs of the bakery are variable, as the bakery will have to hire more workers if the production of bread increases. The relation between fixed cost and variable cost can be modelled by an analytical formula.

In management accounting, fixed costs are defined as expenses that do not change as a function of the activity of a business, within the relevant period. For example, a retailer must pay rent and utility bills irrespective of sales. In marketing, it is necessary to know how costs divide between variable and fixed costs. This distinction is crucial in forecasting the earnings generated by various changes in unit sales and thus the financial impact of proposed marketing campaigns. In a survey of nearly 200 senior marketing managers, 60 percent responded that they found the "variable and fixed costs" metric very useful.

Description

Fixed costs are not permanently fixed; they will change over time, but are fixed in relation to the quantity of production for the relevant period. For example, a company may have unexpected and unpredictable expenses unrelated to production, such as warehouse costs and the like that are fixed only over the time period of the lease. By definition, there are no fixed costs in the long run, because the long run is a sufficient period of time for all short-run fixed inputs to become variable. Investments in facilities, equipment, and the basic organization that can't be significantly reduced in a short period of time are referred to as committed fixed costs. Discretionary fixed costs usually arise from annual decisions by management to spend on certain fixed cost items. Examples of discretionary costs are advertising, machine maintenance, and research & development expenditures. Discretionary fixed costs can be expensive.

In business planning and management accounting, usage of the terms fixed costs, variable costs and others will often differ from usage in economics, and may depend on the context. Some cost accounting practices such as activity-based costing will allocate fixed costs to business activities for profitability measures. This can simplify decision-making, but can be confusing and controversial. In accounting terminology, fixed costs will broadly include almost all costs (expenses) which are not included in cost of goods sold, and variable costs are those captured in costs of goods sold. The implicit assumption required to make the equivalence between the accounting and economics terminology is that the accounting period is equal to the period in which fixed costs do not vary in relation to production. In practice, this equivalence does not always hold, and depending on the period under consideration by management, some overhead expenses (e.g., sales, general and administrative expenses) can be adjusted by management, and the specific allocation of each expense to each category will be decided under cost accounting.

Total Cost

In economics and cost accounting, total cost (TC) describes the total economic cost of production and is made up of variable costs, which vary according to the quantity of a good produced and include inputs such as labor and raw materials, plus fixed costs, which are independent of the quantity of a good produced and include inputs (capital) that cannot be varied in the short term, such as buildings and machinery.

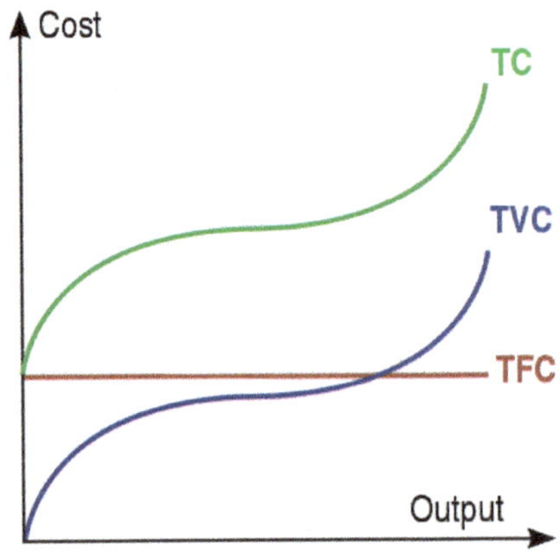

The total cost curve, if non-linear, can represent increasing and diminishing marginal returns.

Total cost in economics includes the total opportunity cost of each factor of production as part of its fixed or variable costs.

The rate at which total cost changes as the amount produced changes is called marginal cost. This is also known as the marginal unit variable cost.

If one assumes that the unit variable cost is constant, as in cost-volume-profit analysis developed and used in cost accounting by the accountants, then total cost is linear in volume, and given by: total cost = fixed costs + unit variable cost * amount.

The total cost of producing a specific level of output is the cost of all the factors of input used. Conventionally, economists use models with two inputs: capital, K; and labor, L. Capital is assumed to be the fixed input, meaning that the amount of capital used does not vary with the level of production. The rental price per unit of capital is denoted r. Thus, the total fixed costs equal Kr. Labor is the variable input, meaning that the amount of labor used varies with the level of output. In fact, in the short run, the only way to vary output is by varying the amount of the variable input. Labor is denoted L and the per unit cost, or wage rate, is denoted w, so the total variable costs is Lw. Consequently, total cost is fixed costs (FC) plus variable cost (VC), or TC = FC + VC = Kr +wL.

Other economic models have the total variable cost curve (and therefore total cost curve) illustrate the concepts of increasing, and later diminishing, marginal returns.

In marketing, it is necessary to know how total costs divide between variable and fixed. "This distinction is crucial in forecasting the earnings generated by various changes in unit sales and thus the financial impact of proposed marketing campaigns." In a survey of nearly 200 senior marketing managers, 60 percent responded that they found the "variable and fixed costs" metric very useful.

Calculating Cost

- Average Total Cost (ATC) = Total Cost / Q (Output is quantity produced or 'Q')
- Average Variable Cost (AVC) = Total Variable Cost / Q

- Average Fixed Cost (AFC) = ATC – AVC
- Total Cost (TC) = (AVC + AFC) X Output (Which is Q)
- Total Variable Cost (TVC) = AVC X Output
- Total Fixed Cost (TFC) = TC – TVC
- Marginal Cost (MC) = Change in Total Costs / Change in Output
- Marginal Product (MP) = Change in Total Product / Change in Variable Factor
- Marginal Revenue (MR) = Change in Total Revenue / Change in Q
- Average Product (AP) = TP / Variable Factor
- Total Revenue (TR) = Price X Quantity
- Average Revenue (AR) = TR / Output
- Total Product (TP) = AP X Variable Factor
- Economic Profit = TR – TC > 0
- A Loss = TR – TC < 0
- Break Even Point = AR = ATC
- Profit Maximizing Condition = MR = MC

Fixed and Variable Costs

Cost	In Total	Per Unit
Variable	Changes as activity level increases.	Remains constant as activity level increases
Fixed	Remains constant as activity level increases	Reduces as Activity level increases

Semi-Variable Cost

These costs contain both fixed and variable components and thus partly affected by fluctuation in the level of activity.

Examples of semi variable costs are telephone bill, electricity, Maintenance.

Example

A company has prepared budget for July and Aug 2013.

Particulars	1000 Units	2000 Units
Direct Material	50000	100000
Direct Labour	28000	56000
Rent of the factory	75000	75000

Power	35000	50000
Maintenance	17000	26000

Differential Costs

Differential cost is the difference between any two alternatives. Differential costs are equal to the additional variable expenses incurred in respect of the additional output, plus the increase in fixed costs if any.

Opportunity Cost

In microeconomic theory, the opportunity cost, also known as *alternative cost,* is the value (not a benefit) of the choice of a best alternative cost while making a decision. A choice needs to be made between several mutually exclusive alternatives; assuming the best choice is made, it is the "cost" incurred by not enjoying the *benefit* that would have been had by taking the second best available choice. The *New Oxford American Dictionary* defines it as "the loss of potential gain from other alternatives when one alternative is chosen." Opportunity cost is a key concept in economics, and has been described as expressing "the basic relationship between scarcity and choice." The notion of opportunity cost plays a crucial part in attempts to ensure that scarce resources are used efficiently. Thus, opportunity costs are not restricted to monetary or financial costs: the real cost of output forgone, lost time, pleasure or any other benefit that provides utility should also be considered an opportunity cost.

History

The term was coined in 1914 by Austrian economist Friedrich von Wieser in his book *Theorie der gesellschaftlichen Wirtschaft*. The idea had been anticipated by previous writers including Benjamin Franklin and Frédéric Bastiat. Franklin coined the phrase "Time is Money", and spelt out the associated opportunity cost reasoning in his "Advice to a Young Tradesman" (1746): "Remember that Time is Money. He that can earn Ten Shillings a Day by his Labour, and goes abroad, or sits idle one half of that Day, tho' he spends but Sixpence during his Diversion or Idleness, ought not to reckon That the only Expence; he has really spent or rather thrown away Five Shillings besides."

Bastiat's 1848 essay "What Is Seen and What Is Not Seen" used opportunity cost reasoning in his critique of the broken window fallacy, and of what he saw as spurious arguments for public expenditure.

Opportunity Costs in Production

Explicit Costs

Explicit costs are opportunity costs that involve direct monetary payment by producers. The explicit opportunity cost of the factors of production not already owned by a producer is the price that the producer has to pay for them. For instance, if a firm spends $100 on electrical power consumed, its explicit opportunity cost is $100. This cash expenditure represents a lost opportunity to purchase something else with the $100.

Implicit Costs

Implicit costs (also called implied, imputed or notional costs) are the opportunity costs that are not reflected in cash outflow but implied by the failure of the firm to allocate its existing (owned) resources, or factors of production to the best alternative use. For example: a manufacturer has previously purchased 1000 tons of steel and the machinery to produce a widget. The implicit part of the opportunity cost of producing the widget is the revenue lost by not selling the steel and not renting out the machinery instead of using it for production.

One example of opportunity cost is in the evaluation of "foreign" (to the US) buyers and their allocation of cash assets in real estate or other types of investment vehicles. With the recent downturn (circa June/July 2015) of the Chinese stock market, more and more Chinese investors from Hong Kong and Taiwan are turning to the United States as an alternative vessel for their investment dollars; the opportunity cost of leaving their money in the Chinese stock market or Chinese real estate market is too high relative to yields available in the US real estate market.

Evaluation

Note that opportunity cost is not the *sum* of the available alternatives when those alternatives are, in turn, mutually exclusive to each other. It is the *next best* alternative given up selecting the best option. The opportunity cost of a city's decision to build the hospital on its vacant land is the loss of the land for a sporting center, or the inability to use the land for a parking lot, or the money the city could have made by selling the land. Use for any one of those purposes precludes all the others.

If someone loses the opportunity to earn money, that is part of the opportunity cost. If someone chooses to spend money, that money could be used to purchase other goods and services so the spent money is part of the opportunity cost as well. Add the value of the next best alternatives and you have the total opportunity cost. If you miss work to go to a concert, your opportunity cost is the money you would have earned if you went to work plus the cost of the concert.

Example

Question

> Suppose you have a free ticket to a concert by *Band X*. The ticket has no resale value. On the night of the concert your next-best alternative entertainment is a performance by *Band Y* for which the tickets cost $40. You like *Band Y* and would usually be willing to pay $50 for a ticket to see them. What is the *opportunity cost* of using your free ticket and seeing *Band X* instead of *Band Y*?

Answer

> The benefit you forgo (that is, the value to you) is $10: the $50 benefit of seeing *Band Y* less the ticket cost of $40.

Marginal Cost

In economics, marginal cost is the change in the opportunity cost that arises when the quantity produced is incremented by one unit, that is, it is the cost of producing one more unit of a good. In general terms, marginal cost at each level of production includes any additional costs required to produce the next unit. For example, if producing additional vehicles requires building a new factory, the marginal cost of the *extra* vehicles includes the cost of the new factory. In practice, this analysis is segregated into short and long-run cases, so that, over the longest run, all costs become marginal. At each level of production and time period being considered, marginal costs include all costs that vary with the level of production, whereas other costs that do not vary with production are considered fixed.

The graph is plotted with Price, Cost and Revenue on the Y-axis and Quantity on the X-axis.

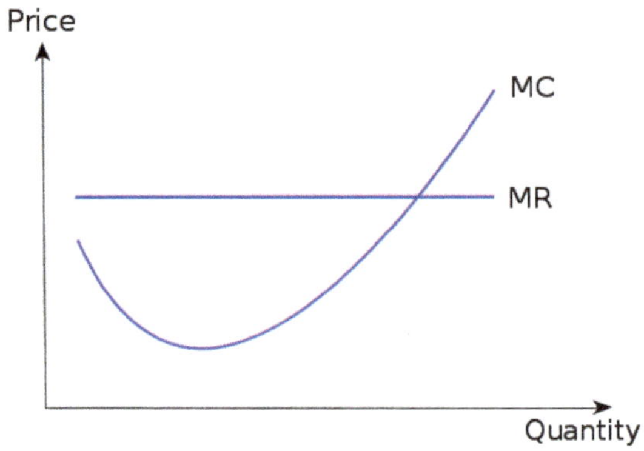

A typical marginal cost curve with marginal revenue overlaid

If the good being produced is infinitely divisible, the size of a marginal cost will change with volume; so a non-linear and non-proportional cost function includes the following:

- variable terms dependent on volume,
- constant terms independent on volume and occurring with the respective lot size,
- jump fix cost increase or decrease dependent on steps of volume increase.

In practice the above definition of marginal cost as the change in total cost as a result of an increase in output of one unit is inconsistent with the differential definition of marginal cost for virtually all non-linear functions. This is as the definition finds the tangent to the total cost curve at the point q which assumes that costs increase at the same rate as they were at q. A new definition may be useful for marginal unit cost (MUC) using the current definition of the change in total cost as a result of an increase of one unit of output defined as: TC(q+1)-TC(q) and re-defining marginal cost to be the change in total as a result of an infinitesimally small increase in q which is consistent with its use in economic literature and can be calculated differentially.

If the cost function is differentiable joining, the marginal cost is the cost of the next unit produced referring to the basic volume.

$$\text{Marginal Cost (MC)} = \frac{dC}{dQ}$$

If the cost function is not differentiable, the marginal cost can be expressed as follows.

$$MC = \frac{\Delta C}{\Delta Q}$$

A number of other factors can affect marginal cost and its applicability to real world problems. Some of these may be considered market failures. These may include information asymmetries, the presence of negative or positive externalities, transaction costs, price discrimination and others.

Cost Functions and Relationship to Average Cost

In the simplest case, the total cost function and its derivative are expressed as follows, where Q represents the production quantity, VC represents variable costs, FC represents fixed costs and TC represents total costs.

Since (by definition) fixed costs do not vary with production quantity, it drops out of the equation when it is differentiated. The important conclusion is that marginal cost *is not related to* fixed costs. This can be compared with average total cost or ATC, which is the total cost divided by the number of units produced and *does* include fixed costs.

$$ATC = \frac{C_0 + \Delta C}{Q}$$

For discrete calculation without calculus, marginal cost equals the change in total (or variable) cost that comes with each additional unit produced. In contrast, incremental cost is the composition of total cost from the surrogate of contributions, where any increment is determined by the contribution of the cost factors, not necessarily by single units.

For instance, suppose the total cost of making 1 shoe is $30 and the total cost of making 2 shoes is $40. The marginal cost of producing the second shoe is $40 – $30 = $10.

Marginal cost is not the cost of producing the "next" or "last" unit. As Silberberg and Suen note, the cost of the last unit is the same as the cost of the first unit and every other unit. In the short run, increasing production requires using more of the variable input — conventionally assumed to be labor. Adding more labor to a fixed capital stock reduces the marginal product of labor because of the diminishing marginal returns. This reduction in productivity is not limited to the additional labor needed to produce the marginal unit – the productivity of every unit of labor is reduced. Thus the costs of producing the marginal unit of output has two components: the cost associated with producing the marginal unit and the increase in average costs for all units produced due to the "damage" to the entire productive process $(\partial AC/\partial q)q$. The first component is the per unit or average cost. The second unit is the small increase in costs due to the law of diminishing marginal returns which increases the costs of all units of sold.

Marginal costs can also be expressed as the cost per unit of labor divided by the marginal product of labor.

$$MC = \frac{\Delta VC}{\Delta Q}$$

$$\Delta VC = w\Delta L$$

$$MC = \frac{w\Delta L}{\Delta Q}$$

Because $\frac{\Delta L}{\Delta Q}$ is the change in quantity of labor that affects a one unit change in output, this implies that this equals $\frac{1}{MPL}$.

where MPL is ratio of increase in the quantity produced per unit increase in labour i.e. ΔQ/ΔL. Therefore, $MC = \frac{W}{MPL}$ Since the wage rate is assumed constant, marginal cost and marginal product of labor have an inverse relationship—if marginal cost is increasing (decreasing) the marginal product of labor is decreasing (increasing).

Economies of Scale

Economies of scale applies to the long run, a span of time in which all inputs can be varied by the firm so that there are no fixed inputs or fixed costs. Production may be subject to economies of scale (or diseconomies of scale). Economies of scale are said to exist if an additional unit of output can be produced for less than the average of all previous units— that is, if long-run marginal cost is below long-run average cost, so the latter is falling. Conversely, there may be levels of production where marginal cost is higher than average cost, and average cost is an increasing function of output. For this generic case, minimum average cost occurs at the point where average cost and marginal cost are equal (when plotted, the marginal cost curve intersects the average cost curve from below); this point will *not* be at the mimum for marginal cost if fixed costs are greater than 0.

Perfectly Competitive Supply Curve

The portion of the marginal cost curve above its intersection with the average variable cost curve is the supply curve for a firm operating in a perfectly competitive market. (the portion of the MC curve below its intersection with the AVC curve is not part of the supply curve because a firm would not operate at price below the shut down point) This is not true for firms operating in other market structures. For example, while a monopoly "has" an MC curve it does not have a supply curve. In a perfectly competitive market, a supply curve shows the quantity a seller's willing and able to supply at each price – for each price there is a unique quantity that would be supplied. The one-to-one relationship simply is absent in the case of a monopoly. With a monopoly there could be an infinite number of prices associated with a given quantity. It all depends on the shape and position of the demand curve and its accompanying marginal revenue curve.

Decisions Taken Based on Marginal Costs

In perfectly competitive markets, firms decide the quantity to be produced based on marginal costs and sale price. If the sale price is higher than the marginal cost, then they supply the unit and sell it. If the marginal cost is higher than the price, it would not be profitable to produce it. So the production will be carried out until the marginal cost is equal to the sale price. In other words, firms refuse to sell if the marginal cost is greater than the market price.

Relationship to Fixed Costs

Marginal costs are not affected by changes in fixed cost. Marginal costs can be expressed as ΔC(q)/ΔQ.

Since fixed costs do not vary with (depend on) changes in quantity, MC is ΔVC/ΔQ. Thus if fixed cost were to double, the cost of MC would not be affected, and consequently the profit maximizing quantity and price would not change. This can be illustrated by graphing the short run total cost curve and the short run variable cost curve. The shape of the curves are identical. Each curve initially increases at a decreasing rate, reaches an inflection point, then increases at an increasing rate. The only difference between the curves is that the SRVC curve begins from the origin while the SRTC curve originates on the y-axis. The distance of the origin of the SRTC above the origin represents the fixed cost – the vertical distance between the curves. This distance remains constant as the quantity produced, Q, increases. MC is the slope of the SRVC curve. A change in fixed cost would be reflected by a change in the vertical distance between the SRTC and SRVC curve. Any such change would have no effect on the shape of the SRVC curve and therefore its slope at any point – MC.

Externalities

Externalities are costs (or benefits) that are not borne by the parties to the economic transaction. A producer may, for example, pollute the environment, and others may bear those costs. A consumer may consume a good which produces benefits for society, such as education; because the individual does not receive all of the benefits, he may consume less than efficiency would suggest. Alternatively, an individual may be a smoker or alcoholic and impose costs on others. In these cases, production or consumption of the good in question may differ from the optimum level.

Negative Externalities of Production

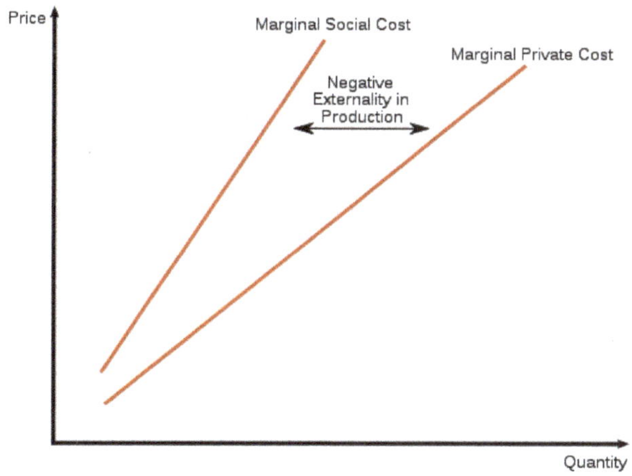

Negative Externalities of Production

Much of the time, private and social costs do not diverge from one another, but at times social costs may be either greater or less than private costs. When marginal social costs of production are greater than that of the private cost function, we see the occurrence of a negative externality of production. Productive processes that result in pollution are a textbook example of production that creates negative externalities.

Such externalities are a result of firms externalising their costs onto a third party in order to reduce their own total cost. As a result of externalising such costs we see that members of society will be negatively affected by such behavior of the firm. In this case, we see that an increased cost of production on society creates a social cost curve that depicts a greater cost than the private cost curve.

In an equilibrium state we see that markets creating negative externalities of production will over-produce that good. As a result, the socially optimal production level would be lower than that observed.

Positive Externalities of Production

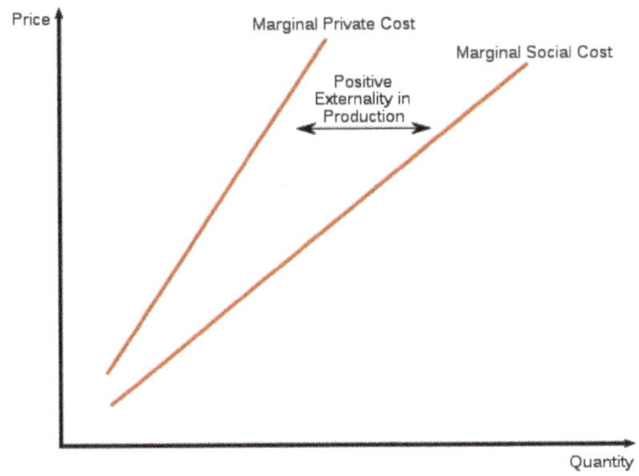

Positive Externalities of Production

When marginal social costs of production are less than that of the private cost function, we see the occurrence of a positive externality of production. Production of public goods are a textbook example of production that create positive externalities. An example of such a public good, which creates a divergence in social and private costs, includes the production of education. It is often seen that education is a positive for any whole society, as well as a positive for those directly involved in the market.

Examining the relevant diagram we see that such production creates a social cost curve that is less than that of the private curve. In an equilibrium state we see that markets creating positive externalities of production will under produce that good. As a result, the socially optimal production level would be greater than that observed.

Social Costs

Of great importance in the theory of marginal cost is the distinction between the marginal *private* and *social* costs. The marginal private cost shows the cost associated to the firm in question. It is the marginal private cost that is used by business decision makers in their profit maximization goals. Marginal social cost is similar to private cost in that it includes the cost of private enterprise but *also* any other cost (or offsetting benefit) to society to parties having no direct association with purchase or sale of the product. It incorporates all negative and positive externalities, of both production and consumption. Examples might include a social cost from air pollution affecting third parties or a social benefit from flu shots protecting others from infection.

Average Cost

In economics, average cost and/or unit cost is equal to total cost divided by the number of goods produced (the output quantity, Q). It is also equal to the sum of average variable costs (total variable costs divided by Q) plus average fixed costs (total fixed costs divided by Q). Average costs may be dependent on the time period considered (increasing production may be expensive or impossible in the short term, for example). Average costs affect the supply curve and are a fundamental component of supply and demand.

$$AC = \frac{TC}{Q}$$

Short-run Average Cost

Average cost is distinct from the price, and depends on the interaction with demand through elasticity of demand and an average cost due to marginal cost pricing.

Short-run average cost will vary in relation to the quantity produced unless fixed costs are zero and variable costs constant. A cost curve can be plotted, with cost on the y-axis and quantity on the x-axis. Marginal costs are often shown on these graphs, with marginal cost representing the cost of the last unit produced at each point; marginal costs are the slope of the cost curve or the first derivative of total or variable costs.

A typical average cost curve will have a U-shape, because fixed costs are all incurred before any production takes place and marginal costs are typically increasing, because of diminishing marginal productivity. In this "typical" case, for low levels of production marginal costs are below average costs, so average costs are decreasing as quantity increases. An increasing marginal cost curve will intersect a U-shaped average cost curve at its minimum, after which point the average cost curve begins to slope upward. For further increases in production beyond this minimum, marginal cost is above average costs, so average costs are increasing as quantity increases. An example of this typical case would be a factory designed to produce a specific quantity of widgets per period: below a certain production level, average cost is higher due to under-utilized equipment, while above that level, production bottlenecks increase the average cost.

Long-run Average Cost

The long run is a time frame in which the firm can vary the quantities used of all inputs, even physical capital. A long-run average cost curve can be upward sloping or downward sloping at relatively low levels of output and upward sloping at relatively high levels of output, with an in-between level of output at which the slope of long-run average cost is zero. The typical long-run average cost curve is U-shaped, by definition reflecting increasing returns to scale where negatively sloped and decreasing returns to scale where positively sloped.

If the firm is a perfect competitor in all input markets, and thus the per-unit prices of all its inputs are unaffected by how much of the inputs the firm purchases, then it can be shown that at a particular level of output, the firm has economies of scale (i.e., is operating in a downward sloping region of the long-run average cost curve) if and only if it has increasing returns to scale. Likewise, it has diseconomies of scale (is operating in an upward sloping region of the long-run average cost curve) if and only if it has decreasing returns to scale, and has neither economies nor diseconomies of scale if it has constant returns to scale. In this case, with perfect competition in the output market the long-run market equilibrium will involve all firms operating at the minimum point of their long-run average cost curves (i.e., at the borderline between economies and diseconomies of scale).

If, however, the firm is not a perfect competitor in the input markets, then the above conclusions are modified. For example, if there are increasing returns to scale in some range of output levels, but the firm is so big in one or more input markets that increasing its purchases of an input drives up the input's per-unit cost, then the firm could have diseconomies of scale in that range of output levels. Conversely, if the firm is able to get bulk discounts of an input, then it could have economies of scale in some range of output levels even if it has decreasing returns in production in that output range.

In some industries, the LRAC is always declining (economies of scale exist indefinitely). This means that the largest firm tends to have a cost advantage, and the industry tends naturally to become a monopoly, and hence is called a natural monopoly. Natural monopolies tend to exist in industries with high capital costs in relation to variable costs, such as water supply and electricity supply.

Long run average cost is the unit cost of producing a certain output when all inputs are variable. The behavioral assumption is that the firm will choose that combination of inputs that will produce the desired quantity at the lowest possible cost.

Relationship to Marginal Cost

When average cost is declining as output increases, marginal cost is less than average cost. When average cost is rising, marginal cost is greater than average cost. When average cost is neither rising nor falling (at a minimum or maximum), marginal cost equals average cost.

Other special cases for average cost and marginal cost appear frequently:

- Constant marginal cost/high fixed costs: each additional unit of production is produced at constant additional expense per unit. The average cost curve slopes down continuously, approaching marginal cost. An example may be hydroelectric generation, which has no fuel expense, limited maintenance expenses and a high up-front fixed cost (ignoring irregular maintenance costs or useful lifespan). Industries where fixed marginal costs obtain, such as electrical transmission networks, may meet the conditions for a natural monopoly, because once capacity is built, the marginal cost to the incumbent of serving an additional customer is always lower than the average cost for a potential competitor. The high fixed capital costs are a barrier to entry.
- Two popular pricing mechanisms are Average Cost Pricing (or Rate of Return Regulation) and Marginal Cost Pricing. A monopoly will produce where their average cost curve meets the market demand curve under Average Cost Pricing, referred to as the Average Cost Pricing Equilibrium. Conversely, the same assertion can be made for Marginal Cost Pricing.
- Minimum efficient scale / maximum efficient scale: marginal or average costs may be non-linear, or have discontinuities. Average cost curves may therefore only be shown over a limited scale of production for a given technology. For example, a nuclear plant would be extremely inefficient (very high average cost) for production in small quantities; similarly, its maximum output for any given time period may essentially be fixed, and production above that level may be technically impossible, dangerous or extremely costly. The long run elasticity of supply will be higher, as new plants could be built and brought on-line.
- Zero fixed costs (long-run analysis) / constant marginal cost: since there are no economies

of scale, average cost will be equal to the constant marginal cost.

Relationship Between AC, AFC, AVC and MC

1. The Average Fixed Cost curve (AFC) starts from a height and goes on declining continuously as production increases.
2. The Average Variable Cost curve, Average Cost curve and the Marginal Cost curve start from a height, reach the minimum points, then rise sharply and continuously.
3. The Average Fixed Cost curve approaches zero asymptotically. The Average Variable Cost curve is never parallel to or as high as the Average Cost curve due to the existence of positive Average Fixed Costs at all levels of production; but the Average Variable Cost curve asymptotically approaches the Average Cost curve from below.
4. The Marginal Cost curve always passes through the minimum points of the Average Variable Cost and Average Cost curves, though the Average Variable Cost curve attains the minimum point prior to that of the Average Cost curve.

Product Cost

Product Cost is the cost incurred to make or manufacture the product and sell it. These are also known as inventoriable costs.

Eg. Direct Material, Direct Labour, Direct Expenses, Power (if Identifiable to product)

Period Costs

Period Costs are the costs which are charged as expenses against the revenue of the period in which they are incurred. These costs are not assigned to product/ project, but are treated as expenses of the period in which they are incurred.

References

- Schwartz, Robert (2010). Micro Markets: A Market Structure Approach to Microeconomic Analysis. Hoboken, New Jersey: John Wiley & Sons, 2010. p. 202. ISBN 0-470-44765-6
- Monden, Yasuhiro & Kazuki Hamada (1991). "Target costing and kaizen costing in Japanese automobile companies". Journal of Management Accounting Research
- Clifton, Bird, Albano & Townsend (2004). Target Costing; Market-Driven Product Design. Marcel Dekker, Inc. ISBN 0-8247-4611-2
- Gittins, Ross (19 April 2014). "At the coal face economists are struggling to measure up". The Sydney Morning Herald. Retrieved 23 April 2014
- Khandwalla, Pradip (Autumn 1972). "The Effect of Different Types of Competition on the Use of Management Controls". Journal of Accounting Research. 10 (2): 275–285
- Chew, Lynsie; Parkinson, Alan (2013). Making Sense of Accounting for Business. Harlow: Pearson. ISBN 9781782369295
- Gelles, Gregory M., and Mitchell, Douglas W., "Returns to scale and economies of scale: Further observations," Journal of Economic Education 27, Summer 1996, 259-261

- Guide to the Project Management Body of Knowledge (PMBOK Guide) Third Edition, An American National Standard, ANSI/PMI 99-001-2004, Project Management Institute, Inc, 2004, ISBN 1-930699-45-X
- Accounting Information Systems: Information on Collection, Storage and Processing of Financial and Accounting Data. Accounting Information Systems. Retrieved 7 December 2012
- Dr Alex, Suleman. "A controversial-issues approach to enhance management accounting education". Journal of Accounting Education. 1994: 59–75
- Standard Estimating Practice Sixth Edition, American Society of Professional Estimators, Bni Publications, Inc, 2004, ISBN 1557014817
- "Definition of Management Accounting" (PDF). Institute of Management Accountants. 2008. Retrieved 4 December 2012s

2

Forms of Cost Accumulation

Direct costs are prices which are directly accountable to objects which have costs assigned to them. Indirect costs are costs that are not directly accountable to the object concerned. Cost allocation, total absorption costing, balanced scorecard and activity based costing are some of the other topics discussed in the following section. Cost accounting is best understood in confluence with the major topics listed in the following chapter.

Cost Accumulation

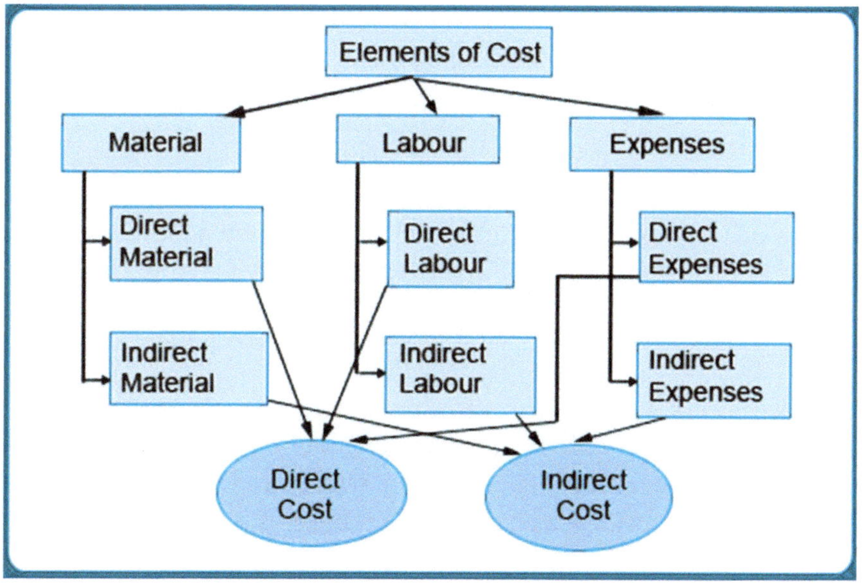

Direct Costs

Direct costs are costs which are directly accountable to a cost object (such as a particular project, facility, function or product). Some overhead costs which can be directly attributed to a project (e.g. a designated project manager) may also be classified as a direct cost.

Direct costs are directly attributable to the object. In construction, the costs of materials, labor, equipment, etc., and all directly involved efforts or expenses for the cost object are direct costs. In manufacturing or other non-construction industries, the portion of operating costs which is directly assignable to a specific product or process is a direct cost. Direct costs are those for activities or services that benefit specific projects, for example salaries for project staff and materials required for a particular project. Because these activities are easily traced to projects, their costs are usually charged to projects on an item-by-item basis.

Direct costs typically include:

- Direct materials used in manufacturing
- Direct labour
- Direct expenses, e.g. a royalty payment to a patent holder for a specific production process.

Direct Material Cost

- Includes the cost of materials and reasonable allowances for scrap and defective units.
- The cost considered for material include freight and related charges but exclude purchase discounts.

Direct Labour Cost

- Consists the cost of the labour that is used in the actual manufacture of the product or that is used to provide the service.
- It also includes the cost associated with the nonproductive time that is considered unavoidable and normal.

Direct Expenses

It includes all expenses other than direct material or direct labour which are specially incurred for a particular cost object and can be identified in an economically feasible way.

Indirect Costs

Indirect costs are costs that are not directly accountable to a cost object (such as a particular project, facility, function or product). Indirect costs may be either fixed or variable. Indirect costs include administration, personnel and security costs. These are those costs which are not directly related to production. Some indirect costs may be overhead. But some overhead costs can be directly attributed to a project and are direct costs.

There are two types of indirect costs. One are the fixed indirect costs which contains activities or costs that are fixed for a particular project or company like transportation of labor to the working site, building temporary roads, etc. The other are recurring indirect costs which contains activities that repeat for a particular company like maintenance of records or payment of salaries.

Indirect vs Direct Costs

Most cost estimates are broken down into direct costs and indirect costs.

Direct costs are directly attributable to the object. In construction, the costs of materials, labor, equipment, etc., and all directly involved efforts or expenses for the cost object are direct costs. In manufacturing or other non-construction industries the portion of operating costs that is directly assignable to a specific product or process is a direct cost. Direct costs are those for activities or services that benefit specific projects, for example salaries for project staff and materials required for a particular project. Because these activities are easily traced to projects, their costs are usually charged to projects on an item-by-item basis.

Indirect costs are not directly attributable to a cost object. Indirect costs are typically allocated to a cost object on some basis. In construction, all costs which are required for completion of the installation, but are not directly attributable to the cost object are indirect, such as overhead. In manufacturing, costs not directly assignable to the end product or process are indirect. These may be costs for management, insurance, taxes, or maintenance, for example. Indirect costs are those for activities or services that benefit more than one project. Their precise benefits to a specific project are often difficult or impossible to trace. For example, it may be difficult to determine precisely how the activities of the director of an organization benefit a specific project. Indirect costs do not vary substantially within certain production volumes or other indicators of activity, and so they may sometimes be considered to be fixed costs.

It is possible to justify the handling of almost any kind of cost as either direct or indirect. Labor costs, for example, can be indirect, as in the case of maintenance personnel and executive officers; or they can be direct, as in the case of project staff members. Similarly, materials such as miscellaneous supplies purchased in bulk—pencils, pens, paper—are typically handled as indirect costs, while materials required for specific projects are charged as direct costs.

Examples

Be cautious here, because the nature of the cost depends on the industry. For example, fuel cost in a telecom is usually allocated as an indirect cost, while for an airliner it is a direct cost.

Costs Usually Charged Directly

- Project staff
- Consultants
- Project supplies
- Publications
- Travel
- Labor
- Direct materials
- Electricity (only if electricity is the principal source)
- Clothes

It is to be noted that if electricity is not used as primary source for production then electricity cost will be treated as utility and is always indirect. For example, electricity is required to run boiler which in turn generates steam, so then electricity will be treated as utility which needs to be allocated.

Costs Either Charged Directly or Allocated Indirectly

- Directors Salary (this is usually an indirect cost)
- Electricity (mostly if it needs allocation it is always indirect)

Costs Usually Allocated Indirectly

- Electricity & other utilities
- Administration cost
- Selling & distribution cost
- Office cost

Indirect Material Cost

- Refers to the cost of materials used in manufacturing that are not physically a part of finished good.
- E.g.: supplies used by manufacturing employees, materials required by machines such as lubricants.

Indirect Labour Cost

- Includes the costs associated with quality control, supervision, support cost associated with manufacturing, inspection, purchase and receiving costs.

Indirect Expenses

Other Indirect Expenses include depreciation on machines and plant, property taxes, utilities, carriage outward, etc.

Cost Object

A cost object is a term used primarily in cost accounting to describe something to which costs are assigned. Common examples of cost objects are: product lines, geographic territories, customers, departments or anything else for which management would like to quantify cost.

The use of cost objects is common within activity based costing and Grenzplankostenrechnung systems.

Cost Centre (Business)

A cost centre is a department within a business to which costs can be allocated. The term includes departments which does not produce directly but incurs costs to the business, when the manager and employees of the cost centre are not accountable for the profitability and investment decisions of the business but they are responsible for some of its costs.

Types

There are two main types of cost centres:

- Production cost centres: This is where the products are manufactured or processed. Example of this is an assembly area.
- Service cost centres: This is where a service is provided to other cost centres. Example of this is the personnel department or the canteen.

Examples

- Marketing Department
- Human resources
- Research and Development
- Work office
- Quality Assurance
- Engineering

Function-specific Cost

The main function of a cost centre is the tracing of all expenses linked with a certain function. For example, by considering a call centre as an independent unit, the firm can calculate how much it is spending each year for its 1-800 support service. If a cost centre is not considered independent then it would take a lot of effort in measuring the cost of providing this service because it will include dividing up the company's entire personnel and phone bills by department each month.

Benefits

There are numerous benefits of a cost centre which include:

- Monitoring efficiency – Cost centres are beneficial as they allow the effectiveness of all aspects within a company to be monitored closely.
- Boosts employees confidence – The delegation of authority that takes place when making employees accountable for cost centre is a good way to improve confidence.
- Preventing loss – Cost centres try to update processes, be more effective and save money so that they can reduce the expenses. Cost centres try to cover all of their costs with offsetting revenue by reducing expenses and producing unpredicted revenue, thus preventing loss.
- Increasing profit – If one of the cost centres is removed from a firm then it has a negative impact on the profit margin of that firm. For example, if an HR department was removed

then basic employment functions and essential business processes cannot be performed which will affect the firm's profit negatively.

- Makes the manager more efficient – Managers compare cost data from different time periods in order to see whether the cost centre is becoming more or less profitable. Generally a specific person (a cost centre manager) is held accountable for costs incurring in the cost centre under his or her control, in which case, collecting and comparing costs may motivate the manager to be more productive.

Drawbacks

There are a few drawbacks of cost centre which include:

- Negative effects on other departments - although the cost of operating a specific department is simple to calculate, cost centres are a source of encouragement for managers to underfund their elements so that it can benefit the cost centre, which can have a harmful effect on other departments within the firm.
- Hard to monitor efficiency- It is hard to keep a track of how efficient these centres are.
- Profit can not be controlled- Divisional performance can only be evaluated in terms of cost because profit is not in control of the manager.
- Efficiency and productivity cannot be assessed properly - in a cost centre, the result of a decision is calculated by cost alone; the achievements of the cost centre are not measured in financial terms, therefore it is hard to assess efficiency and productivity properly.

Difference between a Cost Centre and a Profit Centre

A cost centre adds to a firm's cost whereas a profit centre adds to the firm's cost and profit. Furthermore, the main objective of a cost centre is to minimise cost whereas the main objective of a profit centre is to maximise profit. Profit centres provide a wider and more general measurement of performance than the cost centre. In cost centre, the manager is only responsible for the cost whereas in a profit centre, the manager is responsible for cost and profit. In situations like this when manager is responsible for both, profit and cost, the contribution of each manager to the goal of the firm becomes easier to measure.

Manufacturing Overhead Costs

Manufacturing overhead costs (MOH cost) are all manufacturing costs that are related to the cost object (work in process and then finished goods) but cannot be traced to that cost object in an economically feasible way.

Examples include supplies, indirect materials such as lubricants, indirect manufacturing labor such as plant maintenance and cleaning labor, plant rent, plant insurance, property taxes on the plant, plant depreciation, and the compensation of plant managers.

This cost category is also referred to as Factory overhead cost (FO cost).

Items of the Overhead

Manufacturing overhead includes other costs in manufacturing that are neither direct materials costs nor direct labor costs. It might also be referred as the factory burden or production overhead. Its value is essential for determining the cost of products to be manufactured.

This category of costs includes expenses like:

1. Electricity for the equipment and lighting.
2. Cleaning costs of equipment.
3. Material handling like forklifts
4. Maintenance of the equipment.
5. Wages of employees in the factory who for example work on record keeping and inspection of materials.
6. Computing the operation of the process of manufacturing the product.
7. Insurance
8. Safety and quality cost.

Factory Overhead

Factory overhead, also called manufacturing overhead or work overhead, is the total cost involved in operating all production facilities of a manufacturing business. It generally applies to indirect labor and indirect cost, it also includes all costs involved in manufacturing with the exception of the cost of raw materials and direct labor. Factory overhead also includes certain costs such as quality assurance costs, cleanup costs, and property insurance premiums.

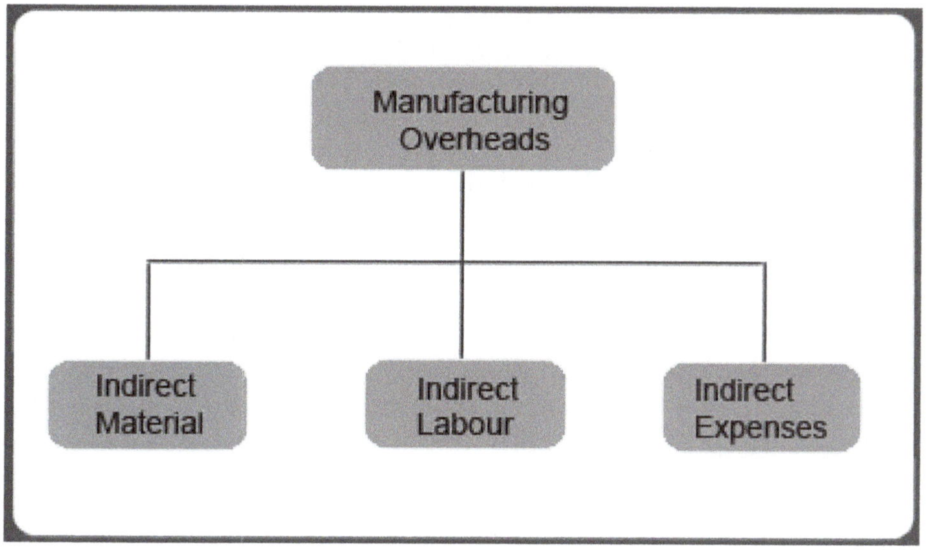

Manufacturing Cost Flow

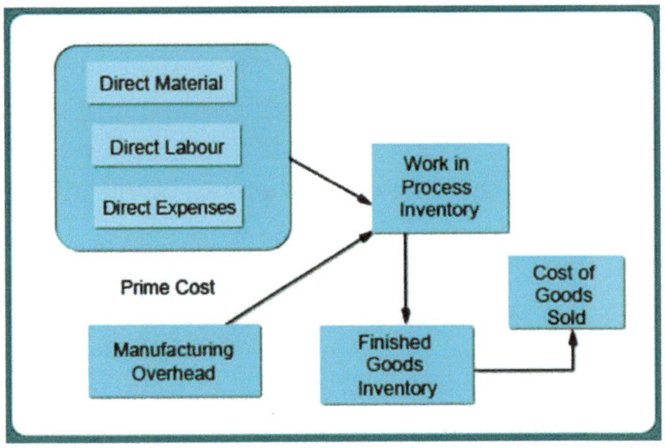

Cost Allocation

Cost allocation is a process of providing relief to shared service organization's cost centers that provide a product or service. In turn, the associated expense is assigned to internal clients' cost centers that consume the products and services. For example, the CIO may provide all IT services within the company and assign the costs back to the business units that consume each offering.

The core components of a cost allocation system consist of a way to track which organizations provides a product and/or service, the organizations that consume the products and/or services, and a list of portfolio offerings (e.g. service catalog). Depending on the operating structure within a company, the cost allocation data may generate an internal invoice or feed an ERP system's chargeback module. Accessing the data via an invoice or chargeback module are the typical methods that drive personnel behavior. In return, the consumption data becomes a great source of quantitative information to make better business decisions. Today's organizations face growing pressure to control costs and enable responsible financial management of resources. In this environment, an organization is expected to provide services cost-effectively and deliver business value while operating under tight budgetary constraints. One way to contain costs is to implement a cost allocation methodology, where your business units become directly accountable for the services they consume.

An effective cost allocation methodology enables an organization to identify what services are being provided and what they cost, to allocate costs to business units, and to manage cost recovery. Under this model, both the service provider and its respective consumers become aware of their service requirements and usage and how they directly influence the costs incurred. This information, in turn, improves discipline within the business units and financial discipline across the entire organization. With the organization articulating the costs of services provided, the business units become empowered – and encouraged – to make informed decisions about the services and availability levels they request. They can make trade-offs between service levels and costs, and they can benchmark internal costs against outsourced providers.

Types of Costs

Every organization must define their costs, like how funding runs through the organization, who touches it, what they do and how they do it serves as a foundation for this understanding. According to the Office of Management and Budget's (OMB) Uniform Guidance, there are only three types of costs – Indirect, Indirect-Admin (Overhead) and Direct. By correctly defining and allocating costs, true cost of service can be fully captured.

1. Direct costs - are those that can be associated specifically to a final cost objective. You know what you spend on programs. You know what expenses go directly to your mission. Most importantly, you know what expenses go directly to those benefitting from your service.
2. Indirect costs - are things that you need to do for the sake of the organizational health & operations, but don't tie back to a specific program. For instance, the actual time (resources) that need to be dedicated when working with your Internet provider to fix the organization's connection is important, but it 's unlikely that the time spent can be tied to one particular function in a program.
3. Indirect-Admin (Overhead) costs - are defined as those that are not Direct but are necessary for the immediate support of the program. Indirect-Admin costs or Overhead are very important to nonprofits since unlike government, they do not necessarily have separate buckets of funding. If Direct costs are the foundation, the Overhead costs are one touch away. So, when you are working on managing a program, leading those working for a program in their work or simply accounting for program expenses and revenues, you are only one touch away and are, in effect, performing direct activities. These activities can be attributed to your Direct Costs for purposes of expense reimbursement.

Total Absorption Costing

Total absorption costing (TAC) is a method of Accounting cost which entails the full cost of manufacturing or providing a service. TAC includes not just the costs of materials and labour, but also of all manufacturing overheads (whether 'fixed' or 'variable').The cost of each cost center can be direct or indirect cost. The direct cost can be easily identified with individual cost centers. whereas the indirect cost can't be easily identified with the cost center. The distribution of overhead among the departments is called apportionment.

Primary Apportionment or Distribution of Overheads

The selection of the base on which overheads are or should be apportioned depends on the following principles:

- Service or use basis: If the benefit obtained by various departments from the overheads can be measured, overheads can be apportioned on that basis.
- survey basis: If amount of overhead can't be measured survey basis can be applied. For example, if it can be noted that a supervisor is giving 60% of his time to one department and 40% to another his wages can be apportioned on that basis.

- Ability to pay basis: In this case the apportionment may depend on the factors like total sale/profitability. This may not be a fair case always as some departments may have to take most of the burden.

Secondary Apportionment

With the process of primary apportionment or distribution, the loading of overheads for all the departments i.e. production as well as service departments can be obtained. The next step is to transfer the overheads of non-production departments to the production departments, as the various cost centers move through the production departments only.

Absorption

Each job while moving through the production department should get its share of overhead. This process of distribution of overheads is called absorption. There can be a number of methods of absorption of overheads, consideration should be given to the type of industry, manufacturing process, nature of industry etc. The various methods of absorption are

- Direct material cost percentage rate
- Direct labour cost percentage rate
- Prime cost percentage rate
- Labour hour rate
- Machine hour rate

Direct Material Cost Percentage Rate

In this method overhead is calculated as a percentage of the material cost. This is used where the material cost is high and of prime importance. Here other costs are negligible or are dependent on the material cost. This is calculated as (Amount of overhead/Material cost)x 100 If the production overhead is 3,000 and the material cost is 10,000 then the absorption rate will be (3000/10000) x 100 = 30%

Now for a product if the material cost is 1000 then the overhead cost is 300. so the total cost would be 1300. The classic example of and industry using this type of absorption are gold jewelers the typical absorption rate varies from 2-5% of the cost of the gold. If the cost of the material fluctuates this method cannot be used. For this type of absorption the material cost should be stable. If in the same industry material of different cost is used the calculation becomes unjustified, especially when the cost of the material differ too much.

Direct Labour Cost Percentage Rate

In this method cost is absorbed as a percent of the labour cost or the wages. (Overhead cost/Labour cost)x 100 If the Labour cost is 5000 and the overhead cost is 1000 then the absorption cost is 20%. If the labour cost of one job is 500 it will have to absorb 20% i.e. 100 as the overhead cost making the total cost to be 600. This method can be used in service industry where the major input is the skilled or unskilled labour. For the proper calculation labour rates need to be constant and the skill and efficiency of the labourer need to be identical.

Prime Cost Percentage Rate

In this method both material cost as well as labour cost is the base for calculating the overhead absorption. It is calculated as (Overhead Cost/Prime cost)x 100. Prime cost is nothing but the sum of direct material cost and direct labour cost.

Labour Hour Rate

This method is mostly used if the industry is labour-intensive and the labour is mostly unskilled or semiskilled. It is calculated as (overhead cost/ Labour hours required for production) if the labour hour required is 1000 and the overhead to be absorbed is 250 then the rate is .25 per labour hour. if 20 labour hours are required to complete a job then the overhead will be 5.

Machine Hour Rate

If the industry considered is having high degree of automation and mechanization then this method can be used. Here the major chunk of the cost comes from the utilization of the machines. it is calculated as (overhead cost/ number of machine hours) This is very useful if the running cost of the machines including rent are the dominant part of the cost of the product.

One of the main reasons for absorbing overheads into the cost of is for inventory valuation purposes. Absorption costing is permissible under GAAP.

Traditional TAC was developed in the age of manufacturing and mostly used to arrive at the full manufacturing cost of producing goods; an alternative method of arriving at full cost known as activity-based costing (ABC) is often thought to be more appropriate for services. Absorption costing is a means of incorporating a fair share of indirect cost or overheads into the cost of a unit of product or service provided.

Absorption Costing

A costing method that includes all manufacturing costs—direct materials, direct labour, and both overhead—in unit product costs. According to the ICMA London "Absorption costing is a principle whereby fixed as well as variable costs are allocated to cost unit the term may be applied where production costs only or costs of all function are so allocated".

Cost Apportionment

- At this stage, those items of estimated overheads which cannot be directly allocated to various cost centers or departments are apportioned.
- Apportionment implies the allotment of proportions of items of cost to cost centers or departments. It implies that unallocable expenses are to be spread over the cost centers or departments on an equitable basis.

- After this stage, all the overhead costs would have been either allocated to or apportioned over various departments.

Cost Driver

A cost driver is the unit of an activity that causes the change in activity's cost.

Cost driver is any factor which causes a change in the cost of an activity

—*Chartered Institute of Management Accountants*

"Cost drivers are the structural determinants of the cost of an activity, reflecting any linkages or interrelationships that affect it". Therefore we could assume that the cost drivers determine the cost behavior within the activities, reflecting the links that these have with other activities and relationships that affect them.

The Activity Based Costing (ABC) approach relates indirect cost to the activities that drive them to be incurred. Activity Based Costing is based on the belief that activities cause costs and therefore a link should be established between activities and product. The cost drivers thus are the link between the activities and the cost.

Generally, the cost driver for short term indirect variable costs may be the volume of output/activity; but for long term indirect variable costs, the cost drivers will not be related to volume of output/activity.

In traditional costing the cost driver to allocate indirect cost to cost objects was volume of output. With the change in business structures, technology and thereby cost structures it was found that the volume of output was not the only cost driver. John Shank and Vijay Govindarajan list cost drivers into two categories: Structural cost drivers that are derived from the business strategic choices about its underlying economic structure such as scale and scope of operations, complexity of products, use of technology, etc., and Executional cost drivers that are derived from the execution of the business activities such as capacity utilization, plant layout, work-force involvement, etc. Resource cost Driver is measure of quantity of resources consumed by an activity. It is used to assign cost of a resource to activity or cost pool. Activity Cost Driver is measure of frequency and intensity of demand placed on activities by cost object. It is used to assign activity costs to cost objects.

To carry out a value chain analysis, ABC is a necessary tool. To carry out ABC, it is necessary that cost drivers are established for different cost pools.

Examples

Some examples of indirect costs and their drivers are: indirect costs for maintenance, with the possible driver of this cost being the number of machine hours; or, the indirect cost of handling raw-material cost, which may be driven by the number of orders received; or, inspection costs that are driven by the number of inspections or the hours of inspection or production runs. In marketing, cost drivers are Number of advertisements, Number of sales personnel etc. In Customer service, cost drivers are Number of service calls attended, number of staff in service department, number of warranties handled, Hours spent on servicing etc..

Balanced Scorecard

The balanced scorecard (BSC) is a strategy performance management tool – a semi-standard structured report, supported by design methods and automation tools, that can be used by managers to keep track of the execution of activities by the staff within their control and to monitor the consequences arising from these actions.

The phrase 'balanced scorecard' is commonly used in two broad forms:

1. As individual scorecards that contain measures to manage performance, those scorecards may be operational or have a more strategic intent; and
2. As a Strategic Management System, as originally defined by Kaplan & Norton.

The critical characteristics that define a balanced scorecard are:

- its focus on the strategic agenda of the organization concerned
- the selection of a small number of data items to monitor
- a mix of financial and non-financial data items.

Use

Balanced scorecard is an example of a closed-loop controller or cybernetic control applied to the management of the implementation of a strategy. Closed-loop or cybernetic control is where actual performance is measured, the measured value is compared to a reference value and based on the difference between the two corrective interventions are made as required. Such control requires three things to be effective:

- a choice of data to measure,
- the setting of a reference value for the data,
- the ability to make a corrective intervention.

Within the strategy management context, all three of these characteristic closed-loop control elements need to be derived from the organisation's strategy and also need to reflect the ability of the observer to both monitor performance and subsequently intervene – both of which may be constrained. Initially, Balanced Scorecard emerged as a performance management system, over a period of time it has come to be known as a strategy management system, with its ultimate aim being the achievement of long term financial performance. Balanced scorecard is seen as a strategic management system enabling business leaders to meet the challenge of strategy execution.

Two of the ideas that underpin modern balanced scorecard designs concern facilitating the creation of such a control – through making it easier to select which data to observe, and ensuring that the choice of data is consistent with the ability of the observer to intervene.

History

Organizations have used systems consisting of a mix of financial and non-financial measures to track progress for quite some time. One such system was created by Art Schneiderman in 1987 at Analog Devices, a mid-sized semi-conductor company; the Analog Devices Balanced Scorecard. Schneiderman's design was similar to what is now recognised as a "First Generation" Balanced Scorecard design.

In 1990 Art Schneiderman participated in an unrelated research study led by Robert S. Kaplan in conjunction with US management consultancy Nolan-Norton, and during this study described his work on performance measurement. Subsequently, Kaplan and David P. Norton included anonymous details of this balanced scorecard design in a 1992 article. Kaplan and Norton's article wasn't the only paper on the topic published in early 1992 but the 1992 Kaplan and Norton paper was a popular success, and was quickly followed by a second in 1993. In 1996, the two authors published a book *The Balanced Scorecard*. These articles and the first book spread knowledge of the concept of balanced scorecard widely, and has led to Kaplan and Norton being seen as the creators of the concept.

While the "corporate scorecard" terminology was coined by Art Schneiderman, the roots of performance management as an activity run deep in management literature and practice. Management historians such as Alfred Chandler suggest the origins of performance management can be seen in the emergence of the complex organisation – most notably during the 19th Century in the USA. More recent influences may include the pioneering work of General Electric on performance measurement reporting in the 1950s and the work of French process engineers (who created the *tableau de bord* – literally, a "dashboard" of performance measures) in the early part of the 20th century. The tool also draws strongly on the ideas of the 'resource based view of the firm' proposed by Edith Penrose. However it should be noted that none of these influences is explicitly linked to original descriptions of balanced scorecard by Schneiderman, Maisel, or Kaplan & Norton.

Kaplan and Norton's first book remains their most popular. The book reflects the earliest incarnations of balanced scorecards – effectively restating the concept as described in the second Harvard Business Review article. Their second book, *The Strategy Focused Organization*, echoed work by others (particularly a book published the year before by Olve et al. in Scandinavia) on the value of visually documenting the links between measures by proposing the "Strategic Linkage Model" or strategy map.

As the title of Kaplan and Norton's second book highlights, even by 2000 the focus of attention among thought-leaders was moving from the design of Balanced Scorecards themselves, towards the use of Balanced Scorecard as a focal point within a more comprehensive strategic management system. Subsequent writing on Balanced Scorecard by Kaplan & Norton has focused on uses of Balanced Scorecard rather than its design (e.g. "The Execution Premium" in 2008), however many others have continued to refine the device itself (e.g. Abernethy et al.).

Characteristics

The characteristics of the balanced scorecard and its derivatives is the presentation of a mixture of financial and non-financial measures each compared to a 'target' value within a single concise report. The report is not meant to be a replacement for traditional financial or operational reports but a succinct summary that captures the information most relevant to those reading it. It is the method by which this 'most relevant' information is determined (i.e., the design processes used to select the content) that most differentiates the various versions of the tool in circulation. The balanced scorecard indirectly also provides a useful insight into an organisation's strategy – by requiring general strategic statements (e.g. mission, vision) to be precipitated into more specific/tangible forms.

The first versions of balanced scorecard asserted that relevance should derive from the corporate strategy, and proposed design methods that focused on choosing measures and targets associated with the main activities required to implement the strategy. As the initial audience for this were the readers of the Harvard Business Review, the proposal was translated into a form that made sense to a typical reader of that journal – managers of US commercial businesses. Accordingly, initial designs were encouraged to measure three categories of non-financial measure in addition to financial outputs – those of "customer," "internal business processes" and "learning and growth." These categories were not so relevant to non-profits or units within complex organizations (which might have high degrees of internal specialization), and much of the early literature on balanced scorecard focused on suggestions of alternative 'perspectives' that might have more relevance to these groups.

Modern balanced scorecards have evolved since the initial ideas proposed in the late 1980s and early 1990s, and the modern performance management tools including Balanced Scorecard are significantly improved – being more flexible (to suit a wider range of organisational types) and more effective (as design methods have evolved to make them easier to design, and use).

Design

Design of a balanced scorecard is about the identification of a small number of financial and non-financial measures and attaching targets to them, so that when they are reviewed it is possible to determine whether current performance 'meets expectations'. By alerting managers to areas where performance deviates from expectations, they can be encouraged to focus their attention on these areas, and hopefully as a result trigger improved performance within the part of the organization they lead.

The original thinking behind a balanced scorecard was for it to be focused on information relating to the implementation of a strategy, and over time there has been a blurring of the boundaries between conventional strategic planning and control activities and those required to design a balanced scorecard. This is illustrated well by the four steps required to design a balanced scorecard included in Kaplan & Norton's writing on the subject in the late 1990s:

1. Translating the vision into operational goals;
2. Communicating the vision and link it to individual performance;
3. Business planning; index setting
4. Feedback and learning, and adjusting the strategy accordingly.

These steps go far beyond the simple task of identifying a small number of financial and non-financial measures, but illustrate the requirement for whatever design process is used to fit within broader thinking about how the resulting balanced scorecard will integrate with the wider business management process.

Although it helps focus managers' attention on strategic issues and the management of the implementation of strategy, it is important to remember that the balanced scorecard itself has no role in the formation of strategy. In fact, balanced scorecards can co-exist with strategic planning systems and other tools.

First Generation

The first generation of balanced scorecard designs used a "4 perspective" approach to identify what measures to use to track the implementation of strategy. `The original four "perspectives" proposed were:

- Financial: encourages the identification of a few relevant high-level financial measures. In particular, designers were encouraged to choose measures that helped inform the answer to the question "How do we look to shareholders?" Examples: cash flow, sales growth, operating income, return on equity.
- Customer: encourages the identification of measures that answer the question "What is important to our customers and stakeholders?" Examples: percent of sales from new products, on time delivery, share of important customers' purchases, ranking by important customers.
- Internal business processes: encourages the identification of measures that answer the question "What must we excel at?"Examples: cycle time, unit cost, yield, new product introductions.
- Learning and growth: encourages the identification of measures that answer the question "How can we continue to improve, create value and innovate?". Examples: time to develop new generation of products, life cycle to product maturity, time to market versus competition.

The idea was that managers used these perspective headings to prompt the selection of a small number of measures that informed on that aspect of the organisation's strategic performance. The perspective headings show that Kaplan and Norton were thinking about the needs of non-divisional commercial organisations in their initial design. These headings are not very helpful to other kinds of organisations (e.g. multi-divisional or multi-national commercial organisations, governmental organisations, non-profits, non-governmental organisations, government agencies etc.), and much of what has been written on balanced scorecard since has, in one way or another, focused on the identification of alternative headings more suited to a broader range of organisations, and also suggested using either additional or fewer perspectives (e.g. Butler et al. (1997), Ahn (2001), Elefalke (2001), Brignall (2002), Irwin (2002), Radnor et al. (2003)).

These suggestions were notably triggered by a recognition that different but equivalent headings would yield alternative sets of measures, and this represents the major design challenge faced with this type of balanced scorecard design: justifying the choice of measures made. "Of all the measures you could have chosen, why did you choose these?" These issues contribute to dis-satisfaction with early Balanced Scorecard designs, since if users are not confident that the measures within the Balanced Scorecard are well chosen, they will have less confidence in the information it provides.

Although less common, these early-style balanced scorecards are still designed and used today.

In short, first generation balanced scorecards are hard to design in a way that builds confidence that they are well designed. Because of this, many are abandoned soon after completion.

Second Generation

In the mid-1990s, an improved design method emerged. In the new method, measures are selected based on a set of "strategic objectives" plotted on a "strategic linkage model" or "strategy map". With this modified approach, the strategic objectives are distributed across the four measurement perspectives, so as to "connect the dots" to form a visual presentation of strategy and measures.

In this modified version of balanced scorecard design, managers select a few strategic objectives within each of the perspectives, and then define the cause-effect chain among these objectives by drawing links between them to create a "strategic linkage model". A balanced scorecard of strategic performance measures is then derived directly by selecting one or two measures for each strategic objective. This type of approach provides greater contextual justification for the measures chosen, and is generally easier for managers to work through. This style of balanced scorecard has been commonly used since 1996 or so: it is significantly different in approach to the methods originally proposed, and so can be thought of as representing the "2nd generation" of design approach adopted for balanced scorecard since its introduction.

Third Generation

In the late 1990s, the design approach had evolved yet again. One problem with the "second generation" design approach described above was that the plotting of causal links amongst twenty or so medium-term strategic goals was still a relatively abstract activity. In practice it ignored the fact that opportunities to intervene, to influence strategic goals are, and need to be, anchored in current and real management activity. Secondly, the need to "roll forward" and test the impact of these goals necessitated the creation of an additional design instrument: the Vision or Destination Statement. This device was a statement of what "strategic success", or the "strategic end-state", looked like. It was quickly realized that if a Destination Statement was created at the beginning of the design process, then it was easier to select strategic activity and outcome objectives to respond to it. Measures and targets could then be selected to track the achievement of these objectives. Design methods that incorporate a Destination Statement or equivalent (e.g. the results-based management method proposed by the UN in 2002) represent a tangibly different design approach to those that went before, and have been proposed as representing a "third generation" design method for balanced scorecards.

Design methods for balanced scorecards continue to evolve and adapt to reflect the deficiencies in the currently used methods, and the particular needs of communities of interest (e.g. NGO's and government departments have found the third generation methods embedded in results-based management more useful than first or second generation design methods).

This generation refined the second generation of balanced scorecards to give more relevance and functionality to strategic objectives. The major difference is the incorporation of Destination

Statements. Other key components are strategic objectives, strategic linkage model and perspectives, measures and initiatives.

Popularity

In 1997, Kurtzman found that 64 percent of the companies questioned were measuring performance from a number of perspectives in a similar way to the balanced scorecard. Balanced scorecards have been implemented by government agencies, military units, business units and corporations as a whole, non-profit organizations, and schools.

Balanced scorecard has been widely adopted, and has been found to be the most popular performance management framework in a recent survey.

Many examples of balanced scorecards can be found via web searches. However, adapting one organization's balanced scorecard to another is generally not advised by theorists, who believe that much of the benefit of the balanced scorecard comes from the design process itself. Indeed, it could be argued that many failures in the early days of balanced scorecard could be attributed to this problem, in that early balanced scorecards were often designed remotely by consultants. Managers did not trust, and so failed to engage with and use, these measure suites created by people lacking knowledge of the organization and management responsibility.

Variants

Since the balanced scorecard was popularized in the early 1990s, a large number of alternatives to the original 'four box' balanced scorecard promoted by Kaplan and Norton in their various articles and books have emerged. Most have very limited application, and are typically proposed either by academics as vehicles for expanding the dialogue beyond the financial bottom line – e.g. Brignall (2002) or consultants as an attempt at differentiation to promote sales of books and / or consultancy (e.g. Bourne (2002); Niven (2002)).

Many of the structural variations proposed are broadly similar, and a research paper published in 2004 attempted to identify a pattern in these variations – noting three distinct types of variation. The variations appeared to be part of an evolution of the balanced scorecard concept, and so the paper refers to these distinct types as "generations". Broadly, the original 'measures in boxes' type design (as proposed by Kaplan & Norton) constitutes the 1st generation balanced scorecard design; balanced scorecard designs that include a 'strategy map' or 'strategic linkage model' (e.g. the Performance Prism, later Kaplan & Norton designs the Performance Driver model of Olve, Roy & Wetter (English translation 1999, 1st published in Swedish 1997)) constitute the 2nd Generation of Balanced Scorecard design; and designs that augment the strategy map / strategic linkage model with a separate document describing the long-term outcomes sought from the strategy (the "destination statement" idea) comprise the 3rd generation balanced scorecard design.

Variants that feature adaptations of the structure of balanced scorecard to suit better a particular viewpoint or agenda are numerous. Examples of the focus of such adaptations include the triple bottom line, decision support, public sector management, and health care management. The performance management elements of the UN's Results Based Management system have strong design and structural similarities to those used in the 3rd Generation Balanced Scorecard design approach.

Balanced scorecard is also often linked to quality management tools and activities. Although there are clear areas of cross-over and association, the two sets of tools are complementary rather than duplicative.

A common use of balanced scorecard is to support the payments of incentives to individuals, even though it was not designed for this purpose and is not particularly suited to it.

Criticism

The balanced scorecard has attracted criticism from a variety of sources. Most have come from the academic community, who dislike the empirical nature of the framework: Kaplan and Norton notoriously failed to include any citation of earlier articles in their initial papers on the topic. Some of this criticism focuses on technical flaws in the methods and design of the original balanced scorecard proposed by Kaplan and Norton,. Other academics have simply focused on the lack of citation support.

A second kind of criticism is that the balanced scorecard does not provide a bottom line score or a unified view with clear recommendations: it is simply a list of metrics (e.g. Jensen 2001). These critics usually include in their criticism suggestions about how the 'unanswered' question postulated could be answered, but typically the unanswered question relate to things outside the scope of balanced scorecard itself (such as developing strategies) (e.g. Brignall).

A third kind of criticism is that the model fails to fully reflect the needs of stakeholders – putting bias on financial stakeholders over others. Early forms of Balanced Scorecard proposed by Kaplan & Norton focused on the needs of commercial organisations in the USA – where this focus on investment return was appropriate. This focus was maintained through subsequent revisions. Even now over 20 years after they were first proposed, the four most common perspectives in Balanced Scorecard designs mirror the four proposed in the original Kaplan & Norton paper. However, as noted earlier in this article, there have been many studies that suggest other perspectives might better reflect the priorities of organisations – particularly but not exclusively relating to the needs of organisations in the public and Non Governmental sectors. For instance, the balanced scorecard does not address important aspects of nonprofit strategy such as social dimensions, human resource elements, political issues and the distinctive nature of competition and collaboration in nonprofit settings. Thus, the model seems to be less effective in nonprofit organisations as the model's strategy, cause-and-effect relationships and its four linked perspectives are incompatible to the unique nonprofit environment. More modern design approaches such as 3rd Generation Balanced Scorecard and the UN's Results Based Management methods explicitly consider the interests of wider stakeholder groups, and perhaps address this issue in its entirety.

There are few empirical studies linking the use of balanced scorecards to better decision making or improved financial performance of companies, but some work has been done in these areas. However, broadcast surveys of usage have difficulties in this respect, due to the wide variations in definition of 'what a balanced scorecard is' noted above (making it hard to work out in a survey if you are comparing like with like). Single organization case studies suffer from the 'lack of a control' issue common to any study of organizational change – what the organization would have achieved if the change had not been made isn't known, so it is difficult to attribute changes observed over time to a single intervention (such as introducing a balanced scorecard). However, such studies as have been done have typically found balanced scorecard to be useful.

A few studies go further, trying to explain PMS size differences in terms of cause and effect. For example, Hvolby and Thorstenson (2000) and McAdam (2000) suggest that the Balanced Scorecard is completely unsuitable for SMEs because of their lack of a longer-term strategic focus. They also argue that the characteristics of SMEs make most, if not all, PM models inappropriate although they do not develop the argument in terms of causality. Similarly, Rompho's (2011) study of a failed implementation of the Balanced Scorecard in an SME attributed the cause to too many changes to the organisation's strategy. Others have suggested that SMEs have limited knowledge about performance measurement in general (Rantanen and Holtari 2000) and do not understand the benefits of PMS implementation (McAdam 2000; Bourne 2001), but none of these studies attempts to theorise the reasons behind their findings.

Software Tools

It is important to recognize that the balanced scorecard by definition is not a complex thing – typically no more than about 20 measures spread across a mix of financial and non-financial topics, and easily reported manually (on paper, or using simple office software).

The processes of collecting, reporting, and distributing balanced scorecard information can be labor-intensive and prone to procedural problems (for example, getting all relevant people to return the information required by the required date). The simplest mechanism to use is to delegate these activities to an individual, and many Balanced Scorecards are reported via ad-hoc methods based around email, phone calls and office software.

In more complex organizations, where there are multiple balanced scorecards to report and/or a need for co-ordination of results between balanced scorecards (for example, if one level of reports relies on information collected and reported at a lower level) the use of individual reporters is problematic. Where these conditions apply, organizations use balanced scorecard reporting software to automate the production and distribution of these reports.

Recent surveys have consistently found that roughly one third of organizations used office software to report their balanced scorecard, one third used software developed specifically for their own use, and one third used one of the many commercial packages available.

Economic Value Added

In corporate finance, economic value added (EVA) is an estimate of a firm's economic profit, or the value created in excess of the required return of the company's shareholders. EVA is the net profit less the equity cost of the firm's capital. The idea is that value is created when the return on the firm's economic capital employed exceeds the cost of that capital. This amount can be determined by making adjustments to GAAP accounting. There are potentially over 160 adjustments but in practice only several key ones are made, depending on the company and its industry. EVA is a service mark of Stern Value Management.

Calculation

EVA is net operating profit after taxes (or NOPAT) less a capital charge, the latter being the product of the cost of capital and the economic capital. The basic formula is:

$$\begin{aligned} EVA &= (ROIC - WACC) \cdot (\text{total assets} - \text{current liability}) \\ &= NOPAT - WACC \cdot (\text{total assets} - \text{current liability}) \end{aligned}$$

where:

- $ROIC = \dfrac{NOPAT}{\text{total assets} - \text{current liability}}$, is the return on invested capital;
- $(WACC)$ is the weighted average cost of capital (WACC);
- $(\text{total assets} - \text{current liability})$ is the economic capital employed (total assets – current liability);
- NOPAT is the net operating profit after tax, with adjustments and translations, generally for the amortization of goodwill, the capitalization of brand advertising and other non-cash items.

EVA calculation:

EVA = net operating profit after taxes – a capital charge [the residual income method]

therefore EVA = NOPAT – (c × capital), or alternatively

EVA = (r × capital) – (c × capital) so that

EVA = (r – c) × capital *[the spread method, or excess return method]*

where

r = rate of return, and

c = cost of capital, or the weighted average cost of capital (WACC).

NOPAT is profits derived from a company's operations after cash taxes but before financing costs and non-cash bookkeeping entries. It is the total pool of profits available to provide a cash return to those who provide capital to the firm.

Capital is the amount of cash invested in the business, net of depreciation. It can be calculated as the sum of interest-bearing debt and equity or as the sum of net assets less non-interest-bearing current liabilities (NIBCLs).

The capital charge is the cash flow required to compensate investors for the riskiness of the business given the amount of economic capital invested.

The cost of capital is the minimum rate of return on capital required to compensate investors (debt and equity) for bearing risk, their opportunity cost.

Another perspective on EVA can be gained by looking at a firm's return on net assets (RONA). RONA is a ratio that is calculated by dividing a firm's NOPAT by the amount of capital it employs (RONA = NOPAT/Capital) after making the necessary adjustments of the data reported by a conventional financial accounting system.

$$\text{EVA} = (\text{RONA} - \text{required minimum return}) \times \text{net investments}$$

If RONA is above the threshold rate, EVA is positive.

Comparison with Other Approaches

Other approaches along similar lines include residual income valuation (RI) and residual cash flow. Although EVA is similar to residual income, under some definitions there may be minor technical differences between EVA and RI (for example, adjustments that might be made to NOPAT before it is suitable for the formula below). Residual cash flow is another, much older term for economic profit. In all three cases, *money cost of capital* refers to the amount of money rather than the proportional cost (% cost of capital); at the same time, the adjustments to NOPAT are unique to EVA.

Although in concept, these approaches are in a sense nothing more than the traditional, common-sense idea of "profit", the utility of having a more precise term such as EVA is that it makes a clear separation from dubious accounting adjustments that have enabled businesses such as Enron to report profits while actually approaching insolvency.

Other measures of shareholder value include:

- Added value
- Market value added
- Total shareholder return

Market Value Added

The firm's market value added, or MVA, is the discounted sum (present value) of all future expected economic value added:

$$\text{MVA} = V - K_0 = \sum_{t=1}^{\infty} \frac{\text{EVA}_t}{(1+c)^t}$$

Note that MVA = PV of EVA.

More enlightening is that since MVA = NPV of free cash flow (FCF) it follows therefore that the

NPV of FCF = PV of EVA;

since after all, EVA is simply the re-arrangement of the FCF formula.

Process-based Costing

In 2012, Mocciaro Li Destri, Picone & Minà proposed a performance and cost measurement system that integrates the EVA criteria with process-based costing (PBC). The EVA-PBC methodology allows us to implement the EVA management logic not only at the firm level, but also at lower levels of the organization. EVA-PBC methodology plays an interesting role in bringing strategy back into financial performance measures.

Overhead (Business)

Overheads and direct costs, when combined, equals total expenses endured by a business.

In business, overhead or overhead expense refers to an ongoing expense of operating a business; it is also known as an *operating expense*. Overheads are the expenditure which cannot be conveniently traced to or identified with any particular cost unit. Therefore, overheads cannot be immediately associated with the products or services being offered, thus do not directly generate profits. However, overheads are still vital to business operations as they provide critical support for the business to carry out profit making activities. For example, overhead costs such as the rent for a factory allows workers to manufacture products which can then be sold for a profit. Such expenses are incurred for output generally and not for particular work order; e.g., wages paid to watch and ward staff, heating and lighting expenses of factory, etc. Overheads are also very important cost element along with direct materials and direct labor.

Overheads are often related to accounting concepts such as fixed costs and indirect costs.

Overhead expenses are all costs on the income statement except for direct labour, direct materials, and direct expenses. Overhead expenses include accounting fees, advertising, insurance, interest, legal fees, labor burden, rent, repairs, supplies, taxes, telephone bills, travel expenditures, and utilities.

There are essentially two types of business overheads. Administrative overheads and manufacturing overheads.

Administrative Overheads

Administrative overheads include items such as utilities, strategic planning, and various supporting functions. These costs are treated as overheads due to the fact that they aren't directly related to any particular function of the organization nor does it directly result in generating any profits. Instead, these costs simply take on the role of supporting all of the business' other functions.

Universities regularly charge administrative overhead rates on research. In the U.S. the average overhead rate is 52%, which is spent on building operation, administrative salaries and other areas not directly tied to research. Academics have argued against these charges. For example, Benjamin Ginsberg showed how overhead rates are primarily used to subsidize ballooning administrative salaries and building depreciation, neither of which directly benefit research; although it does benefit the administrators that determine university policy in his book The Fall of Faculty. An article written by Joshua Pearce in Science (journal) argued that overhead accounting practices hurt science by removing funds from research and discouraging the use of less-expensive open source hardware. He went into detail on the accounting showing how millions were wasted each year on overhead cash grabs by university administrators in ZME Science.

Examples

Employee Salaries

This includes mainly monthly and annual salaries that are agreed upon. They are considered overheads as these costs must be paid regardless of sales and profits of the company. In addition, salary differs from wage as salary is not affected by working hours and time, therefore will remain constant. In particular, this would more commonly apply to more senior staff members as they are typically signed to longer tenure contracts, meaning that their salaries are more commonly predetermined.

Office Equipment and Supplies

This includes office equipment such as printer, fax machine, computers, refrigerator, etc. They are equipments that do not directly result in sales and profits as they are only used for supporting functions that they can provide to business operations. However, equipments can vary between administrative overheads and manufacturing overheads based on the purpose of which they are using the equipments. For example, for a printing company a printer would be considered a manufacturing overhead.

External Legal and Audit Fees

A Google Company Car

This includes the cost of hiring external law and audit firms on behalf of the company. This would not apply if company has own internal lawyers and audit plans. Due to regulations and necessary annual audits to ensure a satisfactory work place environment, these costs often cannot be avoided. Also, since these costs do not necessarily contribute directly to sales, they are considered as indirect overheads. Although in most cases necessary, these costs can sometimes be avoided and reduced.

Company Cars

Many companies provide usage of company cars as a perk for their employees. Since these cars do not contribute directly to sales and profits, they are considered an overhead. Similar company perks that are a one-off or constant payment such as partner contract fees with a gym will also fall under administrative overheads.

Travel and Entertainment Costs

This will include company-paid business travels and arrangements. As well as refreshments, meals, and entertainment fees during company gatherings. Although one might argue that these costs motivate workers to become more productive and efficient, the majority of economists agree that these costs are not direct contributes to sales and profits, therefore shall be categorized as an administrative overhead. Despite these costs occurring periodically and sometimes without prior preparation, they are usually one-off payments and are expected to be within the company's budget for travel and entertainment.

Manufacturing Overheads

Manufacturing overheads are all costs endured by a business that is within the physical platform in which the product or service is created. Difference between manufacturing overheads and administrative overheads is that manufacturing overheads are categorized within a factory or office in which the sale takes place. Whilst administrative overheads is typically categorized within some sort of back-office or supporting office. Although there are cases when the two physical buildings may overlap, it is the usage of the overheads that separates them.

Examples

Employee Salaries

Although the general concept is identical to the example under administrative overheads, the key difference is the role of the employee. In the case of manufacturing overheads, employees would have roles such as maintenance personnel, manufacturing managers, materials management staff, and quality control staff. It would also include the set wages for janitorial staff members. Once again, the key difference lies in the nature of their respective jobs and the physical location in which their jobs are carried out.

Depreciation of Assets and Equipment

This refers to the reduction in value of equipments as it becomes older and more obsolete. For example, if a printer has a potential useful life span of 5 years, the amount that it can be sold for will decrease each year. Therefore, this value in depreciation is calculated as a manufacturing overhead. Moreover, this also applies to vehicles as they tend to depreciate in value significantly after the first year. When calculating manufacturing overheads, accountants mainly use two methods: straight-line method and declining balance method.

Property Taxes on Production Facilities

Every single property unless government owned is subject to some form of property tax. Therefore, the taxes on production factories are categorized as manufacturing overheads as they are costs which cannot be avoided nor cancelled. In addition, property taxes do not change in relation to the business's profits or sales and will likely remain the same unless a change by the government administration.

The rent for factory buildings is considered a manufacturing overhead

Rent of Factory Building

Unless the business decides to purchase land and build its own factory, it will be subject to some sort of rent due to the amount of capital required to build a privately owned factory. Therefore, this rent must be paid to the land lord on a regular basis regardless of the performance of the business. Although the rent for the building provides the physical platform for the company to produce its products and services, it is not a direct contributor.

Utilities for Factory

This would vary depending on how the utility bill is structured. In the case of it being an overhead, the utility bill is pre-negotiated meaning that the monthly utility bill will be the same regardless of the amount in which the factory actually consumes. This will only be relevant in various countries where there is an option for standardized utility bills. However, due to the vast consumption of electricity, gas, and water in most factories, most companies tend to not have standardized utility bills as it tends to be more expensive. Standardized utility bills are also oftentimes discouraged by governments as it leads to wastage of resources and negative externalities of production.

Application of Business Overheads

For most businesses, business overheads are calculated by accountants for budgeting purposes but also often so the business has an idea of how much they must charge consumers in order to make a profit. The following are common accounting tools which take account of business overheads.

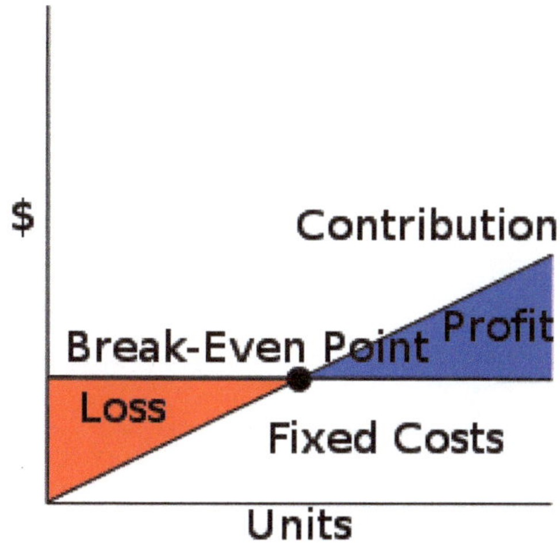

A standard break-even analysis chart

Break-even Analysis

The break-even analysis determines the point which the business's revenue is equivalent to the costs required to receive that revenue. It first calculates a margin of safety (the point which the revenue exceeds the break-even point) as that is the "safe" amount which the revenue can fall whilst still remaining to be above the break-even point. The graph on the right shows a typical break-even chart. Contribution refers to sales of the product or service, it can also be interpreted as the business's revenue stream. Fixed costs in this case serves the same purpose as business overheads, it will simply be shown as a straight horizontal line on the graph as shown.

Shut-down Graph

In economics, revenue curves are often illustrated to show whether or not a business should stay in business, or shut down. In theory, if a business is able cover variable operational costs but unable to cover business overheads in the short run, the business should remain in business. On the other hand, if the business is not even able to cover operational costs, it should shut down. Although this rule largely differs depending on the size of the business, the business's cash-flow, and the competitive nature of the business, it serves as a model rule for most small competitive businesses to operate on.

Balance Sheet

Balance sheet is a financial statement which outlines a company's financial assets, liabilities, and shareholder's equity at a specific time. Both assets and liabilities are separated into two categories depending on their time frame; current and long-term. Business overheads in particular fall under current liabilities as they are costs in which the company must pay for on a relatively short-term/

immediate basis. Although balance sheet by itself do not offer much information, it is a useful piece of financial information when combined with other documents such as the income statement or ratio analysis as it offers a diverse and well-rounded description of the company's financial position.

Methods of Absorbing Overheads

- Percentage of direct material.
- Percentage of prime cost.
- Percentage of direct labour cost.
- Labour hour rate.
- Machine hour rate.

Pre-Determined Overhead Rate

Pre-determined Overhead rate is a rate, based on budgeted factory overhead cost and budgeted activity, which is calculated before a period begins.

A pre-determined overhead rate normally applies for a a single, plant-wide base to calculate and apply overhead.

Overhead is then applied by multiplying the pre-determined overhead rate by the actual driver units.

Predetermined Overhead	Budgeted yearly Factory
Rate	Overheads

Budgeted Yearly Activity (direct labor-hours, etc.)

Steps for Calculating Pre-Determined Overhead Rate

Step 1: Estimate the amount of the activity base will be required to support operations in the coming period.

Step 2: Estimate the total manufacturing cost at that level of activity.

Step 3: Compute the predetermined overhead rate by dividing the estimated total manufacturing overhead costs by the estimated total amount of cost driver or activity base. (Note: Common activity bases used in the calculation include direct labour costs, direct labour hours, or machine hours).

Over and Under Application of Overheads

- Through the use of pre-determined overhead rate, overheads are applied into actual production throughout accounting period.
- Since the pre-determined rates are based on expected overheads to be incurred and estimated production, usually the overheads absorbed into the production cost may not fully agree with actual overheads.

- If the overheads absorbed are higher than actual incurred then it is called Over Application.
- If the overheads absorbed are lesser than actual incurred for the accounting period, it is called Under Application.

Reasons

- The actual hours worked can be more or less than the estimated hours.
- The actual overhead costs are different from budgeted overhead.
- The application method used may not be correct.
- Both actual overhead costs and actual activity levels are different from the budgeted costs and level.
- Extra-ordinary expenses might have been incurred during the accounting period.
- Seasonal variations in the overhead expenses from period to period.
- Major changes might have taken place for example replacement of manual labour with machines, replacement of general purpose machine with automatic high speed machine etc.

Treatment of Over/Under Absorbed Overheads in Cost Accounting

Application of supplementary rate: The supplementary rate is calculated by dividing the under or over application amount by the actual base. In case of under application, by applying the supplementary rate the uncovered amount will be adjusted and vice versa.

Write off to costing profit and loss account: If the under or over absorbed overheads is small, the it will be written off by transferring it to the costing P&L Account.

Carry forward to subsequent year: By treating the under or over absorbed as seasonal fluctuations, we can carry forward it to subsequent accounting year.

This may be transferred to Overhead Suspense A/c or Overhead Reserve A/c.

Efficiency-based Absorption Costing

Efficiency-based absorption costing (EBAC) is the discipline of accounting, which is concerned with establishing methods or techniques to allocate fixed costs to each product or service an organization produces. EBAC (Samuel et al. 2009) is an alternative or even improved technique of absorption compared to previous established techniques as it takes into account the different level of overhead use efficiency of products. EBAC highlights the problem with use of the single standard absorption rate to allocate fixed costs to products. The single standard absorption rate was used for simplicity purposes (Steve R. and Ken 1994; Gunasekaran et al. 1999). However, it ignores the different level of efficiency of each product or service in incurring the fixed cost and as a result, a high degree of cross subsidization occurs between more efficient and less efficient products and services. In a nutshell, EBAC focuses on the efficiency aspect by identifying the products' different level of overhead utilization efficiency.

The EBAC first coined by Samuel et al. (2009) uses efficiency as the main determinant to calculate the absorption rate. Efficiency is defined here as the ratio of input required to produce an output. An output or product or service is efficient if it requires lesser input to produce a given number of outputs. For example if Product A needs 200 set ups to produce 100 of its units and Product B needs 50 set ups to produce 100 of its units, Product B is more efficient. This is because Product B needs lesser input or drivers to produce a given number of outputs.

EBAC is a methodology that is both easy and convenient to apply. Firms using ABC could instantly explore the alternative and improved EBAC as no new data collection effort is required. The use of EBAC as compared to earlier established methods results in key changes in host of pertinent cost control and decision making scenario business face like to make or buy, to accept or reject a special order, to continue or shut down a cost/revenue centre, how much to price products and services and how much resources to allocate to different products and establish output volume levels.

Example

Given below is an illustrative example on the working of EBAC and its comparison with the traditional absorption costing system (TCS) and Activity-based costing (ABC).

Firm Samuel Plc produces two products, A and B. Details of the cost information of product A and B are as follow:

	Product A	Product B
Direct material	20	30
Direct labour	10	15
Variable cost	30	45
Total labour hours	10,000	20,000
Total units produced	5,000	10,000

	Cost pool	Cost driver		
Fixed costs:	$		A	B
Rental	20,000	Square feet	3,000	1,000
Maintenance costs	30,000	Number of maintenance	40	20
Inspection costs	10,000	Number of maintenance	5	20
	60,000			

a)The direct labour hour is used as the base to absorb fixed cost in the Traditional Absorption Costing System (TCS). b)The cost drivers and cost pools are used as the base to absorb fixed cost in the Activity Based Costing (ABC) method. c)The cost drivers, cost pools and the efficiency rate are used as the base to absorb fixed cost in the Efficiency Based Absorption Costing (EBAC) method. d)Samuel Plc applies a standard mark up of 10% for its products to arrive at the selling price.

Calculation of TCS overhead absorption rate – Samuel Plc

Cost Pool	RM	Driver	Absorption rate (AR)
Total overhead costs	60,000	Direct labour hours	60,000/ 30,000 = 2 per hour

Calculation of ABC overhead absorption rate – Samuel Plc

Cost Pool	RM	Driver	AR/Driver	A	Overhead/ unit	B	Overhead/ unit
Rental	20,000	Square feet – 4,000	5.00	(5 × 3,000) /5,000	3.00	5 × 1,000) /10,000	0.5
Maintenance cost	30,000	No. of maintenance – 60	500.00	(500 × 40) / 5,000	4.00	(500 × 20) / 10,000	1.00
Inspection cost	10,000	No. of inspections – 25	400.00	4.00	0.4	(400 × 20) / 10,000	0.80
	60,000						

Calculation of EBAC overhead absorption rate – Samuel Plc

Cost pool	RM	Driver	A	No of units	ER	Overhead/ unit	B	No of units	ER	Overhead/ unit	Total ER
Rental	20,000	Square feet	3,000	5,000	0.60	[(0.6/0.7) × 20,000] /5,000 = 3.4	1,000	10,000	0.10	[(0.1/0.7) × 20,000]/ 10,000 = 0.3	0.70
Main-tenance cost	30,000	Number of maintenance	40	5,000	0.008	[(0.008/0.01) × 30,000] / 5,000 = 4.8	20	10,000	0.002	[(0.002/0.01) × 30,000] / 10,000 = 0.6	0.01
Inspec-tion cost	10,000	Number of inspections	5	5,000	0.001	[(0.001/0.003) × 10,000] / 5,000 = 0.7	25	10,000	0.002	[(0.002/0.003) × 10,000] / 10,000 = 0.7	0.003
	60,000										

Cost and profitability of A and B under different costing methods – Samuel Plc

	A			B		
	$	$	$	$	$	$
	TCS	ABC	EBAC	TCS	ABC	EBAC
Variable costs	30	45	30	45	30	45
Fixed Costs	4			4		
Rental		3.00	0.5	3.4	0.5	0.30
Maintenance cost		4.00	4.80		1.00	0.60
Inspection cost		0.4	0.70		0.8	0.70
Total costs	34	37.4	38.90	49	47.3	46.55
20% Mark Up	6.80	7.48	7.78	9.80	9.46	9.31
Price	40.8	44.88	46.67	58.8	56.76	55.86

References

- Muralidharan, Raman (2004). "A framework for designing strategy content controls". International Journal of Productivity and Performance Management. 53 (7): 590–601. doi:10.1108/17410400410561213
- Gowthorpe, Catherine (2005). Management Accounting for non-specialists. London: Thomson Learning. p. 302. ISBN 978 1 84480 206 7
- Rigby, D.; Bilodeau B. (2013). "Bain and Company's Management Tools and Trends Survey 2013". Bain & Company. Archived from the original on 7 April 2014. Retrieved 28 May 2014
- Ouchi, W. G. (1977). "The relationship between organisational structure and organisational control". Administrative Science Quarterly. 2 (1): 95–113. JSTOR 2391748. doi:10.2307/2391748
- Maisel, L. S. (1992). "Performance measurement: the Balanced Scorecard approach". Journal of Cost Management. 6 (2): 47–52
- Kaplan, Robert S; Norton, D. P. (1996). The Balanced Scorecard: Translating Strategy into Action. Boston, MA.: Harvard Business School Press. ISBN 978-0-87584-651-4
- "How do I link corporate and individual performance management systems?" (PDF). 2GC Active Management. Archived from the original (PDF) on 1 May 2014. Retrieved 28 May 2014
- Butler, A.; Letza S. R.; Neale B. (1997). "Linking the Balanced Scorecard to Strategy". Long Range Planning. 30 (2): 242–253. doi:10.1016/s0024-6301(96)00116-1
- Malina, M. A.; Selto, F. H. (2001). "Communicating and Controlling Strategy: An Empirical Study of the Effectiveness of the Balanced Scorecard". Journal of Management Accounting Research. 13: 47–90. doi:10.2308/jmar.2001.13.1.47
- Bourne, Mike; Bourne P. (29 November 2002). Balanced Scorecard in a Week. London: Hodder & Stoughton. ISBN 978-0-340-84945-3
- Kaplan, Robert S.; Norton D. P. (1996). "Linking the Balanced Scorecard to Strategy". California Management Review. 39 (1): 53–79. doi:10.2307/41165876
- Irwin, D (2002). "Strategy Mapping in the Public Sector". International Journal of Strategic Management. 35 (6): 563–672
- Niven, Paul R. (18 April 2002). Balanced Scorecard Step-by-step: Maximizing Performance and Maintaining Results. New York: John Wiley & Sons. ISBN 978-0-471-07872-2
- Northcott, Deryl; Taulapapa, Tuivaiti Ma'amora (2012). "sing the balanced scorecard to manage performance in public sector organizations". The International Journal of Public Sector Management. 25 (3): 166–191. doi:10.1108/09513551211224234
- Schneiderman, Arthur M. (2006). "Analog Devices: 1986–1992, The First Balanced Scorecard". Arthur M. Schneiderman. Archived from the original on 25 December 2013. Retrieved 28 May 2014
- Gunasekaran, A., Marri, H., & Yusuf, Y. (1999). Application of activity-based costing: some case experiences. Managerial Auditing Journal , 14(6), pp. 286–293
- Norreklit, Hanne (2000). "The balance on the balanced scorecard – a critical analysis of some of its assumptions". Management Accounting Research. 11 (1): 65–88. doi:10.1006/mare.1999.0121

3

Understanding Manufacturing Cost

Job costing calculates overhead costs of raw material, means of production and cost of labor, all of which are part of manufacturing cost. Process costing calculates costs incurred in the manufacture of one unit of a commodity. The aspects elucidated in this chapter are of vital importance, and provide a better understanding of cost accounting.

Job Costing

Job costing is accounting which tracks the costs and revenues by "job" and enables standardized reporting of profitability by job. For an accounting system to support job costing, it must allow job numbers to be assigned to individual items of expenses and revenues. A job can be defined to be a specific project done for one customer, or a single unit of product manufactured, or a batch of units of the same type that are produced together.

To apply job costing in a manufacturing setting involves tracking which "job" uses various types of direct expenses such as direct labour and direct materials, and then allocating overhead costs (indirect labor, warranty costs, quality control and other overhead costs) to the jobs. A job profitability report is like an overall profit & loss statement for the firm, but is specific to each job number.

Job costing may assess all costs involved in a construction "job" or in the manufacturing of goods done in discrete batches. These costs are recorded in ledger accounts throughout the life of the job or batch and are then summarized in the final trial balance before the preparing of the job cost or batch manufacturing statement.

Job Costing vs. Process Costing

Job costing (known by some as job order costing) is fundamental to managerial accounting. It differs from Process costing in that the flow of costs is tracked by job or batch instead of by process.

The distinction between job costing and process costing hinges on the nature of the product and, therefore, on the type of production process:

- Process costing is used when the products are more homogeneous in nature. Conversely, job costing systems assign costs to distinct production jobs that are significantly different. An average cost per unit of product is then calculated for each job.
- Process costing systems assign costs to one or more production processes. Because all units

are identical or very similar, average costs for each unit of product are calculated by dividing the process costs by the number of units produced.

- Many businesses produce products with some unique features and some common processes. These businesses use costing systems that have both job and process costing features.

Using Job Costing

Job Costing is the process of determining the labor and materials cost for each job in a systematic way, and then using this information to create a quote for the customer. Job costing or cost accounting can be used in virtually any industry (especially service industry) to ensure that the product pricing covers actual costs, overhead and provides a profit. The purpose of any business is to make money, and job costing is the most effective way to ensure that occurs.In a job costing system, costs may be accumulated either by job or by batch. For a typical job, direct material, labor, subcontract costs, equipment, and other direct costs are tracked at their actual values. These are accrued until the job or batch is completed. Overhead or "burden" may be applied either by using a rate based on direct labor hours or by using some other Activity Based Costing (ABC) cost driver. In either case, once overhead/burden is added, the total cost for the job can be determined. If the accountant is using a general ledger accounting system, which lacks true job costing functionality, the costs must be manually transferred out of Work in Process to Finished Goods (Cost of Goods Sold for service industries). Of course, in the days of computerized job costing software, journaling costs manually is an obsolete process. Such hand-journaling is mandatory for companies that continue to use general accounting software to do job costing. Enlightened accountants are moving forward and using job costing software, thereby improving cost control, reducing risk, and increasing the chance of profitability.

Using Cost Codes in Budgeting

In a true job cost accounting system, a Budget is set up in advance of the job. As actual costs are accrued, they are compared to budgeted costs, to determine variances for each phase of each job. Cost Codes are used for each phase, allowing "mini-budgets" to be generated and tracked. In the construction industry, the Construction Specifications Institute (CSI) has established an industry standard Cost Coding system.job costing system consists of various cost driver that drives job cost, moreover it.

Example

These examples will assume that overhead is allocated on the basis of Direct Labor Hours. Direct Material is abbreviated DM, Direct Labor as DL, and Overhead as OH.

XYZ corporation manufactures airplanes. 1 order was completed (#110), 2 received further work (#111, 112), and 1 new order was received (#113). Overhead is allocated at a rate of $100/DL Hour. All employees earn $20/hour. Beginning Work In Process Balances are as follows: #110, $25,000; #111, $10,000; #112, $12,000; #113 $0 (New Order). Below are the amounts of DM and DL used.

- #110 $2,000 DM, 25 DL hours. Therefore, $5,000 in new cost is added ($2,000 DM, $500 DL, $2,500 OH). The job had a total cost of $30,000. this amount is transferred out of Work in Process to Finished Goods or Cost of Goods Sold.

- #111 $3,000 DM, 30 DL hours. Therefore, $6,600 in new cost is added ($3,000 DM, $600 DL, $3,000 OH). The job has a new total cost of $16,600. This amount remains in Work in Process until completion.
- #112 $5,000 DM, 100 DL hours. Therefore, $17,000 in new cost is added ($5,000 DM, $2,000 DL, $10,000 OH). The job has a new total cost of $29,000. This amount remains in Work in Process until completion.
- #113 $1,000 DM, 10 DL hours. Therefore, $2,200 in new cost is added ($1,000 DM, $200 DL, $1000 OH). The job has a new total cost of $2,200. This amount remains in Work in Process until completion.

Caution: Remember, overhead is allocated on the basis of DL hours. While in this case, allocating overhead on the basis of DL cost ($5 of overhead for every $1 DL cost) would produce the same result, this may not always be the case. Since rates are developed based on a budget, if employees are actually paid a different rate from the budgeted rate, allocating at a $5 to $1 ratio would produce a different cost from the stated $100/DL hour allocation. Companies use slightly different overhead allocation methods.

Usually Cost sheet is prepared to record and report the costs. It may be prepared for a job or for some period.

Cost Sheet for June

Particulars	Total Cost	Per Unit
Direct Material		
Opening Stock of Raw Material		
Add: Purchase		
Less: Closing stock of Raw material		
Direct Labour		
Direct Expenses		
Prime Cost		
Add: Factory Overheads		
Works Cost		
Add: Opening Work in Progress		
Less: Closing Work in Progress		
Factory Cost		
Add: Office and Administration Exp		
Cost of Production		
Add: Opening stock of Finished Goods		
Less: Closing stock of Finished Goods		
Cost of goods Sold		

Add: Selling and Distribution Exp		
Cost of Sales		
Add: Profit		
Sales		

Loss

- Loss of material is inherent during certain production processes.
- There are two types of material losses viz. (i) Normal Loss (ii) Abnormal Loss.
- Normal Loss: It is defined as the loss of material which is inherent in the nature of work. Such a loss can be reasonably anticipated from the nature of material, Nature of operation, the experience and technical data.
- Abnormal Loss: It is defined as the loss in excess of the pre determined loss. This type of loss may occur due to carelessness of workers, a bad plant design or operation etc.

Process Costing

Process costing is an accounting methodology that traces and accumulates direct costs, and allocates indirect costs of a manufacturing process. Costs are assigned to products, usually in a large batch, which might include an entire month's production. Eventually, costs have to be allocated to individual units of product. It assigns average costs to each unit, and is the opposite extreme of Job costing which attempts to measure individual costs of production of each unit. Process costing is usually a significant chapter. It is a method of assigning costs to units of production in companies producing large quantities of homogeneous products.

Process costing is a type of operation costing which is used to ascertain the cost of a product at each process or stage of manufacture. CIMA defines process costing as "The costing method applicable where goods or services result from a sequence of continuous or repetitive operations or processes. Costs are averaged over the units produced during the period". Process costing is suitable for industries producing homogeneous products and where production is a continuous flow. A process can be referred to as the sub-unit of an organization specifically defined for cost collection purpose.

The Importance of Process Costing

Costing is an important process that many companies engage in to keep track of where their money is being spent in the production and distribution processes. Understanding these costs is the first step in being able to control them. It is very important that a company chooses the appropriate type of costing system for their product type and industry. One type of costing system that is used in certain industries is process costing that varies from other types of costing (such as job costing) in some ways. In process costing unit costs are more like averages, the process-costing system requires less bookkeeping than does a job-order costing system. Thus, some companies often prefer to use the process-costing system.

When Process Costing is Applied?

Process costing is appropriate for companies that produce a continuous mass of like units through series of operations or process. Also, when one order does not affect the production process and a standardization of the process and product exists. However, if there are significant differences among the costs of various products, a process costing system would not provide adequate product-cost information. Costing is generally used in such industries such as petroleum, coal mining, chemicals, textiles, paper, plastic, glass, food, banks, courier, cement, and soap.

Reasons for Use

Companies need to allocate total product costs to units of product for the following reasons:

- A company may manufacture thousands or millions of units of product in a given period of time.
- Products are manufactured in large quantities, but products may be sold in small quantities, sometimes one at a time (automobiles, loaves of bread), a dozen or two at a time (eggs, cookies), etc.
- Product costs must be transferred from Finished Goods to Cost of Goods Sold as sales are made. This requires a correct and accurate accounting of product costs per unit, to have a proper matching of product costs against related sales revenue.
- Managers need to maintain cost control over the manufacturing process. Process costing provides managers with feedback that can be used to compare similar product costs from one month to the next, keeping costs in line with projected manufacturing budgets.
- A fraction-of-a-cent cost change can represent a large dollar change in overall profitability, when selling millions of units of product a month. Managers must carefully watch per unit costs on a daily basis through the production process, while at the same time dealing with materials and output in huge quantities.
- Materials part way through a process (e.g. chemicals) might need to be given a value, process costing allows for this. By determining what cost the part processed material has incurred such as labor or overhead an "equivalent unit" relative to the value of a finished process can be calculated.

Process Cost Procedures

There are four basic steps in accounting for Process cost:

- Summarize the flow of physical units of output.
- Compute output in terms of equivalent units.
- Summarize total costs to account for and Compute equivalent unit costs.
- Assign total costs to units completed and to units in ending work in process inventory.

The journal entries for process costing are the same as those for job-order costing with one exception. The entry to transfer cost from one work-in-process account to another is:

Work-in-process inventory-second department Debit (Left)

Work-in-process-first department Credit (Right)

e.g.(1) Micro Labs Company produces house paint in two processing departments: the Mixing Department which mixes the paint colors and the Finishing Department which puts the paint in containers and labels them. The following information related to the company's operation for October follows:

A) Raw materials were issued for use in production: Mixing department, $551,000, and the Finishing department, $629,000. B) Direct labor costs incurred: Mixing department $230,000, and Finishing department $270,000. C) Manufacturing overhead cost applied: Mixing department $665,000, and Finishing department, $405,000. D) The cost of the mixed paint transferred from the Mixing department to the Finishing department was $1,850,000. E) Paint that had been prepared for shipping was transferred from the Finishing department to Finished Goods. Cost of the transferred paint was $3,200,000.

Required: Prepare journal entries to record items A) through E) above.

Solution(1):

-Work in Process - Mixing	551,000	
-Work in Process - Finishing	629,000	
-Raw Materials		1,180,000
-Work in Process - Mixing	230,000	
-Work in Process - Finishing	270,000	
-Wages and Salaries Payable		500,000
-Work in Process - Mixing	665,000	
-Work in Process - Finishing	405,000	
-Manufacturing Overhead		1,070,000
-Work in Process - Finishing	1,850,000	
-Work in Process - Mixing		1,850,000
-Finished Goods	3,200,000	
-Work in Process - Finishing		3,200,000

e.g.(2) Larney Corporation uses process costing. A number of transactions that occurred in June are listed below. As follows:

A) Raw materials that cost $38,200 are withdrawn from the storeroom for use in the Mixing Department. B) Direct labor costs incurred $36,500,in the Mixing Department. C) Manufacturing overhead of $42,100 is applied in the Mixing Department. D) Units with a carrying cost of $112,400 finish processing in the Mixing Department and are transferred to the Drying Department for further processing. E) Units with a carrying cost of $143,800 finish processing in the Drying Department, the final step in the production process, and are transferred to the finished goods warehouse. F) Finished goods with a carrying cost of $138,500

Required: Prepare journal entries to record items A) through F).

Solution (2):

-work in process-mixing department	$38,200	
—raw materials		$38,200
-work in process	$36,500	
-salaries/wages payable		$36,500
-work in process-mixing department	$42,100	
-manufacturing overhead		$42,100
-work in process-drying department.	$112,400	
-work in process mixing department		$112,400
-finished goods	$143,800	
-work in process-drying department		$143,800
-costs of goods sold	$138,500	
-finished goods		$138,500

Operation Cost in Batch Manufacturing

Batch costing is a modification of job costing. When production is repetitive nature and consists of a definite number of articles, batch is used. In batch costing, the most important problem is to determine the optimum size of the batch that follows the fact that production of two elements of costs:

- Set up costs which are generally fixed per batch.
- Carrying costs which vadetermination of batch quantity requires considerations of some factors:
- setting up costs per batch.
- cost of manufacturing such as (direct materials cost + direct wages + direct overhead) per piece.
- cost of storage.

- rate of interest on the capital invested in product and rate of demand for product.

Usually Process Accounts are prepared for some period to record and report the costs.

The cost of each process comprises the cost of:

1. Direct Material.
2. Direct Labour.
3. Direct Expenses.
4. Production Overheads.

Direct Materials Cost

Direct materials cost the cost of direct materials which can be easily identified with the unit of production. For example, the cost of glass is a direct materials cost in light bulb manufacturing.

The manufacture of products or goods required material as the prime element. In general, these materials are divided into two categories. These categories are direct materials and indirect materials.

Direct materials are also called productive materials, raw materials, raw stock, stores and only materials without any descriptive title.

Direct Materials Cost Estimation

Steps to estimate the direct material costs:

1. Find the total amount to be produced. This is usually noted as the order size.
2. Calculate the total amount of raw materials required to produce the order size.
3. Multiply that amount by the cost associated with the raw materials.
4. If there is a waste or scrap, its cost should be added to the costs in step 3.
5. If the waste or scrap can be sold at salvage value, this value should be subtracted from the costs in step 4.

Direct Labor Cost

Direct labor cost is a part of wage-bill or payroll that can be specifically and consistently assigned to or associated with the manufacture of a product, a particular work order, or provision of a service. Also, we can say it is the cost of the work done by those workers who actually make the product on the production line.

Determination of the Direct Labor Cost

- Planning the work to be performed.

- Describing the job content of the work, by indicating the skill, knowledge, etc.
- Matching the jobs with the employees.

Usage

The direct labor cost is part of the manufacturing cost.

Calculation of Direct Labor Cost

In the direct labor cost we need to have the job time and wage we will pay it to the worker to calculate the direct labor cost as in this formulation:-

$$\text{Direct labor cost} = \text{job time} \times \text{wage}$$

Wage

The wage is the payment rendered to the worker per hour as a compensation for the work done.

Calculating Job Time

The job time needs to be measured by one of the following ways:

1. time study
2. work sampling
3. Predetermined motion time system

Production Line

Doughnut production line

A production line is a set of sequential operations established in a factory where materials are put through a refining process to produce an end-product that is suitable for onward consumption; or components are assembled to make a finished article.

Typically, raw materials such as metal ores or agricultural products such as foodstuffs or textile source plants (cotton, flax) require a sequence of treatments to render them useful. For metal, the processes include crushing, smelting and further refining. For plants, the useful material has to be separated from husks or contaminants and then treated for onward sale.

History

Early production processes were constrained by the availability of a source of energy, with wind mills and water mills providing power for the crude heavy processes and manpower being used for activities requiring more precision. In earlier centuries, with raw materials, power and people often being in different locations, production was distributed across a number of sites. The concentration of numbers of people in manufactories, and later the factory as exemplified by the cotton mills of Richard Arkwright, started the move towards co-locating individual processes.

Introduction of the Steam Engine

With the development of the steam engine in the latter half of the 18th century, the production elements became less reliant on the location of the power source, and so the processing of goods moved to either the source of the materials or the location of people to perform the tasks. Separate processes for different treatment stages were brought into the same building, and the various stages of refining or manufacture were combined.

Industrial Revolution

With increasing use of steam power, and increasing use of machinery to supplant the use of people, the integrated use of techniques in production lines spurred the industrial revolutions of Europe and North America.

Assembly Line

Thus, from the processing of raw materials into useful goods, the next step was the concept of the assembly line, as introduced by Eli Whitney. This was taken to the next stage at the Ford Motor Company in 1913, where Henry Ford introduced the innovation of continuously moving the cars being assembled past individual work stations. This introduced the idea of standardization.

The assembly line was a contraption of many chains and links that moved to place different parts into various places throughout the car. The chassis of the car was along the 45 metre line by a chain conveyor and then 140 workers applied their assigned parts to the chassis. Other workers brought additional parts to the car builders to keep them stocked. The assembly line decreased the assembly time per vehicle. The production time for a single car dropped from over twelve hours to just 93 minutes.

Process Costing Concepts

From the following data prepare process a/c of 1, 2 and 3.

The output of each process is treated as input for next process. Direct Costs are:

	Pr 1	Pr 2	Pr 3
Material	70000	15000	30000
Wages	38000	40000	25000
Expenses	11000	12000	15000

Factory overheads of Rs. 40000 to be apportioned on the basis of wages paid. There was no opening or closing stock.

15000 units have been introduced in 1st process and the output and normal loss for each process are as follows:

	Output	Normal Loss
Process 1	14550	3%
Process 2	13500	6%
Process 3	13300	2%

Solution

Process 1 A/c					
Particular	Units	Total Cost	Particular	Units	Total Cost
Material	15000	70000	Normal Loss	450	0
Wages		38000	Transfer to Process 1	14550	133737
Other Expenses		11000			
Factory Overheads		14757			
	15000	133737		15000	133737

Process 2 A/c					
Particular	Units	Total Cost	Particular	Units	Total Cost
Transfer from Process 1	14550	133757	Normal Loss	873	0
Material		15000	Abnormal Loss	177	2799
Wages		40000	Transfer to Pr2	13500	213492
Other Expenses		12000			
Factory Overheads		15534			
	14550	216291		14550	216291

Process 3 A/c					
Particular	Units	Total Cost	Particular	Units	Total Cost
Transfer from Process 1	13500	213492	Normal Loss	270	0
Material		30000	Finished Stock	13300	294752
Wages		25000			
Other Expenses		15000			
Factory Overheads		9709			
Abnormal Gain	70	1551			
	13570	294752		13570	294752

Equivalent Units

Thus, in Process Costing

Cost per unit = Cost/Output Units

What can be done when partially produced units remain in stock ?

To ascertain the cost of each completed unit it is necessary to ascertain the cost of work in progress in the beginning and at the end of the process. Hence the method of converting partly finished units to equivalent finished units is used.

Equivalent production means converting the incomplete production units into their completed units.

Equivalent completed units = {Actual number of units in the process} X {percentage of work completed}

- Conversion + direct material applied: The term equivalent unit cost refers to conversion and direct-material applied to physical units after adjusting the stage of completion.
- Physical and equivalent units equal in completed batch: If a batch of goods has been completed, the number of physical units and equivalent units will be the same.
- Work-in-Process only partially completed: The units in ending Work-in-Process Inventory are only partially completed and may be in different stages of production.
- Example: 100% of materials may be present in the product, but only 50% of the conversion work (labor and overhead) may have been done.
- Conversion costs added continuously: Conversion costs are usually added continuously throughout the process.
- Example: If 100 units are 60% of the way through the process, 60 equivalent units have been produced. Notice that none of the units are completed—the firm is said to have done the work equivalent to manufacturing 60 finished units.
- Direct material added at specific points: Direct materials are usually added at discrete points in the process in text problems.

- Consider when material added: When considering materials, determine at what point the ending in-process costs are and evaluate whether or not the materials have been added.
- Once added 100% complete: If added, the units are 100% complete with respect to materials; if not, the units are 0% complete.
- Unit cost based on equivalent units: When computing the cost of a unit, the related calculations are based on equivalent units, not physical units.

The procedure states fully-completed units on the same measurement scale as partially-completed units, thus avoiding the addition (combination) of "apples and oranges."

Next divide costs by equivalent units: Next, the cost of direct materials and conversion is divided by the proper number of equivalent units for each of these production elements.

Product Cost Management

Product cost management (PCM) is a set of tools, processes, methods, and culture used by firms who develop and manufacture products to ensure that a product meets its profit (or cost) target.

Scope

There is not an agreed-upon definition for product cost management or an agreed scope for what it encompasses. Some people argue that PCM is a synonym for target costing. However, others argue that PCM is different, because target costing is a pricing method, whereas, PCM is focused on the maximum profit or minimum cost of a product, regardless of the price at which the product is sold to the end customer. Some analysts seem to equate PCM to design-to-cost.

Some practitioners of PCM are mostly concerned with the cost of the product up until the point that the customer takes delivery (e.g. manufacturing costs + logistics costs) or the total cost of acquisition. They seek to launch products that meet profit targets at launch rather than reducing the costs of a product after production. Other people believe that PCM extends to a total cost of ownership or lifecycle costing (Manufacturing + Logistics + operational costs + disposal). Depending on the practitioner, PCM may include any combination of organizational or /cultural change, processes, team roles, and tools. Many believe that PCM must encompass all four aspects to be successful and have shown how the four parts work together.

Processes and Activities

Depending on the scope the practitioner assigns to PCM, it may include one or more of the following processes.

- Change management and building a cost/profit-conscious culture.
- Building cost management into the Product Lifecycle Management processes
- DFM – Design for Manufacturing

- DFA – Design for assembly
- DTC – Design to Cost
- DFP – Design for Procurement
- VA/VE – Value Analysis / Value engineering
- DFSS – Design for Six Sigma
- Cost targeting
- Should Cost / Price
- Make Buy
- Capital asset justification
- Commodity Pricing
- Spend analysis

Tools

Initially, PCM was done with pencil and paper. However, with the advent of computers, companies started to create internal software for predicting, controlling, minimizing, recording, and sharing product costs. With the invention of spreadsheets, PCM tools got a major boost in ease of use and adoption. In the late 1970s, specialized third-party software was developed that could do some of the activities included in PCM. Today, there are several tools that directly or indirectly promote themselves as "Product Cost Management" software solutions. Some of these tools also state that they can help users with problems of target costing, as well.

However, despite the creation of third-party tools, spreadsheets, specifically Microsoft Excel may still be, overwhelmingly, the most popular tool for PCM practitioners.

Is PCM a Software Category?

In the mid-2000s, there was some discussion of whether PCM (sometimes referred to as Enterprise Cost Management) would become a separate software category or be part of one or more of the existing enterprise software categories of enterprise resource planning (ERP), product lifecycle management (PLM), or supply chain management (SCM). The vendors who make specialized PCM software have not yet gained the revenue necessary for the major industry analysts to proclaim PCM as its own category. However, there has been at least one analyst report focusing on product cost analytics. It is unknown whether PCM will become part of a bigger enterprise software category. At least one of the major ERP vendors and two of the major PLM vendors have products that they bill as Product Cost Management or analytics solutions.

Purposes

The strategic purpose of PCM has been to maximize the profit of products through making a product the most cost efficient. Tactically, this has been accomplished by using the various PCM techniques and tools discussed above in a predictive way. That is, the tools are used to estimate a cost that is used as an absolute value for what a cost should be, or to relatively evaluate the cost of one design or manufacturing process or supplier versus another. In 2012, some experts in the PCM field have advocated that the purpose of PCM is not only to predict the most accurate cost, but also as a tool for leverage in negotiation.

Activity-based Costing

Activity-based costing (ABC) is a costing methodology that identifies activities in an organization and assigns the cost of each activity with resources to all products and services according to the actual consumption by each. This model assigns more indirect costs (overhead) into direct costs compared to conventional costing.

CIMA (Chartered Institute of Management Accountants) defines ABC as an approach to the costing and monitoring of activities which involves tracing resource consumption and costing final outputs. Resources are assigned to activities, and activities to cost objects based on consumption estimates. The latter utilize cost drivers to attach activity costs to outputs.

Objectives

With ABC, a company can soundly estimate the cost elements of entire products, activities and services. That may help inform a company's decision to either:

- Identify and eliminate those products and services that are unprofitable and lower the prices of those that are overpriced (product and service portfolio aim)
- Or identify and eliminate production or service processes that are ineffective and allocate processing concepts that lead to the very same product at a better yield (process re-engineering aim)

In a business organization, the ABC methodology assigns an organization's resource costs through activities to the products and services provided to its customers. ABC is generally used as a tool for understanding product and customer cost and profitability based on the production or performing processes. As such, ABC has predominantly been used to support strategic decisions such as pricing, outsourcing, identification and measurement of process improvement initiatives.

Prevalence

Following initial enthusiasm, ABC lost ground in the 1990s, to alternative metrics, such as Kaplan's balanced scorecard and economic value added. An independent 2008 report concluded that manually driven ABC was an inefficient use of resources: it was expensive and difficult to implement for small gains, and a poor value, and that alternative methods should be used. Other reports show the broad band covered with the ABC methodology.

However, application of an activity based recording may be applied as an addition to activity based accounting, not as a replacement of any *costing* model, but to transform concurrent process accounting into a more authentic approach.

Historical Development

Traditionally, cost accountants had arbitrarily added a broad percentage of analysis into the indirect cost. In addition, activities include actions that are performed both by people and machine.

However, as the percentages of indirect or overhead costs rose, this technique became increasingly inaccurate, because indirect costs were not caused equally by all products. For example, one product might take more time in one expensive machine than another product—but since the amount of direct labor and materials might be the same, additional cost for use of the machine is not being recognized when the same broad 'on-cost' percentage is added to all products. Consequently, when multiple products share common costs, there is a danger of one product subsidizing another.

ABC is based on George Staubus' Activity Costing and Input-Output Accounting. The concepts of ABC were developed in the manufacturing sector of the United States during the 1970s and 1980s. During this time, the *Consortium for Advanced Management-International*, now known simply as *CAM-I*, provided a formative role for studying and formalizing the principles that have become more formally known as Activity-Based Costing.

Robin Cooper and Robert S. Kaplan, proponents of the Balanced Scorecard, brought notice to these concepts in a number of articles published in *Harvard Business Review* beginning in 1988. Cooper and Kaplan described ABC as an approach to solve the problems of traditional cost management systems. These traditional costing systems are often unable to determine accurately the actual costs of production and of the costs of related services. Consequently, managers were making decisions based on inaccurate data especially where there are multiple products.

Instead of using broad arbitrary percentages to allocate costs, ABC seeks to identify cause and effect relationships to objectively assign costs. Once costs of the activities have been identified, the cost of each activity is attributed to each product to the extent that the product uses the activity. In this way ABC often identifies areas of high overhead costs per unit and so directs attention to finding ways to reduce the costs or to charge more for costly products.

Activity-based costing was first clearly defined in 1987 by Robert S. Kaplan and W. Bruns as a chapter in their book *Accounting and Management: A Field Study Perspective*. They initially focused on manufacturing industry where increasing technology and productivity improvements have reduced the relative proportion of the direct costs of labor and materials, but have increased relative proportion of indirect costs. For example, increased automation has reduced labor, which is a direct cost, but has increased depreciation, which is an indirect cost.

Like manufacturing industries, financial institutions have diverse products and customers, which can cause cross-product, cross-customer subsidies. Since personnel expenses represent the largest single component of non-interest expense in financial institutions, these costs must also be attributed more accurately to products and customers. Activity based costing, even though originally developed for manufacturing, may even be a more useful tool for doing this.

Activity-based costing was later explained in 1999 by Peter F. Drucker in the book *Management Challenges of the 21st Century*. He states that traditional cost accounting focuses on what it costs to *do something*, for example, to cut a screw thread; activity-based costing also records the cost of *not doing*, such as the cost of waiting for a needed part. Activity-based costing records the costs that traditional cost accounting does not do.

The overhead costs assigned to each activity comprise an activity cost pool.

Alternatives

Lean accounting methods have been developed in recent years to provide relevant and thorough accounting, control, and measurement systems without the complex and costly methods of manually driven ABC. However lean accounting is a snapshot concept for capturing just partial derivatives or differentials of selected cost functions. Lean accounting takes an opposite direction from ABC by working to eliminate peculiar cost allocations rather than apply complex methods of resource allocation.

Lean accounting is primarily used within lean manufacturing. The approach has proven useful in many service industry areas including healthcare, construction, financial services, governments, and other industries.

Application of Theory of constraints (TOC) is analysed in a study showing interesting aspects of productive coexistence of TOC and ABC application. Identifying cost drivers in ABC is described as somewhat equivalent to identifying bottlenecks in TOC. However the more thorough insight into cost composition for the inspected processes justifies the study result: ABC may deliver a better structured analysis in respect to complex processes, and this is no surprise regarding the necessarily spent effort for detailed ABC reporting.

Methodology

Methodology of ABC focuses on cost allocation in operational management. ABC helps to segregate

- Fixed cost
- Variable cost
- Overhead cost

The split of cost helps to identify cost drivers, if achieved. Direct labour and materials are relatively easy to trace directly to products, but it is more difficult to directly allocate indirect costs to products. Where products use common resources differently, some sort of weighting is needed in the cost allocation process. The cost driver is a factor that creates or drives the cost of the activity. For example, the cost of the activity of bank tellers can be ascribed to each product by measuring how long each product's transactions (cost driver) takes at the counter and then by measuring the number of each type of transaction. For the activity of running machinery, the driver is likely to be machine operating hours. That is, machine operating hours drive labor, maintenance, and power cost during the running machinery activity.

Application

ABC has proven its applicability beyond academic discussion.

- is applicable throughout company financing, costing and accounting:
- is a modeling process applicable for full scope as well as for partial views.
- helps to identify inefficient products, departments and activities.
- helps to allocate more resources on profitable products, departments and activities.
- helps to control the costs at any per-product-level level and on a departmental level.
- helps to find unnecessary costs that may be eliminated.
- helps fixing the price of a product or service with any desired analytical resolution.

A report summarizes reasons for implementing ABC as mere unspecific and mainly for case study purposes (in alphabetical order):

- Better Management
- Budgeting, performance measurement
- Calculating costs more accurately
- Ensuring product /customer profitability
- Evaluating and justifying investments in new technologies
- Improving product quality via better product and process design
- Increasing competitiveness or coping with more competition
- Management
- Managing costs
- Providing behavioral incentives by creating cost consciousness among employees
- Responding to an increase in overheads
- Responding to increased pressure from regulators
- Supporting other management innovations such as TQM and JIT systems

Beyond such selective application of the concept, ABC may be extended to accounting, hence proliferating a full scope of cost generation in departments or along product manufacturing. Such extension, however requires a degree of automatic data capture that prevents from cost increase in administering costs.

Implementation

According to Velmurugan, Activity-based costing must be implemented in the following ways:

1. Identify and assess ABC needs - Determine viability of ABC method within an organization.
2. Training requirements - Basic training for all employees and workshop sessions for senior managers.

3. Define the project scope - Evaluate mission and objectives for the project.
4. Identify activities and drivers - Determine what drives what activity.
5. Create a cost and operational flow diagram – How resources and activities are related to products and services.
6. Collect data – Collecting data where the diagram shows operational relationship.
7. Build a software model, validate and reconcile.
8. Interpret results and prepare management reports.
9. Integrate data collection and reporting.

Integrating EVA and Process based Costing

Recently, Mocciaro Li Destri, Picone & Minà (2012) proposed a performance and cost measurement system that integrates the Economic Value Added (EVA) criteria with Process Based Costing (PBC).

Authors note that activity-based costing system is introspective and focuses on a level of analysis which is too low. On the other hand, they undescore the importance to consider the cost of capital in order to bring strategy back into performance measures.

Limitations

Applicability of ABC is bound to cost of required data capture. That drives the prevalence to slow processes in services and administrations, where staff time consumed per task defines a dominant portion of cost. Hence the reported application for production tasks do not appear as a favorized scenario.

Treating Fixed Costs As Variable

The key problem with ABC, like other cost allocation approaches, is that in essence it treats fixed costs as if they were variable, thereby presenting an inaccurate picture that will lead to wrong decisions. Allocating PPE to individual products, for example, may lead to discontinuation of products that seem unprofitable after the allocation, even if in fact their discontinuation will negatively affect the bottom line.

Tracing Costs

Even in ABC, some overhead costs are difficult to assign to products and customers, such as the chief executive's salary. These costs are termed 'business sustaining' and are not assigned to products and customers because there is no meaningful method. This lump of unallocated overhead costs must nevertheless be met by contributions from each of the products, but it is not as large as the overhead costs before ABC is employed.

Although some may argue that costs untraceable to activities should be "arbitrarily allocated" to products, it is important to realize that the only purpose of ABC is to provide information to management. Therefore, there is no reason to assign any cost in an arbitrary manner.

Transition to Automated Activity-based Costing Accounting

The prerequisite for lesser cost in performing ABC is automating the data capture with an accounting extension that leads to the desired ABC model. Known approaches for event based accounting simply show the method for automation. Any transition of a current process from one stage to the next may be detected as a relevant event. Paired events easily form the respective activity.

The state of the art approach with authentication and authorization in IETF standard RADIUS gives an easy solution for accounting all workposition based activities. That simply defines the extension of the *Authentication and Authorization* (AA) concept to a more advanced *AA and Accounting* (AAA) concept. Respective approaches for AAA get defined and staffed in the context of mobile services, when using smart phones as e.a. intelligent agents or smart agents for automated capture of accounting data .

Public Sector Usage

When ABC is reportedly used in the public administration sector, the reported studies do not provide evidence about the success of methodology beyond justification of budgeting practise and existing service management and strategies.

Usage in the US Marine Corps started in 1999. Its use by the UK Police has been mandated since the 2003-04 UK tax year as part of England and Wales' National Policing Plan, specifically the Policing Performance Assessment Framework.

Treatment of Costs Under ABC

In ABC, products are assigned the overhead costs that are supposed to be related to the allocation base.

- Non-manufacturing costs.
- Manufacturing costs.
- Plant wide Overhead Rate.
- Departmental Overhead Rates.
- Costs of idle capacity.

ABC's Basic Steps

- Analyze activities.
- Gather cost data.
- Trace costs to activities.
- Establish output measures.
- Analyze costs.

ABC's Basic Benefits

- Makes it possible to determine production cost traced to outputs.
- Targets areas needing management attention.
- Encourages the consideration of alternative methods of production.
- Highlights operational efficiency.
- Identifies financial benchmarks for activity performance.
- Generates more information to measure and reward performance, and prioritizes activities for cost reductions.
- Provides a common managerial framework among support activities.

Limitations of ABC

- Trade-off between expense and accuracy.
- Need for more precise data.
- Need of full support of top level management, and support of ABC based performance review.
- Cases of overstated costs and under-stated margins and mistakes in pricing and other critical decisions.

Activity based Management

- Activity based management involves any use of ABC information to support the organization's strategy, improve operations, or manage activities and their resulting costs.
- Activity Based Costing

  establishes relationships between overhead costs and activities so that we can better allocate overhead costs.
- Activity-based management

  focuses on managing activities to reduce costs.

Activity-based Management

Activity-based management (ABM) is a method of identifying and evaluating activities that a business performs using activity-based costing to carry out a value chain analysis or a re-engineering initiative to improve strategic and operational decisions in an organization.

Activity-based Costing

Activity-based costing establishes relationships between overhead costs and activities so that overhead costs can be more precisely allocated to products, services, or customer segments. Activity-based management focuses on managing activities to reduce costs and improve customer value. Kaplan and Cooper divide ABM into operational and strategic:

- *Operational ABM* is about *doing things right*, using ABC information to improve efficiency. Those activities which add value to the product can be identified and improved. Activities that don't add value are the ones that need to be reduced to cut costs without reducing product value.
- *Strategic ABM* is about *doing the right things*, using ABC information to decide which products to develop and which activities to use. This can also be used for customer profitability analysis, identifying which customers are the most profitable and focusing on them more.

Risks

A risk with ABM is that some activities have an implicit value, not necessarily reflected in a financial value added to any product. For instance, a particularly pleasant workplace can help attract and retain the best staff, but may not be identified as adding value in operational ABM. A customer that represents a loss based on committed activities, but that opens up leads in a new market, may be identified as a low value customer by a strategic ABM process.

Managers should interpret these values and use ABM as a "common, yet neutral, ground ... this provides the basis for negotiation". ABM can give middle managers an understanding of costs to other teams to help them make decisions that benefit the whole organization, not just their activities' bottom line.

Eliminating Non-value Added Costs using ABM

- Identifying Activities.
- Identifying non-value added activities.
- Understanding activity linkage, root causes and triggers.
- Establishing performance measures.
- Reporting non value added costs.

ABM Seeks to Satisfy Following Customers Needs

- Lower costs.
- Higher quality.
- Faster response time.
- Greater innovation.

Profitability Analysis

In cost accounting, profitability analysis is an analysis of the profitability of an organisation's output. Output of an organisation can be grouped into products, customers, locations, channels and/ or transactions.

Description

In order to perform a profitability analysis, all costs of an organisation have to be allocated to output units by using intermediate allocation steps and drivers. This process is called costing. When the costs have been allocated, they can be deducted from the revenues per output unit. The remainder shows the unit margin of a product, client, location, channel or transaction.

After calculating the profit per unit, managers or decision makers can use the outcome to substantiate management decisions. Managers can decide to stop selling loss making products, to reduce costs for loss making customers or to increase sales in profitable locations.

Pareto Analysis

In profitability analysis it is possible to perform a Pareto analysis by ranking output units from most profitable to least profitable. By doing so it is possible to create a so-called 'Whale Curve', graphically showing the potential margin of an organisation.

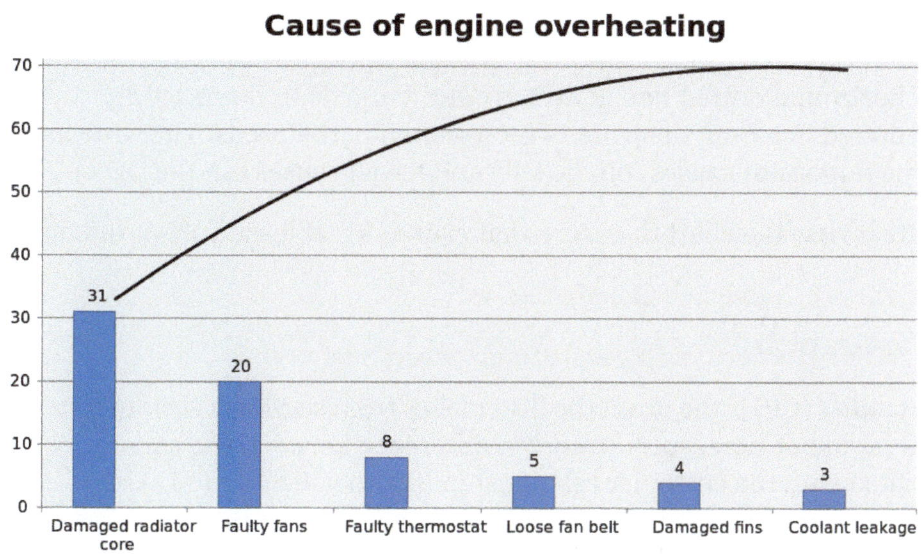

A Pareto analysis in a diagram showing which cause should be addressed first.

Pareto analysis is a formal technique useful where many possible courses of action are competing for attention. In essence, the problem-solver estimates the benefit delivered by each action, then selects a number of the most effective actions that deliver a total benefit reasonably close to the maximal possible one.

Pareto analysis is a creative way of looking at causes of problems because it helps stimulate thinking and organize thoughts. However, it can be limited by its exclusion of possibly important problems which may be small initially, but which grow with time. It should be combined with other analytical tools such as failure mode and effects analysis and fault tree analysis for example.

This technique helps to identify the top portion of causes that need to be addressed to resolve the majority of problems. Once the predominant causes are identified, then tools like the Ishikawa diagram or Fish-bone Analysis can be used to identify the root causes of the problems. While it is common to refer to pareto as "80/20" rule, under the assumption that, in all situations, 20% of causes determine 80% of problems, this ratio is merely a convenient rule of thumb and is not nor should it be considered immutable law of nature.

The application of the Pareto analysis in risk management allows management to focus on those risks that have the most impact on the project.

Steps to Identify the Important Causes using 80/20 Rule

1. Form an explicit table listing the causes and their frequency of occurrence as a percentage
2. Arrange the rows in decreasing order of importance of the causes (i.e., the most important cause first)
3. Add a cumulative percentage column to the table, then plot the information
4. Plot (#1) a curve with causes on *x*- and cumulative percentage on *y*-axis
5. Plot (#2) a bar graph with causes on *x*- and percent frequency on *y*-axis
6. Draw a horizontal dotted line at 80% from the *y*-axis to intersect the curve. Then draw a vertical dotted line from the point of intersection to the *x*-axis. The vertical dotted line separates the important causes (on the left) and trivial causes (on the right)
7. Explicitly review the chart to ensure that causes for at least 80% of the problems are captured

Customer Profitability

Customer profitability (CP) is the profit the firm makes from serving a customer or customer group over a specified period of time, specifically the difference between the revenues earned from and the costs associated with the customer relationship in a specified period. According to Philip Kotler,"a profitable customer is a person, household or a company that overtime, yields a revenue stream that exceeds by an acceptable amount the company's cost stream of attracting, selling and servicing the customer."

Calculating customer profit is an important step in understanding which customer relationships are better than others. Often, the firm will find that some customer relationships are unprofitable. The firm may be better off (more profitable) without these customers. At the other end, the firm will identify its most profitable customers and be in a position to take steps to ensure the continuation of these most profitable relationships. However, abandoning customers is a sensitive practice, and a business should always consider the public relations consequences of such actions.

Purpose

Although CP is nothing more than the result of applying the business concept of profit to a customer relationship, measuring the profitability of a firm's customers or customer groups can often deliver useful business insights.

The purpose of the "customer profit" metric is to identify the profitability of individual customers. Companies commonly look at their performance in aggregate. A common phrase within a company is something like: "We had a good year, and the business units delivered $400,000 in profits." When customers are considered, it is often using an average such as "We made a profit of $2.50 a customer." Although these can be useful metrics, they sometimes disguise an important fact that not all customers are equal and, worse yet, some are unprofitable. Simply put, rather than measuring the "average customer," we can learn a lot by finding out what each customer contributes to our bottom line.

Quite often a very small percentage of the firm's best customers will account for a large portion of firm profit. Although this is a natural consequence of variability in profitability across customers, firms benefit from knowing exactly who the best customers are and how much they contribute to firm profit.

At the other end of the distribution, firms sometimes find that their worst customers actually cost more to serve than the revenue they deliver. These unprofitable customers actually detract from overall firm profitability. The firm would be better off if they had never acquired these customers in the first place.

Construction

Customer profitability is the difference between the revenues earned from and the costs associated with the customer relationship during a specified period. In theory, this is a trouble-free calculation. Find out the cost to serve each customer and the revenues associated with each customer for a given period.

The biggest challenge in measuring customer profitability is the assignment of costs to customers. While it is usually clear what revenue each customer generated, it is often not clear at all what costs the firm incurred serving each customer. Activity Based Costing can sometimes be used to help determine the costs associated with each customer or customer group. For components of cost not directly related to serving customers, the calculation of customer profit must use some method to fully allocate these costs to customers if the total of customer profit is to match the operating profit of the firm. If the firm decides not to allocate these non-customer costs to customers, then the sum of customer profit will be greater than the operating profit of the firm.

Cautions

Like other profit measures, customer profitability is historical. It is a financial summary of what happened in a previous period. And although the past is often indicative of the future, it is easy to imagine situations in which relationships that were unprofitable in the past might become profitable in the future (and vice versa). The forward-looking measure of the value to be derived by serving a customer is called customer lifetime value. Unprofitable customers can have high customer lifetime values (and vice versa).

Cost–Volume–Profit Analysis

Cost–volume–profit (CVP), in managerial economics, is a form of cost accounting. It is a simplified model, useful for elementary instruction and for short-run decisions.

Overview

A critical part of CVP analysis is the point where total revenues equal total costs (both fixed and variable costs). At this break-even point, a company will experience no income or loss. This break-even point can be an initial examination that precedes more detailed CVP analysis.

CVP analysis employs the same basic assumptions as in breakeven analysis. The assumptions underlying CVP analysis are:

- The behavior of both costs and revenues are linear throughout the relevant range of activity. (This assumption precludes the concept of volume discounts on either purchased materials or sales.)
- Costs can be classified accurately as either fixed or variable.
- Changes in activity are the only factors that affect costs.
- All units produced are sold (there is no ending finished goods inventory).
- When a company sells more than one type of product, the product mix (the ratio of each product to total sales) will remain constant.

The components of CVP analysis are:

- Level or volume of activity
- Unit selling prices
- Variable cost per unit
- Total fixed costs

Assumptions

CVP assumes the following:

- Constant sales price;
- Constant variable cost per unit;

- Constant total fixed cost;
- Units sold equal units produced.

These are simplifying, largely linearizing assumptions, which are often implicitly assumed in elementary discussions of costs and profits. In more advanced treatments and practice, costs and revenue are nonlinear and the analysis is more complicated, but the intuition afforded by linear CVP remains basic and useful.

One of the main methods of calculating CVP is profit–volume ratio which is (contribution / sales)*100 = this gives us profit–volume ratio.

- contribution stands for sales minus variable costs.

Therefore, it gives us the profit added per unit of variable costs.

Model

Basic Graph

The assumptions of the CVP model yield the following linear equations for total costs and total revenue (sales):

$$\text{Total costs} = \text{fixed costs} + (\text{unit variable cost} \times \text{number of units})$$

$$\text{Total revenue} = \text{sales price} \times \text{number of units}$$

These are linear because of the assumptions of constant costs and prices, and there is no distinction between units produced and units sold, as these are assumed to be equal. Note that when such a chart is drawn, the linear CVP model is assumed, often implicitly.

In symbols:

$$TC = TFC + V \times X$$

$$TR = P \times X$$

where

- TC = Total costs
- TFC = Total fixed costs
- V = Unit variable cost (variable cost per unit)
- X = Number of units
- TR = S = Total revenue = Sales
- P = (Unit) sales price

Profit is computed as TR-TC; it is a profit if positive, a loss if negative.

Break Down

Costs and sales can be broken down, which provide further insight into operations.

One can decompose total costs as fixed costs plus variable costs:

$$TC = TFC + V \times X$$

Following a matching principle of matching a portion of sales against variable costs, one can decompose sales as contribution plus variable costs, where contribution is "what's left after deducting variable costs". One can think of contribution as "the marginal contribution of a unit to the profit", or "contribution towards offsetting fixed costs".

In symbols:

$$\begin{aligned} TR &= P \times X \\ &= ((P - V) + V) \times X \\ &= (C + V) \times X \\ &= C \times X + V \times X \end{aligned}$$

where

- C = Unit Contribution (Margin)

Subtracting variable costs from both costs and sales yields the simplified diagram and equation for profit and loss.

In symbols:

$$\begin{aligned} PL &= TR - TC \\ &= (C + V) \times X - (TFC + V \times X) \\ &= C \times X - TFC \end{aligned}$$

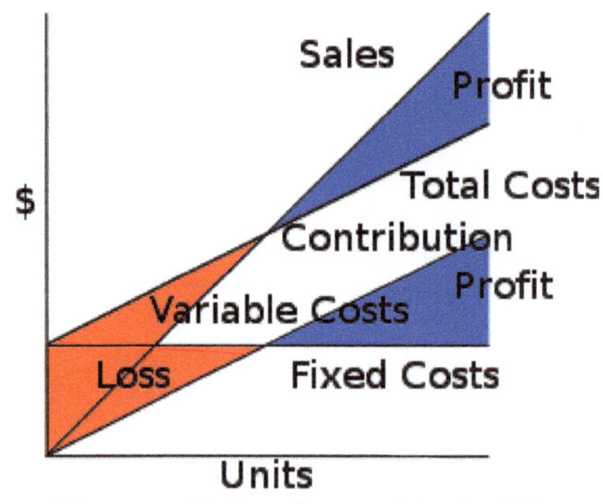

Diagram relating all quantities in CVP.

These diagrams can be related by a rather busy diagram, which demonstrates how if one subtracts variable costs, the sales and total costs lines shift down to become the contribution and fixed costs lines. Note that the profit and loss for any given number of unit sales is the same, and in particular the break-even point is the same, whether one computes by sales = total costs or as contribution = fixed costs. Mathematically, the contribution graph is obtained from the sales graph by a shear, to be precise $\begin{pmatrix} 1 & 0 \\ -V & 1 \end{pmatrix}$, where V are unit variable costs.

Applications

CVP simplifies the computation of breakeven in break-even analysis, and more generally allows simple computation of target income sales. It simplifies analysis of short run trade-offs in operational decisions.

Limitations

CVP is a short run, marginal analysis: it assumes that unit variable costs and unit revenues are constant, which is appropriate for small deviations from current production and sales, and assumes a neat division between fixed costs and variable costs, though in the long run all costs are variable. For longer-term analysis that considers the entire life-cycle of a product, one therefore often prefers activity-based costing or throughput accounting.

When we analyze CVP is where we demonstrate the point at which in a firm there will be no profit nor loss means that firm works in breakeven situation

1. Segregation of total costs into its fixed and variable components is always a daunting task to do. 2. Fixed costs are unlikely to stay constant as output increases beyond a certain range of activity. 3. The analysis is restricted to the relevant range specified and beyond that the results can become unreliable. 4. Aside from volume, other elements like inflation, efficiency, capacity and technology impact on costs 5. Impractical to assume sales mix remain constant since this depends on the changing demand levels. 6. The assumption of linear property of total cost and total revenue relies on the assumption that unit variable cost and selling price are always constant. In real life it is valid within relevant range or period and likely to change.

It is used for forecasting or predicting how the changes in costs and sales volume affect profit. It is also known as 'Break-Even Analysis'.

CVP analysis could be helpful in the following situations:

Budget planning: for forecasting profit by considering cost and profit relation, and volume of production volume. This will help in determining the sales volume required to make a profit.

To make decisions regarding pricing and sales volume.

Determining the sales mix of different products, in what proportions each of the products can be sold.

Preparing flexible budget considering costs at different levels of production.

Objectives of CVP Analysis

- Understand the interaction among

- Prices of products.
- Volume or level of activity.
- Per unit variable cost.
- Total fixed cost.
- Mix of product sold.

Assumptions of CVP Analysis

- Expenses can be classified as either variable or fixed.
- CVP relationships are linear over a wide range of production and sales.
- Sales prices, unit variable cost, and total fixed expenses will not vary within the relevant range.
- Volume is the only cost driver.
- The relevant range of volume is specified.
- Inventory levels will be unchanged.
- The sales mix remains unchanged during the period.

Break-Even (Economics)

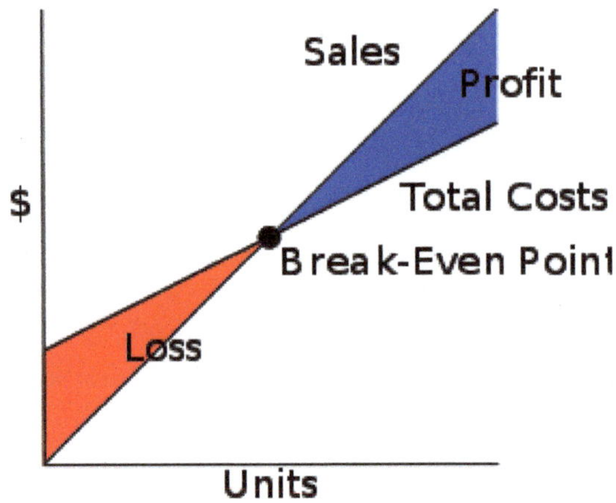

The Break-even Point

The break-even point (BEP) in economics, business—and specifically cost accounting—is the point at which total cost and total revenue are equal. There is no net loss or gain, and one has "broken even," though opportunity costs have been paid and capital has received the risk-adjusted, expected return. In short, all costs that must be paid are paid, and there is neither profit nor loss.

Overview

The break-even point (BEP) or break-even level represents the sales amount—in either unit (quantity) or revenue (sales) terms—that is required to cover total costs, consisting of both fixed and variable costs to the company. Total profit at the break-even point is zero. It is only possible for a firm to Break-even, if the dollar value of sales is higher than the variable cost per unit. This means that the selling price of the good must be higher than what the company paid for the good or its components for them to cover the initial price they paid (variable costs). Once they surpass the break-even price, the company can start making a profit.

The break-even point is one of the most commonly used concepts of financial analysis, and is not only limited to economic use, but can also be used by entrepreneurs, accountants, financial planners, managers and even marketers. Break-even points can be useful to all avenues of a business, as it allows employees to identify required outputs and work towards meeting these.

The Breakeven value is not a generic value and will vary dependent on the individual business. Some businesses may have a higher or lower breakeven point, however it is important that each business develop a break-even point calculation, as this will enable them to see the number of units they need to sell to cover their variable costs. Each sale will also make a contribution to the payment of fixed costs as well.

For example, a business that sells tables needs to make annual sales of 200 tables to break-even. At present the company is selling less than 200 tables and is therefore operating at a loss. As a business, they must consider increasing the number of tables they sell annually in order to make enough money to pay fixed and variable costs.

If the business does not think that they can sell the required amount of units, they could consider the following options:

1. Reduce the fixed costs. This could be done through a number or negotiations, such as reductions in rent, or through better management of bills or other costs.
2. Reduce variable costs by, for example, finding a new supplier that sells tables for less.
3. Increase the quantity of tables they sell.

Any of these options can reduce the break-even point so the business need not sell as many tables as before, and could still pay fixed costs.

Purpose

The main purpose of break-even analysis is to determine the minimum output that must be exceeded for a business to profit. It also is a rough indicator of the earnings impact of a marketing activity. A firm can analyze ideal output levels to be knowledgeable on the amount of sales and revenue that would meet and surpass the break-even point. If a business doesn't meet this level, it often becomes difficult to continue operation.

The break-even point is one of the simplest, yet least-used analytical tools. Identifying a break-even point helps provide a dynamic view of the relationships between sales, costs, and profits. For example, expressing break-even sales as a percentage of actual sales can help managers understand when to expect to break even (by linking the percent to when in the week or month this percent of sales might occur).

The break-even point is a special case of Target Income Sales, where Target Income is 0 (breaking even). This is very important for financial analysis. Any sales made past the breakeven point can be considered profit (after all initial costs have been paid)

Break-even analysis can also provide data that can be useful to the marketing department of a business as well, as it provides financial goals that the business can pass on to marketers so they can try to increase sales.

Break-even analysis can also help businesses see where they could re-structure or cut costs for optimum results. This may help the business become more effective and achieve higher returns. In many cases, if an entrepreneurial venture is seeking to get off of the ground and enter into a market it is advised that they formulate a break-even analysis to suggest to potential financial backers that the business has the potential to be viable and at what points.

Construction

In the linear Cost-Volume-Profit Analysis model (where marginal costs and marginal revenues are constant, among other assumptions), the break-even point (BEP) (in terms of Unit Sales (X)) can be directly computed in terms of Total Revenue (TR) and Total Costs (TC) as:

$$TR = TC$$
$$P \times X = TFC + V \times X$$
$$P \times X - V \times X = TFC$$
$$(P - V) \times X = TFC$$
$$X = \frac{TFC}{P - V}$$

where:

- TFC is Total Fixed Costs,
- P is Unit Sale Price, and
- V is Unit Variable Cost.

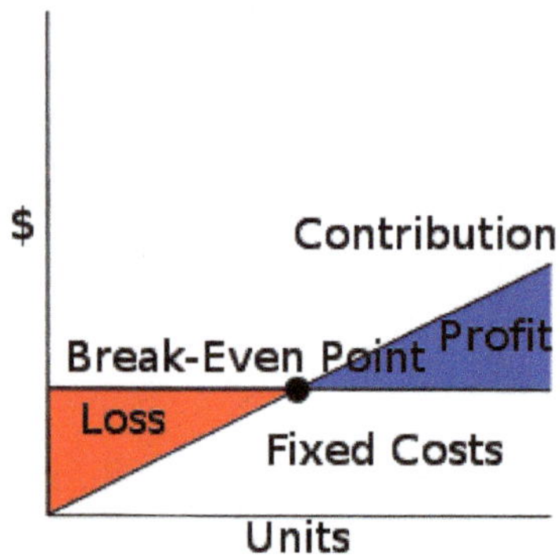

The Break-Even Point can alternatively be computed as the point where Contribution equals Fixed Costs.

The quantity, $(P - V)$, is of interest in its own right, and is called the Unit Contribution Margin (C): it is the marginal profit per unit, or alternatively the portion of each sale that contributes to Fixed Costs. Thus the break-even point can be more simply computed as the point where Total Contribution = Total Fixed Cost:

$$\text{Total Contribution} = \text{Total Fixed Costs}$$
$$\text{Unit Contribution} \times \text{Number of Units} = \text{Total Fixed Costs}$$
$$\text{Number of Units} = \frac{\text{Total Fixed Costs}}{\text{Unit Contribution}}$$

To calculate the break-even point in terms of revenue (a.k.a. currency units, a.k.a. sales proceeds) instead of Unit Sales (X), the above calculation can be multiplied by Price, or, equivalently, the Contribution Margin Ratio (Unit Contribution Margin over Price) can be calculated:

$$\text{Break-even(in Sales)} = \frac{\text{Fixed Costs}}{C / P}.$$

R=C, Where R is revenue generated, C is cost incurred i.e. Fixed costs + Variable Costs or Q * P (Price per unit) = TFC + Q * VC (Price per unit), Q * P - Q * VC = TFC, Q * (P - VC) = TFC, or, Break Even Analysis Q = TFC/c/s ratio=Break Even

Margin of Safety

Margin of safety represents the strength of the business. It enables a business to know what is the exact amount it has gained or lost and whether they are over or below the break-even point. In break-even analysis, margin of safety is the extent by which actual or projected sales exceed the break-even sales.

Margin of safety = (current output - breakeven output)

Margin of safety% = (current output - breakeven output)/current output × 100

When dealing with budgets you would instead replace "Current output" with "Budgeted output." If P/V ratio is given then profit/PV ratio.

Break-even Analysis

By inserting different prices into the formula, you will obtain a number of break-even points, one for each possible price charged. If the firm changes the selling price for its product, from \$2 to \$2.30, in the example above, then it would have to sell only 1000/(2.3 - 0.6)= 589 units to break even, rather than 715.

The break-even points (A,B,C) are the points of intersection between the total cost curve (TC) and a total revenue curve (R1, R2, or R3). The break-even quantity at each selling price can be read off the horizontal axis and the break-even price at each selling price can be read off the vertical axis. The total cost, total revenue, and fixed cost curves can each be constructed with simple formula. For example, the total revenue curve is simply the product of selling price times quantity for each output quantity. The data used in these formula come either from accounting records or from various estimation techniques such as regression analysis.

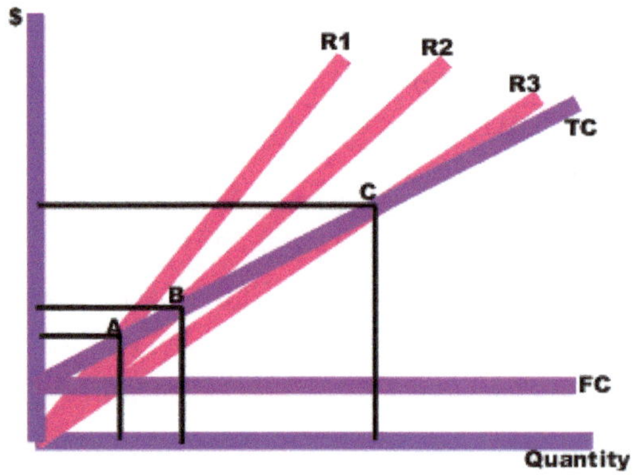

To make the results clearer, they can be graphed. To do this, draw the total cost curve (TC in the diagram), which shows the total cost associated with each possible level of output, the fixed cost curve (FC) which shows the costs that do not vary with output level, and finally the various total revenue lines (R1, R2, and R3), which show the total amount of revenue received at each output level, given the price you will be charging.

Limitations

- Break-even analysis is only a supply-side (i.e., costs only) analysis, as it tells you nothing about what sales are actually likely to be for the product at these various prices.
- It assumes that fixed costs (FC) are constant. Although this is true in the short run, an increase in the scale of production is likely to cause fixed costs to rise.
- It assumes average variable costs are constant per unit of output, at least in the range of likely quantities of sales. (i.e., linearity).
- It assumes that the quantity of goods produced is equal to the quantity of goods sold (i.e., there is no change in the quantity of goods held in inventory at the beginning of the period and the quantity of goods held in inventory at the end of the period).
- In multi-product companies, it assumes that the relative proportions of each product sold and produced are constant (i.e., the sales mix is constant).

Break Even Applications

- New Product decisions :-

  Enables to determine the sale volume required for a firm (or an individual product) to breakeven, given expected sales price and expected costs.

- Pricing decisions:

  Enables to study the effect of changing price and volume relationship on total profits.

- Modernizations or automation decisions:

  Analysis the profit in implication of a modernization or automation programme.

- Expansion Decisions :

  studies the aggregate effect of a general expansion in production and sales.

Formulae

- BEP in units = $\dfrac{Total\ fixed\ cost}{(Sales\ price - variable\ cost\ p.u.)}$

  $\dfrac{Fixed\ cost}{Contribution\ per\ unit}$

- BEP in sales value = $\dfrac{Fixed\ cost}{PV\ Ratio}$

Profit Volume Ratio (PV)

The contribution margin ratio (CMR) i.e. PV ratio is the percentage by which the selling price (or revenue) per unit exceeds the variable cost per unit, or contribution margin as a percentage of revenue.

Example

For Hero1, we could use the forecast information about volume (12,000 bikes) to determine the contribution margin ratio.

- Total revenue = 800 * 12,000

  = 96,00,000

- Total variable cost = 300* 12,000

  = 36,00,000

- Total contribution margin = 9,600,000 - 3,600,000

  = 6,000,000

- Contribution margin ratio = 6,000,000 / 9,600,000

  = 0.625

Relevant Cost

Cost which are relevant for a particular business decision. They are not historical cost but future costs to be associated with different inputs and activities related a particular business decision.

Relevant cost is expected future cost which differs for alternative course. Usually variable costs are relevant while fixed cost are non-relevant.

Ex. Make or Buy, Special Pricing.

However, It is not essential that all variable cost are relevant and all fixed cost are irrelevant. Fixed or variable costs that differ for various alternatives are relevant costs.

Relevant costs draw our alternation to those elements of cost which are relevant for decision.

e.g. 1) Fixed Cost for project X is Rs. 5 lakhs and for alternative project Y it is 7 lakhs.

therefore fixed cost is relevant in this example.

E.g. 2) Direct material under alternative I- Rs. 150 per Kg.

Direct material under alternative II- Rs. 150 per Kg.

therefore variable cost is not relevant in this example.

Sunk Costs

Sunk costs are all costs incurred or committed in the past that cannot be changed by any decision made now or in the future. Sunk costs should not be considered in decisions.

E.g. cost incurred on research of a product will be irrelevant while making decision whether to undertake production or not.

Sunk costs have been incurred and cannot be reversed. Historical costs are sunk costs. They play no role in decision making in the current period.

Sunk Cost do not affect future costs and cannot be changed by any current or future action, hence these costs are irrelevant in decision making.

Ex. Spending on advertising during product launching is sunk for taking a decision on continuance of product.

Make / Buy

Very often make-or-buy decision is the act of making a tactical choice between producing an item internally and buying it from an outside supplier.

Under such circumstances two factors are to be considered:

- whether surplus capacity is available and
- the marginal cost.

Elements of the “Make“ Analysis Include:

- Incremental inventory-carrying costs.
- Direct labor costs.
- Incremental factory overhead costs.
- Delivered purchased material costs.

- Incremental managerial costs.
- Any follow-on costs stemming from quality and related problems.
- Incremental purchasing costs.
- Incremental capital costs.
- Ms. Keshav (Case).

Cost Considerations for the "Buy" Analysis Include

- Purchase price of the part.
- Transportation costs.
- Receiving and inspection costs.
- Incremental purchasing costs.
- Any follow-on costs related to quality or service.

Shutdown Cost

Some times it becomes necessary for a company to temporarily close down the factory or unit because of trade downturn with view to reopening it in the future. In this situation decisions are based on the variable cost analysis.

If selling price is above the variable cost then it better to continue because the losses are minimized.

By closing the manufacturing activity, some extra fixed expenses (e.g. Security) may be incurred and certain fixed expenses can be avoided (e.g. maintenance cost of plant). Such costs are also relevant.

The decision is based on as to whether the contribution is more than the difference between fixed expenses incurred in normal operation and the fixed expenses incurred when the plant is shut down.

Introducing New Product

There are two reasons why a commercial enterprise should undertake the time, effort, and expense of introducing a new product or service:

1. customers have shown interest.
2. demand is sufficient and sustainable enough for the proposed product to make a profit.

In other words, successful enterprises sell what customers want to buy rather than what the entrepreneur wants to sell.

All relevant costs should be recovered over a period of product life.

Joint Product

When two or more products of equivalent importance are produced simultaneously, they are termed as joint products.

In other words two or more products separated in course of the same processing operation, each product being in such proportion that no single product can be designated as a major product.

Joint Products usually require further processing.

Joint Products.

in Coke production, Coal is raw material with Coke, Sulfate of ammonia, light oil asjoint products.

E.g. Refining Process, where crude oil is raw material gives Petrol, Diesel, Gas as Joint Products.

By Product

By Product is product of relatively small total value that is produced simultaneously with a product of greater total value. The product with the greater value (Main product), is usually produced in greater quantities than the By Product.

In other words, when two or more products are separated in course of the same processing operation, where one of the products being in such proportion/ value that it can be designated as a Main product, while others are considered as By Products.

ex. of By-products in coke manufacture - gas and tar in lumber mills - sawdust. Cotton cleaning process - cotton seed coconut oil industry - coca shells.

Terminology

Joint Product Process

A process that results in production of two or more products, which are termed as joint products.

Joint Product Cost

The cost of the raw materials/input and the joint production process.

Split Off Point

The point in the production process where the individual products become separately identifiable.

Joint Cost Allocation: Methods

- Physical units method.
- Relative Sales Value Method.
- Sale value at split off point.
- Net Realisable value method.

References

- Sapp, Richard, David Crawford and Steven Rebishcke "Article title?" Journal of Bank Cost and Management Accounting (Volume 3, Number 2), 1990
- Don R. Hansen and Maryanne M. Mowen (2006). Cost Management Accounting & Control. Ohio: Thomas South-Western. pp. ????. ISBN 0-324-00232-7
- Author(s)? "Article title?" Journal of Bank Cost and Management Accounting (Volume 4, Number 1), 1991
- Kaplan, Robert S. and Bruns, W. Accounting and Management: A Field Study Perspective (Harvard Business School Press, 1987) ISBN 0-87584-186-4
- Velmurugan, Manivannan Senthil. "The Success And Failure of Activity-Based Costing Systems." Journal of Performance Management 23.2 (2010): 3-33. Business Source Complete. Web. 15 Mar. 2012
- Levine, David; Michele Boldrin (2008-09-07). Against Intellectual Monopoly. Cambridge University Press. p. 312. ISBN 978-0-521-87928-6
- Pfeifer, P.E.; M.E. Haskins; and R.M. Conroy (2005). "Customer Lifetime Value, Customer Profitability, and the Treatment of Acquisition Spending," Journal of Managerial Issues, 17 (1), 11-25

4

Fundamentals of Budgeting

A financial plan that is defined as expanding over a period of time is known as budgeting. Types of budgets include flexible budgets, fixed budgets, current budgets, short term budgets, long term budgets, etc. The topics discussed in the chapter are of great importance to broaden the existing knowledge on cost accounting.

Budget

The word budget came from the french word 'budge' which means a small bag of leather . In 1773 the Prime Minister of Britain came with the documents about the plan of expenditure for the year, from then the word budget is used. A budget is a quantitative expression of a financial plan for a defined period of time. It may also include planned sales volumes and revenues, resource quantities, costs and expenses, assets, liabilities and cash flows. It expresses strategic plans of business units, and an organization , activities or events in measurable terms.

A budget is the sum of money allocated for a particular purpose and the summary of intended expenditures along with proposals for how to meet them.

Brooklyn Museum - Comme Sisyphe - Honoré Daumier

Etymology

A budget (derived from old French word *bougette*, purse) is a quantified financial plan for a forthcoming accounting period.

A budget is an important concept in microeconomics, which uses a budget line to illustrate the trade-offs between two or more goods. In other terms, a budget is an organizational plan stated in monetary terms.

Purpose

Budget helps to aid the planning of actual operations by forcing managers to consider how the conditions might change and what steps should be taken now and by encouraging managers to consider problems before they arise. It also helps to co-ordinate the activities of the organization by compelling managers to examine relationships between their own operation and those of other departments. Other essentials of budget include:

- To control resources
- To communicate plans to various responsibility center managers.
- To motivate managers to strive to achieve budget goals.
- To evaluate the performance of managers
- To provide visibility into the company's performance
- For accountability

In summary, the purpose of budgeting tools:

1. Tools provide a forecast of revenues and expenditures, that is, construct a model of how a business might perform financially if certain strategies, events and plans are carried out.
2. Tools enable the actual financial operation of the business to be measured against the forecast.
3. Lastly, tools establish the cost constraint for a project, program, or operation.

Corporate

The budget of a company is often compiled annually, but may not be a finished budget, usually requiring considerable effort, is a plan for the short-term future, typically allows hundreds or even thousands of people in various departments (operations, human resources, IT, etc.) to list their expected revenues and expenses in the final budget.

If the actual figures delivered through the budget period come close to the budget, this suggests that the managers understand their business and have been successfully driving it in the intended direction. On the other hand, if the figures diverge wildly from the budget, this sends an 'out of control' signal, and the share price could suffer. Campaign planners incur two types of cost in any campaign: the first is the cost of human resource necessary to plan and execute the campaign. the second type of expense that campaign planners incur is the hard cost of the campaign itself.

Event Management

A budget is a fundamental tool for an event director to predict with a reasonable accuracy whether the event will result in a profit, a loss or will break-even. A budget can also be used as a pricing tool.

There are two basic approaches or philosophies, when it comes to budgeting. One approach is telling you on mathematical models, and the other on people.

The first school of thought believes that financial models, if properly constructed, can be used to predict the future. The focus is on variables, inputs and outputs, drivers and the like. Investments of time and money are devoted to perfecting these models, which are typically held in some type of financial spreadsheet application.

The other school of thought holds that it's not about models, it's about people. No matter how sophisticated models can get, the best information comes from the people in the business. The focus is therefore in engaging the managers in the business more fully in the budget process, and building accountability for the results. The companies that adhere to this approach have their managers develop their own budgets. While many companies would say that they do both, in reality the investment of time and money falls squarely in one approach or the other.

Government

The budget of a government is a summary or plan of the intended revenues and expenditures of that government. There are three types of government budget : the operating or current budget, the capital or investment budget, and the cash or cash flow budget.

United Kingdom

The budget is prepared by the Treasury team led by the Chancellor of the Exchequer and is presented to Parliament by the Chancellor of the Exchequer on Budget Day. It is customary for the Chancellor to stand on the steps of Number 11 Downing Street with his or her team for the media to get photographic shots of the Despatch Box, immediately prior to them going to the House of Commons. Once presented in the House of Commons it is debated and then voted on. Minor changes may be made however with the budget being written and presented by the party with the majority in the House of Commons (the Government), the Whips will ensure that is it passed as written by the Chancellor.

United States

The federal budget is prepared by the Office of Management and Budget, and submitted to Congress for consideration. Invariably, Congress makes many and substantial changes. Nearly all American states are required to have balanced budgets, but the federal government is allowed to run deficits.

India

The first budget of India was submitted on 18 February 1860 by James Wilson. James Wilson is also known as the father of Indian budget. Finance Minister is the head of the budget making committee. The budget is prepared by the Budget Division Department of Economic Affairs of the Ministry of Finance annually. This includes supplementary excess grants and when a proclamation by the President as to failure of Constitutional machinery is in operation in relation to a State or a Union Territory, preparation of the Budget of such State.

Philippines

The Philippine budget is considered the most complicated in the world, incorporating multiple approaches in one single budget system: line-item (budget execution), performance (budget accountability), and zero-based budgeting. The Department of Budget and Management (DBM) prepares the National Expenditure Program and forwards it to the Committee on Appropriations of the House of Representative to come up with a General Appropriations Bill (GAB). The GAB will go through budget deliberations and voting; the same process occurs when the GAB is transmitted to the Philippine Senate.

After both houses of Congress approves the GAB, the President signs the bill into a General Appropriations Act (GAA); also, the President may opt to veto the GAB and have it returned to the legislative branch or leave the bill unsigned for 30 days and lapse into law. There are two types of budget bill veto: the line-item veto and the veto of the whole budget.

Personal or Family

In a personal or family budget all sources of income (inflows) are identified and expenses (outflows) are planned with the intent of matching outflows to inflows (making ends meet). In consumer theory, the equation restricting an individual or household to spend no more than its total resources is often called the budget constraint.

Elements of a personal or family budget usually include, fixed expenses, monthly payments, insurance, entertainment, and savings.

There are many informational sites and software available for use in personal and family budgeting.

Types

- Sales budget – an estimate of future sales, often broken down into both units and currency. It is used to create company sales goals.
- Production budget - an estimate of the number of units that must be manufactured to meet the sales goals. The production budget also estimates the various costs involved with manufacturing those units, including labor and material. Created by product oriented companies.
- Capital budget - used to determine whether an organization's long-term investments such as new machinery, replacement machinery, new plants, new products, and research development projects are worth pursuing.

- Cash flow/cash budget – a prediction of future cash receipts and expenditures for a particular time period. It usually covers a period in the short-term future. The cash flow budget helps the business to determine when income will be sufficient to cover expenses and when the company will need to seek outside financing.
- Marketing budget – an estimate of the funds needed for promotion, advertising, and public relations in order to market the product or service.
- Project budget – a prediction of the costs associated with a particular company project. These costs include labour, materials, and other related expenses. The project budget is often broken down into specific tasks, with task budgets assigned to each. A cost estimate is used to establish a project budget.
- Revenue budget – consists of revenue receipts of government and the expenditure met from these revenues. Tax revenues are made up of taxes and other duties that the government levies.
- Expenditure budget – includes spending data items.
- "Flexibility budget - it is established for fixed cost and variable rate is determined per activity measure for variable cost.
- ' *Appropriation budget* - a maximum amount is established for certain expenditure based on management judgment.
- Performance budget - it is mostly used by organization and ministries involved in the development activities .This process of budget takes into account the end results.
- Zero based budget - It has clear advantage when the limited resources are to be allocated carefully and objectively.

Setting Up A Budget

Budgeting is a plan for your future income and expenditures that you can use as a guideline for spending and saving. When starting a budget, one must assess their future goals. Set your financial goals for short term, mid-term, and long term. Short term means within the next year, mid-term lies between one to five years, and long term is anytime after. Make sure all goals are S.M.A.R.T. Goals. Specific, Measurable, Achievable, Relevant, and Time-Framed. Using this mindset, you will be setting attainable goals. Second, one must allocate where your income is coming from. Is it a consistent income, monthly, yearly? Is it sporadic and can not be included in a normal budget? Deciding if your income is sporadic or normal, decreases the chances for overspending. Then you must divide the consistent income into normal increments. For example, a semester loan must be divided up into monthly increments to make your budget more maintainable. Next, figure out where one's money is going. How much is going toward rent, groceries, etc? With this, I always keep in mind the 50-20-30 Rule. Fifty percent of your income should go toward living expenses and essentials. This should be the necessities in your life. Twenty percent of your income must go to savings for your future financial goals. This can also go toward debt-reduction to pay off credit card statements and loans as well. Then the remainder can be allocated as flexible spending.

Budget Constraint

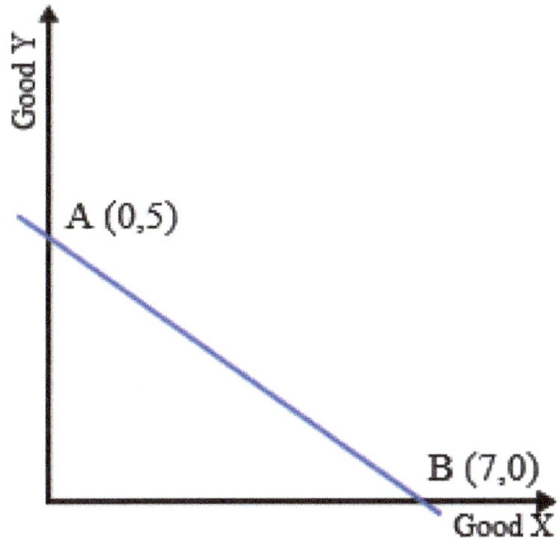

Budget constraint, where $A = \frac{m}{P_y}$ and $B = \frac{m}{P_x}$

A budget constraint represents all the combinations of goods and services that a consumer may purchase given current prices within his or her given income. Consumer theory uses the concepts of a budget constraint and a preference map to analyze consumer choices. Both concepts have a ready graphical representation in the two-good case.

Uses

Individual Choice

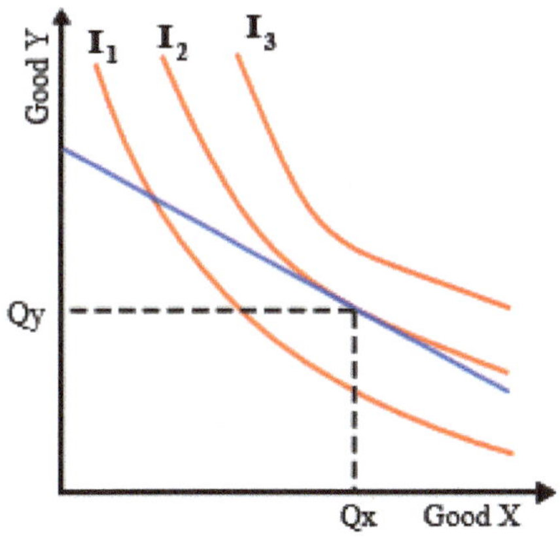

An individual should consume at (Qx, Qy).

Consumer behaviour is a maximisation problem. It means making the most of our limited resources to maximise our utility. As consumers are insatiable, and utility functions grow with quantity, the only thing that limits our consumption is our own budget.

An individual consumer should choose to consume goods at the point where the most preferred available indifference curve on his preference map is tangent to his budget constraint. That is, the indifference curve tangent to the budget constraint represents the maximum utility obtained utilizing the entire budget of the consumer. The tangent point (the xy coordinate) represents the amount of goods x and y the consumer should purchase to fully utilize their budget to obtain maximum utility. A line connecting all points of tangency between the indifference curve and the budget constraint is called the expansion path.

All two dimensional budget constraints are generalized into the equation:

$$P_x x + P_y y = m$$

Where:

- $m =$ money income allocated to consumption (after saving and borrowing)
- $P_x =$ the price of a specific good
- $P_y =$ the price of all other goods
- $x =$ amount purchased of a specific good
- $y =$ amount purchased of all other goods

The equation can be rearranged to represent the shape of the curve on a graph:

$y = (m / P_y) - (P_x / P_y)x$, where (m / P_y) is the y-intercept and $(-P_x / P_y)$ is the slope, representing a downward sloping budget line.

The factors that can shift the budget line are a change in income (m), a change in the price of a specific good (P_x), or a change in the price of all other goods (P_y).

International Economics

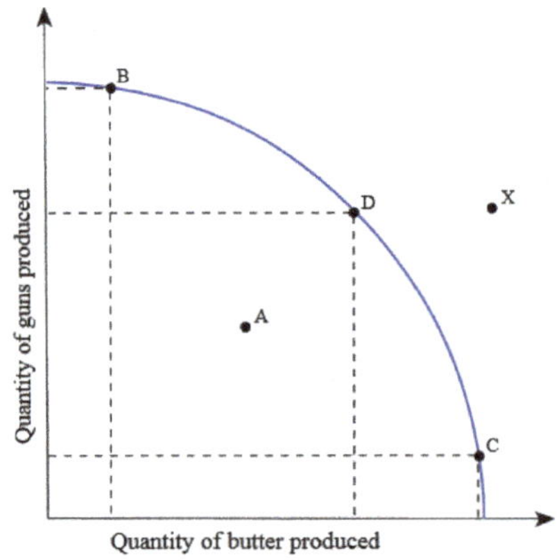

Point X is unobtainable given the current "budget" constraints on production.

A production-possibility frontier is a constraint in some ways analogous to a budget constraint, showing limitations on a country's production of multiple goods based on the limitation of available factors of production. Under autarky this is also the limitation of consumption by individuals in the country. However, the benefits of international trade are generally demonstrated through allowance of a shift in the consumption-possibility frontiers of each trade partner which allows access to a more appealing indifference curve. In the "toolbox" Hecksher-Ohlin and Krugman models of international trade, the budget constraint of the economy (its CPF) is determined by the terms-of-trade (TOT) as a downward-sloped line with slope equal to those TOTs of the economy. (The TOTs are given by the price ratio Px/Py, where x is the exportable commodity and y is the importable).

Many Goods

While low-level demonstrations of budget constraints are often limited to less than two good situations which provide easy graphical representation, it is possible to demonstrate the relationship between multiple goods through a budget constraint.

In such a case, assuming there are n goods, called x_i for $i = 1, \ldots, n$, that the price of good x_i is denoted by p_i , and if W is the total amount that may be spent, then the budget constraint is:

$$\sum_{i=1}^{n} p_i x_i \leq W.$$

Further, if the consumer spends his income entirely, the budget constraint binds:

$$\sum_{i=1}^{n} p_i x_i = W.$$

In this case, the consumer cannot obtain an additional unit of good x_i without giving up some other good. For example, he could purchase an additional unit of good x_i by giving up p_i / p_j units of good x_j.

Budgetary Control

It is a process in which budget is set and actual is compared with budget to analyse variances.

It means the establishment of budgets relating the responsibilities of executives to the prerequisite of policy and the continuous evaluation of actual with budgeted results either to secure by individual action the objective of that policy or to provide a base for its revision.

Objectives of Budget

- Planning:

  A set of targets/goals is often essential to lead and focus individual and group actions. Planning not only motivates the employees but also improves overall decision making.

- Directing:

  Business is very complex and requires more formal direction and coordination. Once the budgets are in place they can be used to direct and coordinate operations in order to achieve the stated targets.

- Controlling:

  The actual performance can be compared with the planned targets. This provides prompt feedback about performance. budget also prevents unplanned adhoc expenditure.

Advantages of Budgetary Control System

- Enables the managers/ administrators to conduct activities in efficient manner.
- Provides yardstick for measuring and evaluating the performance of individuals and their departments.
- Reveals the deviations, from the budget by comparing with actuals; Helps in prompt review process.
- Creates suitable conditions for the implementation of standard costing system.
- Acts as systematic base for framing future policies and targets.
- Inculcates the feeling of cost consciousness and goal orientation.
- Leads to effective utilization of various resources, as the activities are planned and executed effectively.

Components of Budgetary Control System

The policy of a business for a defined period is represented by the master budget, the details of which are given in a number of individual budgets called functional budgets.

These functional budgets are broadly grouped as physical, cost and profit budgets.

- Physical Budgets-

  Those budgets which contains information in terms of physical units about sales, production etc. for example, quantity of sales, quantity of production, inventories and manpower budgets are physical budgets.

- Cost budgets-

  Budgets which provides cost information in respect of manufacturing, selling, administration etc. for example, manufacturing cost, selling cost, administration cost and research and development cost budgets are cost budgets.

- Profit budgets-

  Budgets which enables in the ascertainment of profit, for example, sales budget, profit and loss budget, etc.

Types of Budget

- Fixed Budget.
- Flexible Budget.
- Master Budget.
- Functional Budget.

- Long Term Budget.
- Short Term Budget.
- Current Budget.

Fixed Budget

A fixed budget is the budget designed to remain unchanged irrespective of level of activity actually attained. Such budget is suitable for Fixed Expenses. It is also known as Static budget.

A fixed budget is not suitable in dynamic environment and for a longer period because of its rigidity. It is not suitable where labour cost, material cost and other factors are constantly changing.

Flexible Budget

Flexible budget show the expected results of responsibility centre for several activity level. Flexible budget is the series of static budgets for different level of activity.

While preparing flexible budget the revenues and expenses are classified into Fixed, Variable and Semi-variable categories.

In most cases, the level of activity during the period varies from period to period due to change in demand or seasonal nature or changing circumstances. In such industries/ government organisations flexible budget is suitable.

Functional Budget

Budgets which relate to the individual function/task in an organisation are known as Functional Budgets. For example, purchase budget, sales budget, production budget, plant utilization budget, cash budget.

Master Budget

It is a consolidated summary of the various functional budgets. It is based on goals set. It serves as the basis upon which budgeted P & L A/c and forecasted Balance Sheet are built up.

Long-Term Budget

The budget which are prepared for periods longer than a year are called long-term budget. Such budgets are helpful in business forecasting and strategic planning. E.g. Capital expenditure budget, Research and Development budget.

Short-Term Budget

Budgets which are prepared for periods less than a year are known as short term budgets. E.g. Cash Budget. Such budgets are prepared regular comparison and action to bring variation under control.

Current Budget

A budget which is established for use over a short period of time and is related to the current conditions is called current budget.

Zero-based Budgeting

Zero-based budgeting in the 1970s was primarily concerned with attributing a particular activity of a company to the decision packages, which involves ranking and evaluating the packages for the benefits and costs, and making sure the resources are distributed appropriately. ZBB is a process that can be repeated to review every single dollar in the budget, establish a cost management culture, and also manage financial performance.

ZBB is not a very complex process. Many businesses will budget and plan out things to maintain financials. In the past, businesses would only look at specific things and would assume that everything is already in place and does not need to be double-checked. However, in zero-based budgeting, everything that is to be budgeted needs to be approved. Since zero-based budgeting requires an approval for budgeting, this means that budgets are started from a zero-base and are completely started over every year.

Zero-based budgeting can also be used as a personal way to budget money. The point of a zero-based budget is to make income minus the outgo equal zero spent. This means that money not only needs to be budgeted, but also that one must not spend money that is not there to spend.

Creator and Definition

As an accounting manager for Texas Instruments, Pete Pyhrr created zero-based budgeting. In an interview by *People* magazine, he stated that many line items were historically and traditionally budgeted regardless of the need for the item. Mr. Pyhrr was subsequently asked by Georgia governor Jimmy Carter to manage the Georgia budget process. Pyhrr authored "Zero Based Budgeting: A Practical Management Tool for Evaluating Expenses".

According to Peter Sarant, former director of management analysis training for the US Civil Service Commission, ZBB is "a technique which complements and links to existing planning, budgeting and review processes. It identifies alternative and efficient methods of utilizing limited resources. It is a flexible management approach which provides a credible rationale for reallocating resources by focusing on a systematic review and justification of the funding and performance levels of current programs."

Zero-based budgeting is a method of budgeting in which all expenses must be justified for each new period. Zero-based budgeting starts from a "zero base" and every function within an organization is analyzed for its needs and costs. Budgets are then built around what is needed for the upcoming period regardless of whether the budget is higher or lower than the previous one.

ZBB allows top-level strategic goals to be implemented into the budgeting process by tying them to specific functional areas of the organization. Costs can be first grouped, then measured against previous results and current expectations.

Misconceptions

There are five misconceptions about Zero-Based Budgeting that can make financial advisers shy away from using this type of budgeting.

1. The idea that zero-based budgeting is just starting your budget from a zero sum.

The reality is that zero-based budgeting uses an approach that can facilitate cost viability, cost governance, and cost accountability. Using zero based budgeting correctly can lead to better cost management.

2. Using zero-based budgeting is cutting a budget to ribbons.

The reality is that the amount of budget cutting depends on what the company/government body wants to do. This type of budget cutting also depends on the bodies top-down savings target.

3. Zero-based budgeting can bog down a business and stop it from doing anything else.

The reality is that yes, introducing a new cost management culture within a new business/government body can take some time, it does not always have to create stops. Having a team to implement this type of change can help make the transition easier.

4. Zero-based budgeting only focuses on Selling, General, and Administrative Costs (SG&A)

The reality is that this type of budgeting tool can be used in any type of cost. The main purposes of zero based budgeting is accountability, viability, aligned incentives, and a rigorous process and all of these can be important to any type of costs.

5. Zero-based budgeting was not created for growth oriented companies.

The reality is that zero-based budgeting can be used at any company/government body whether it is being used for cost saving or growth. Zero-based budgeting is not a full slash and burn budgeting technique it can be used in situations to provide strong visibility within a body to create more success.

Advantages

1. Accuracy: This type of budgeting requires companies to look over every department to make sure they are getting the correct amount of money.
2. Efficiency: It helps judge actual need by focusing on current numbers instead of past budgets.
3. Reduction in wasteful spending: It can remove redundant spending by reexamining potentially unnecessary expenditures.
4. Coordination and Communication: It allows for better communication within departments by involving employees in decision-making and budget prioritization.

Disadvantages

1. Bureaucracy: Creating ZBB within a company can take enormous amounts of time, effort, and analysis that would require extra staff. This could cause the process to be counter productive in cutting costs.

2. Corruption: In using ZBB, managers could attempt to skew numbers to make expenditures into vital activities, thus creating a "need" for them. This would cause companies to continue wasting money on things they don't need.

3. Intangible Justifications: This type of budgeting requires departments to justify their budget, which can be difficult on many levels. Departments such as advertising and marketing have to justify expenses they may or may not use in the next year due to the fluctuation of the market. This could cost them profits in the future due to not being able to justify a certain amount.

4. Managerial Time: ZBB comes at the cost of time and extra training for managers. This means extra time every year to do the budget, make adjustments, and receive the proper training to understand how to do ZBB.

5. Slower Response Time: Due to the amount of time and training is required to do ZBB, managerial staff could be less likely to revise the budget in response to a changing market. This means that it will take longer for a company to move money into departments that need it the most at the time. ZBB could potentially leave gaps in a company because the budget might not react to departments' sudden needs.

Use in Public and Private Sectors

Background

Zero-based budgeting (ZBB) in the public sector versus the private sector is a different process. "The use of ZBB in the private sector has been limited primarily to administrative overhead activities (i.e. administrative expenses needed to maintain the organization. In the United States Zero-based budgeting was developed in 1969 at Texas Instrument Inc. Jimmy Carter, Governor of Georgia, was the first to adopt the process of zero-base into the government for the preparation of the fiscal of 1973 budget. Three years later, sponsored by the President and Congress the federal government for the first time implemented zero-base budgeting in The Government Economy and Spending Reform act of 1976.

President Carter later required the adoption of ZBB by the federal government during the late 1970s. "Zero-Base Budgeting (ZBB) was an executive branch budget formulation process introduced into the federal government in 1977. Its main focus was on optimizing accomplishments available at alternative budgetary levels. Under ZBB agencies were expected to set priorities based on the program results that could be achieved at alternative spending levels, one of which was to be below current funding."

For the most part in government, the main users of ZBB are the legislative, executive, and the agency. The legislative includes the congress, state legislature, and city council, and they require more summarization and focusing on public priorities and objectives. Agencies include the agency director and department managers and they require more detailed information and focus on program implementation and efficiency. Lastly, the executive includes the President, governors, mayor/city manager and they focus on the needs of the legislature and agency. Although the legislative, the agency, and the executive have different focuses they all have to address two standard questions:

1. Are the current activities efficient and effective?
2. Should current activities be eliminated or reduced to fund higher-priority new programs? Or to reduce the current budget?

According to Peter Sarant, the former director of management analysis training for the US Civil Service Commission during the Carter ZBB implementation effort, "ZBB means 'different things to different people'." Some definitions imply that zero-based budgeting is the act of starting budgets from scratch or requiring each program or activity to be justified from the ground up. This is not true; the acronym ZBB is a misnomer. ZBB is a misnomer because in many large agencies a complete zero-base review of all program elements during one budget period is not feasible; it would result in excessive paperwork and be an almost impossible task if implemented." In many respects the "common misunderstanding" of ZBB noted above resembles a "sunset review" process more than a traditional public sector ZBB process.

Components of a Public Sector ZBB Analysis

In an overview of zero-based budgeting, there are a total of three elements that make up the concept:

1. Decision Unit Determination
   - This is the building process of the formulation of a budget structure.
2. Decision Package Formulation
   - When compiling and packaging a budget request, this mechanism is utilized.
3. Ranking
   - This process requires the most attention as it requires a company's manager(s) to prioritize out of a group of decision packages that are laid out to them.

In general there are three components that make up public sector ZBB:

1. Identify three alternate funding levels for each decision unit (Traditionally, this has been a zero-base level, a current funding level and an enhanced service level.);
2. Determine the impact of these funding levels on program (decision unit) operations using program performance metrics; and
3. Rank the program "decision packages" for the three funding levels.

In many cases, program staffers were asked to look for alternative service delivery models that could deliver services more efficiently at lower funding level.

The US General Accounting Office (GAO) reviewed past performance budgeting initiatives in 1997 and found that ZBBs "main focus was on optimizing accomplishments available at alternative budgetary levels:

Set priorities based on the program results that could be achieved at alternative spending levels, one of which was to be below current funding.

1. In developing budget forms, these were to be ranked against each other sequentially from the lowest level organizations up through the department and without reference to a past base.

2. In concept, ZBB sought a precise link between budgetary resources and program results."

Further, "ZBB illustrated the usefulness of:

1. Defining and presenting alternative funding levels; and

2. Expanded participation of program managers in the budget process."

The federal ZBB budgeting system had the following components: "Budget requests for each decision unit were to be prepared by their managers, who would (1) identify alternative approaches to achieving the unit's objectives, (2) identify several alternative funding levels, including a "minimum" level normally below current funding, (3) prepare "decision packages" according to a prescribed format for each unit, including budget and performance information, and (4) rank the decision packages against each other."

ZBB was officially eliminated in federal budgeting on August 7, 1981. "Some participants in the budget process as well as other observers attributed certain program efficiencies, arising from the consideration of alternatives, to ZBB. Interestingly, ZBB established within federal budgeting a requirement to:

1. Present alternative levels of funding; and

2. Link (them) to alternative results."

This element of the ZBB budgeting process remained in effect through the Reagan, Bush and early Clinton administrations before being eliminated in 1994.

→Defining the government program zero-base:

There is often considerable confusion over the meaning of zero-base budgeting. There is no evidence that public sector ZBB has ever included "building budgets from the bottom up" and "reviewing every invoice" as part of the analysis. In discussions of ZBB, there is often confusion between a ZBB process and a sunset review process. In a sunset review the entire function is eliminated unless evidence is provided of program effectiveness. This confusion ultimately leads to the question: what is a zero-base?

Sarant's definition of the zero-base based on the federal training experience is: "A minimum level is actually the grass roots funding level necessary to keep a program alive. Therefore, the minimal level is the "program or funding level below which it is not feasible to continue a program... because no constructive contribution can be made toward fulfilling its objective." Identifying this level of program funding has been subjective and problematic.

Consequently, "some states have selected arbitrary percentages to ensure that an amount smaller than last year's request in considered. They do this by stipulating that one alternative must be 50, 80, or 90 percent of last year's request." This equates to analyzing the impact on program operations of a 10, 20 or 50 percent reduction in funding as the "zero base" funding level.

Importance of Performance Measures

Performance measures are a key component of the ZBB process. At the core, ZBB requires quality measures that can be used to analyze the impact of alternative funding scenarios on program operations and outcomes. Without quality measures ZBB simply will not work because decision packages cannot be ranked. To perform a ZBB analysis "alternative decision packages are prepared and ranked, thus allowing marginal utility and comparative analysis."

Traditionally, a ZBB analysis focused on three types of measures. "They (federal agency program staff) were to identify the key indicators to be used in measuring performance and results. These should be "measures of:

1. effectiveness,
2. efficiency, and
3. workload for each decision unit.

Indirect or proxy indicators could be used if these systems did not exist or were under development."

Impact on Government Operations

According to the GAO:

"Agencies believed that inadequate time had been allowed to implement the new initiative. The requirement to compress planning and budgeting functions within the time frames of the budget cycle had proven especially difficult, affecting program managers' ability to identify alternative approaches to accomplishing agency objectives. Some agency officials also believed that the performance information needed for ZBB analysis was lacking."

According to the National Conference of State Legislatures:

"In its original sense, ZBB meant that no past decisions are taken for granted. Every previous budget decision is up for review. Existing and proposed programs are on an equal footing, and the traditional state practice of altering almost all existing budget lines by small amounts every year or two would be swept away. No state government has ever found this feasible. Even Georgia, where Governor Jimmy Carter introduced ZBB to state budgeting in 1971, employed a much modified form.

State programs are not, in practice, amenable to such a radical annual re-examination. Statutes, obligations to local governments, requirements of the federal government, and other past decisions have many times created state funding commitments that are almost impossible to change very much in the short run. Education funding levels are determined in many states partly by state and federal judicial decisions and state constitutional provisions, as well as by statutes. Federal mandates require that state Medicaid funding meet a specific minimum level if Medicaid is to exist at all in a state. Federal law affects environmental program spending, and both state and federal courts help determine state spending on prisons. Much state spending, therefore, cannot usefully be subjected to the kind of fundamental re-examination that ZBB in its original form envisions.

To the extent that ZBB has encouraged governors and legislators to take a hard look at the impact of incremental changes in state spending, it produced a significant improvement in state budgeting. But in its classic form – begin all budget evaluations from zero – ZBB is as unworkable as it ever was."

Use in the Chinese Public Sector

The concept of ZBB was first introduced to China in the beginning of the 1990s and was primarily focused in the Hubei Province area of China. Just as the United States encountered many problems and failures with ZBB, China too ran into them as well. But even with the numerous amount of problems and failures along the way, they have gradually adjusted appropriately since then to become more effective on using ZBB as a budget reform. Western influence on budgeting was non-existent in China before 1993. It was during the 1990s that China began looking out for a new and modern form of budgeting for their country's nationwide budget reform. They ended up settling on ZBB. A new policy was set in place to put ZBB into action, known as the DBR, or the Departmental Budgeting Reform. The DBR and ZBB were first implemented in the Hubei province of China. According to Jun Ma, a professor at the university of Nebraska, the beginning years of ZBB in Hubei were a bit rocky as the DBR had not yet been implemented into all the state departments in Hubei. Only a few departments implemented the budgeting system and the results of multiple departments using multiple budgeting systems were not good. It slowly became clear that using ZBB in a traditional sense would not work out. Officials in the Hubei province and the DBR began looking for ways to incorporate the best parts of ZBB and form a new budgeting system that would work for their needs. The result of this change was a Chinese-styled Target-Based Budgeting system. This form of budgeting required bureaucracies and agencies to submit a simple budget within a pre-set time limit. TBB, as a modified form of ZBB, has worked out moderately okay for the Chinese government in Hubei over the years, but many problems still face the budgeting system.

Some number of issues ranging from the absence of a unified budget and certain expenditures that are somehow exempt from the ZBB process, to the influence or effects of political factors have been widely noted.

1. Absence of a Budget Unification- Though the Hubei Province has developed a thorough budget by combining expenditures and off-budget revenues into the budget, there yet remains certain types of expenses that are still under the control of certain individuals other than the government Finance Department. Because of this, the difficulty of prioritizing all the possible government programs becomes confusing.

2. Political Factor Influences- No matter what the term or whose term it is, political officials have always had a certain plan or change that they would like to implement that would greatly influence the prioritizing process of ZBB. Certain political officials could say they greatly support a certain program and would like the Finance Department to focus more money into that particular program whilst other political officials would think otherwise. Therefore, any real changes or improvements made will always face opposition unless you have a unified political support.

3. Expenditure exemptions- Ranging from operating and personnel expenses to central government policies that are unfunded that start after the budget year, these are just to name

a few things that are excluded from the ZBB process. By not including a large portion of spending into the ZBB process, the effectiveness potential of these reforms becomes greatly reduced.

Two notable reforms to the ZBB process include having departments submit budget requests and the use of sunset legislation.

1. Budget requests- These requests are to reflect (1) a cut of a certain percentage, (2) current level of spending, and (3) an increase of a certain percentage. This allows the opportunity of trading between departments of the funding of a lower priority of one department to a higher priority of another.

2. Sunset legislation- This process places a sense of urgency on certain programs implemented or that are currently being funded as that program shall be placed under review to determine efficiency & effectiveness ,and see whether the public or government really need this program.

Use in Private Sector

3G Capital has become successful using ZBB within their company. Their merger with Kraft Foods Group in 2015 no doubt helped in making its' use successful. This use of ZBB might have continued the misconception that this budgeting style was only for businesses trying to lighten the load of a new company. However, this merger did trigger the use of ZBB within the company and made Kraft Foods Group review and shave down things like cut hundreds of management jobs, jettisoning corporate jets, to requiring employees to ask to make photocopies.

Impact of ZBB on Stockholders

The use of ZBB within 3G Capital has been profitable for stockholders. Their ability to cut costs within Kraft fast caused their stock prices to soar 36% due to the news. This type of budgeting allows for companies like Kraft and others attached to 3G Capital to take out some of the leaner competition that can undercut their prices. Zero based budgeting helps more money to flow to stockholders than into unused departments, over funded programs, and wasteful spending habits.

Capital Budgeting

Capital budgeting, or investment appraisal, is the planning process used to determine whether an organization's long term investments such as new machinery, replacement of machinery, new plants, new products, and research development projects are worth the funding of cash through the firm's capitalization structure (debt, equity or retained earnings). It is the process of allocating resources for major capital, or investment, expenditures. One of the primary goals of capital budgeting investments is to increase the value of the firm to the shareholders.

Many formal methods are used in capital budgeting, including the techniques such as

- Accounting rate of return

- Average accounting return
- Payback period
- Net present value
- Profitability index
- Internal rate of return
- Modified internal rate of return
- Equivalent annual cost
- Real options valuation

These methods use the incremental cash flows from each potential investment, or *project*. Techniques based on accounting earnings and accounting rules are sometimes used - though economists consider this to be improper - such as the *accounting rate of return,* and "return on investment." Simplified and hybrid methods are used as well, such as *payback period* and *discounted payback period.*

Net Present Value

Capital budgeting projects are classified as either Independent Projects or Mutually Exclusive Projects. An Independent Project is a project whose cash flows are not affected by the accept/reject decision for other projects. Thus, all Independent Projects which meet the Capital Budgeting criterion should be accepted.

Mutually exclusive projects are a set of projects from which at most one will be accepted. For example, a set of projects which are to accomplish the same task. Thus, when choosing between "mutually exclusive projects", more than one project may satisfy the capital budgeting criterion. However, only one, i.e., the best, project can be accepted.

Of these three, only the net present value and internal rate of return decision rules consider all of the project's cash flows and the time value of money. As we shall see, only the net present value decision rule will always lead to the correct decision when choosing among mutually exclusive projects. This is because the net present value and internal rate of return decision rules differ with respect to their reinvestment rate assumptions. The net present value decision rule implicitly assumes that the project's cash flows can be reinvested at the firm's cost of capital, whereas the internal rate of return decision rule implicitly assumes that the cash flows can be reinvested at the project's IRR. Since each project is likely to have a different IRR, the assumption underlying the net present value decision rule is more reasonable.

Internal Rate of Return

The internal rate of return (IRR) is defined as the discount rate that gives a net present value (NPV) of zero. It is a commonly used measure of investment efficiency.

The IRR method will result in the same decision as the NPV method for (non-mutually exclusive) projects in an unconstrained environment, in the usual cases where a negative cash flow occurs at the start of the project, followed by all positive cash flows. In most realistic cases, all independent projects that have an IRR higher than the hurdle rate should be accepted. Nevertheless, for mutually exclusive projects, the decision rule of taking the project with the highest IRR - which is often used - may select a project with a lower NPV.

In some cases, several zero NPV discount rates may exist, so there is no unique IRR. The IRR exists and is unique if one or more years of net investment (negative cash flow) are followed by years of net revenues. But if the signs of the cash flows change more than once, there may be several IRRs. The IRR equation generally cannot be solved analytically but only via iterations.

One shortcoming of the IRR method is that it is commonly misunderstood to convey the actual annual profitability of an investment. However, this is not the case because intermediate cash flows are almost never reinvested at the project's IRR; and, therefore, the actual rate of return is almost certainly going to be lower. Accordingly, a measure called Modified Internal Rate of Return (MIRR) is often used.

Despite a strong academic preference for NPV, surveys indicate that executives prefer IRR over NPV, although they should be used in concert. In a budget-constrained environment, efficiency measures should be used to maximize the overall NPV of the firm. Some managers find it intuitively more appealing to evaluate investments in terms of percentage rates of return than dollars of NPV.

Equivalent Annuity Method

The *equivalent annuity* method expresses the NPV as an annualized cash flow by dividing it by the present value of the annuity factor. It is often used when assessing only the costs of specific projects that have the same cash inflows. In this form it is known as the *equivalent annual cost* (EAC) method and is the cost per year of owning and operating an asset over its entire lifespan.

It is often used when comparing investment projects of unequal lifespans. For example, if project A has an expected lifetime of 7 years, and project B has an expected lifetime of 11 years it would be improper to simply compare the net present values (NPVs) of the two projects, unless the projects could not be repeated.

The use of the EAC method implies that the project will be replaced by an identical project.

Alternatively the *chain method* can be used with the NPV method under the assumption that the projects will be replaced with the same cash flows each time. To compare projects of unequal length, say 3 years and 4 years, the projects are *chained together*, i.e. four repetitions of the 3-year project are compare to three repetitions of the 4-year project. The chain method and the EAC method give mathematically equivalent answers.

The assumption of the same cash flows for each link in the chain is essentially an assumption of zero inflation, so a real interest rate rather than a nominal interest rate is commonly used in the calculations.

Real Options

Real options analysis has become important since the 1970s as option pricing models have gotten more sophisticated. The discounted cash flow methods essentially value projects as if they were risky bonds, with the promised cash flows known. But managers will have many choices of how to increase future cash inflows, or to decrease future cash outflows. In other words, managers get to manage the projects - not simply accept or reject them. Real options analysis tries to value the choices - the option value - that the managers will have in the future and adds these values to the NPV.

Ranked Projects

The real value of capital budgeting is to rank projects. Most organizations have many projects that could potentially be financially rewarding. Once it has been determined that a particular project has exceeded its hurdle, then it should be ranked against peer projects (e.g. - highest Profitability index to lowest Profitability index). The highest ranking projects should be implemented until the budgeted capital has been expended.

Funding Sources

Capital budgeting investments and projects must be funded through excess cash provided through the raising of debt capital, equity capital, or the use of retained earnings. Debt capital is borrowed cash, usually in the form of bank loans, or bonds issued to creditors. Equity capital are investments made by shareholders, who purchase shares in the company's stock. Retained earnings are excess cash surplus from the company's present and past earnings.

Need

1. A large sum of money is involved which influences the profitability of the firm making capital budgeting an important task.
2. Long term investments, once made, cannot be reversed without a significant loss of invested capital. The investment becomes sunk, and mistakes, rather than being readily rectified, must often be borne until the firm can be withdrawn through depreciation charges or liquidation. It influences the whole conduct of the business for the years to come.
3. Investment decisions are the based on which the profit will be earned and probably measured through the return on the capital. A proper mix of capital investment is quite important to ensure adequate rate of return on investment, calling for the need of capital budgeting.
4. The implication of long term investment decisions are more extensive than those of short run decisions because of time factor involved, capital budgeting decisions are subject to the higher degree of risk and uncertainty than short run decision.

Payback Period

Payback period in capital budgeting refers to the period of time required to recoup the funds expended in an investment, or to reach the break-even point. For example, a $1000 investment made at the start of year 1 which returned $500 at the end of year 1 and year 2 respectively would have a two-year payback period. Payback period is usually expressed in years. Starting from investment year by calculating Net Cash Flow for each year: Net Cash Flow Year 1 = Cash Inflow Year 1 - Cash Outflow Year 1. Then Cumulative Cash Flow = (Net Cash Flow Year 1 + Net Cash Flow Year 2 + Net

Cash Flow Year 3, etc.) Accumulate by year until Cumulative Cash Flow is a positive number: that year is the payback year.

The time value of money is not taken into account. Payback period intuitively measures how long something takes to "pay for itself." All else being equal, shorter payback periods are preferable to longer payback periods. Payback period is popular due to its ease of use despite the recognized limitations described below.

The term is also widely used in other types of investment areas, often with respect to energy efficiency technologies, maintenance, upgrades, or other changes. For example, a compact fluorescent light bulb may be described as having a payback period of a certain number of years or operating hours, assuming certain costs. Here, the return to the investment consists of reduced operating costs. Although primarily a financial term, the concept of a payback period is occasionally extended to other uses, such as energy payback period (the period of time over which the energy savings of a project equal the amount of energy expended since project inception); these other terms may not be standardized or widely used.

Purpose

Payback period as a tool of analysis is often used because it is easy to apply and easy to understand for most individuals, regardless of academic training or field of endeavor. When used carefully or to compare similar investments, it can be quite useful. As a stand-alone tool to compare an investment to "doing nothing," payback period has no explicit criteria for decision-making (except, perhaps, that the payback period should be less than infinity).

The payback period is considered a method of analysis with serious limitations and qualifications for its use, because it does not account for the time value of money, risk, financing, or other important considerations, such as the opportunity cost. Whilst the time value of money can be rectified by applying a weighted average cost of capital discount, it is generally agreed that this tool for investment decisions should not be used in isolation. Alternative measures of "return" preferred by economists are net present value and internal rate of return. An implicit assumption in the use of payback period is that returns to the investment continue after the payback period. Payback period does not specify any required comparison to other investments or even to not making an investment.

Construction

Payback period is usually expressed in years. Start by calculating Net Cash Flow for each year: Net Cash Flow Year 1 = Cash Inflow Year 1 - Cash Outflow Year 1. Then Cumulative Cash Flow = (Net Cash Flow Year 1 + Net Cash Flow Year 2 + Net Cash Flow Year 3, etc.) Accumulate by year until Cumulative Cash Flow is a positive number: that year is the payback year.

To calculate a more exact payback period: Payback Period = Amount to be Invested/Estimated Annual Net Cash Flow.

It can also be calculated using the formula:

$$\text{Payback Period} = (p - n) \div p + n_y$$
$$= 1 + n_y - n \div p \text{ (unit:years)}$$

Where

n_y= The number of years after the initial investment at which the last negative value of cumulative cash flow occurs.

n= The value of cumulative cash flow at which the last negative value of cumulative cash flow occurs.

p= The value of cash flow at which the first positive value of cumulative cash flow occurs.

This formula can only be used to calculate the soonest payback period; that is, the first period after which the investment has paid for itself. If the cumulative cash flow drops to a negative value some time after it has reached a positive value, thereby changing the payback period, this formula can't be applied. This formula ignores values that arise after the payback period has been reached.

Additional complexity arises when the cash flow changes sign several times; i.e., it contains outflows in the midst or at the end of the project lifetime. The modified payback period algorithm may be applied then. First, the sum of all of the cash outflows is calculated. Then the cumulative positive cash flows are determined for each period. The modified payback is calculated as the moment in which the cumulative positive cash flow exceeds the total cash outflow.

Shortcomings

Payback period doesn't take into consideration the time value of money and therefore may not present the true picture when it comes to evaluating cash flows of a project. This issue is addressed by using DPP, which uses discounted cash flows. Payback also ignores the cash flows beyond the payback period. Most major capital expenditures have a long life span and continue to provide cash flows even after the payback period. Since the payback period focuses on short term profitability, a valuable project may be overlooked if the payback period is the only consideration.

Net Present Value

In finance, the net present value (NPV) or net present worth (NPW) is a measurement of the profitability of an undertaking that is calculated by subtracting the present values (PV) of cash outflows (including initial cost) from the present values of cash inflows over a period of time. Incoming and outgoing cash flows can also be described as benefit and cost cash flows, respectively.

Time value of money dictates that time affects the value of cash flows. In other words, a lender may give you 99 cents for the promise of receiving $1.00 a month from now, but the promise to receive that same dollar 20 years in the future would be worth much less today to that same person (lender), even if the payback in both cases was equally certain. This decrease in the current value of future cash flows is based on the market dictated rate of return. More technically, cash flows of *nominal* equal value over a time series result in different *effective* value cash flows that make future cash flows less valuable over time. If for example there exists a time series of identical cash flows, the cash flow in the present is the most valuable, with each future cash flow becoming less valuable than the previous cash flow. A cash flow today is more valuable than an identical cash flow in the future because a present flow can be invested immediately and begin earning returns, while a future flow cannot.

Net present value (NPV) is determined by calculating the costs (negative cash flows) and benefits (positive cash flows) for each period of an investment. The period is typically one year, but could be measured in quarter-years, half-years or months. After the cash flow for each period is calculated, the present value (PV) of each one is achieved by discounting its future value at a periodic rate of return (the rate of return dictated by the market). NPV is the sum of all the discounted future cash flows. Because of its simplicity, NPV is a useful tool to determine whether a project or investment will result in a net profit or a loss. A positive NPV results in profit, while a negative NPV results in a loss. The NPV measures the excess or shortfall of cash flows, in present value terms, above the cost of funds. In a theoretical situation of unlimited capital budgeting a company should pursue every investment with a positive NPV. However, in practical terms a company's capital constraints limit investments to projects with the highest NPV whose cost cash flows, or initial cash investment, do not exceed the company's capital. NPV is a central tool in discounted cash flow (DCF) analysis and is a standard method for using the time value of money to appraise long-term projects. It is widely used throughout economics, finance, and accounting.

In the case when all future cash flows are positive, or incoming (such as the principal and coupon payment of a bond) the only outflow of cash is the purchase price, the NPV is simply the PV of future cash flows minus the purchase price (which is its own PV). NPV can be described as the "difference amount" between the sums of discounted cash inflows and cash outflows. It compares the present value of money today to the present value of money in the future, taking inflation and returns into account.

The NPV of a sequence of cash flows takes as input the cash flows and a discount rate or discount curve and outputs a price. The converse process in DCF analysis—taking a sequence of cash flows and a price as input and inferring as output a discount rate (the discount rate which would yield the given price as NPV)—is called the yield and is more widely used in bond trading.

Formula

Each cash inflow/outflow is discounted back to its present value (PV). Then all are summed. Therefore, NPV is the sum of all terms,

$$\frac{R_t}{(1+i)^t}$$

where

t – the time of the cash flow

i – the discount rate, i.e. the return that could be earned per unit of time on an investment with similar risk

R_t – the net cash flow i.e. cash inflow – cash outflow, at time t. For educational purposes, R_0 is commonly placed to the left of the sum to emphasize its role as (minus) the investment.

The result of this formula is multiplied with the Annual Net cash in-flows and reduced by Initial Cash outlay the present value but in cases where the cash flows are not equal in amount, then the previous formula will be used to determine the present value of each cash flow separately. Any cash flow within 12 months will not be discounted for NPV purpose, nevertheless the usual initial investments during the first year R_0 are summed up a negative cash flow.

Given the (period, cash flow) pairs (t, R_t) where N is the total number of periods, the net present value NPV is given by:

$$\mathrm{PV}(i,N)=\sum_{t=0}^{N}\frac{R_t}{(1+i)^t}$$

Many computer-based spreadsheet programs have built-in formula for PV and NPV.

The Discount Rate

The rate used to discount future cash flows to the present value is a key variable of this process.

A firm's weighted average cost of capital (after tax) is often used, but many people believe that it is appropriate to use higher discount rates to adjust for risk, opportunity cost, or other factors. A variable discount rate with higher rates applied to cash flows occurring further along the time span might be used to reflect the yield curve premium for long-term debt.

Another approach to choosing the discount rate factor is to decide the rate which the capital needed for the project could return if invested in an alternative venture. If, for example, the capital required for Project A can earn 5% elsewhere, use this discount rate in the NPV calculation to allow a direct comparison to be made between Project A and the alternative. Related to this concept is to use the firm's reinvestment rate. Re-investment rate can be defined as the rate of return for the firm's investments on average. When analyzing projects in a capital constrained environment, it may be appropriate to use the reinvestment rate rather than the firm's weighted average cost of capital as the discount factor. It reflects opportunity cost of investment, rather than the possibly lower cost of capital.

An NPV calculated using variable discount rates (if they are known for the duration of the investment) may better reflect the situation than one calculated from a constant discount rate for the entire investment duration.

For some professional investors, their investment funds are committed to target a specified rate of return. In such cases, that rate of return should be selected as the discount rate for the NPV calculation. In this way, a direct comparison can be made between the profitability of the project and the desired rate of return.

To some extent, the selection of the discount rate is dependent on the use to which it will be put. If the intent is simply to determine whether a project will add value to the company, using the firm's weighted average cost of capital may be appropriate. If trying to decide between alternative investments in order to maximize the value of the firm, the corporate reinvestment rate would probably be a better choice.

Using variable rates over time, or discounting "guaranteed" cash flows differently from "at risk" cash flows, may be a superior methodology but is seldom used in practice. Using the discount rate to adjust for risk is often difficult to do in practice (especially internationally) and is difficult to do well. An alternative to using discount factor to adjust for risk is to explicitly correct the cash flows for the risk elements using rNPV or a similar method, then discount at the firm's rate.

Use in Decision Making

NPV is an indicator of how much value an investment or project adds to the firm. With a particular project, if R_t is a positive value, the project is in the status of positive cash inflow in the time of t. If R_t is a negative value, the project is in the status of discounted cash outflow in the time of t. Appropriately risked projects with a positive NPV could be accepted. This does not necessarily mean that they should be undertaken since NPV at the cost of capital may not account for opportunity cost, i.e., comparison with other available investments. In financial theory, if there is a choice between two mutually exclusive alternatives, the one yielding the higher NPV should be selected. A positive net present value indicates that the projected earnings generated by a project or investment (in present dollars) exceeds the anticipated costs (also in present dollars). Generally, an investment with a positive NPV will be a profitable one and one with a negative NPV will result in a net loss. This concept is the basis for the Net Present Value Rule, which dictates that the only investments that should be made are those with positive NPV values.

If	It means	Then
NPV > 0	the investment would add value to the firm	the project may be accepted
NPV < 0	the investment would subtract value from the firm	the project may be rejected
NPV = 0	the investment would neither gain nor lose value for the firm	We should be indifferent in the decision whether to accept or reject the project. This project adds no monetary value. Decision should be based on other criteria, e.g., strategic positioning or other factors not explicitly included in the calculation.

Interpretation as Integral Transform

The time-discrete formula of the net present value

$$\mathrm{NPV}(i,N)=\sum_{t=0}^{N}\frac{R_t}{1+i^t}$$

can also be written in a continuous variation

$$\mathrm{PV}(i)=\int_{t=0}^{\infty}(1+i)^{-t}\cdot r(t)dt$$

where

$r(t)$ is the rate of flowing cash given in money per time, and $r(t) = 0$ when the investment is over.

Net present value can be regarded as Laplace- respectively Z-transformed cash flow with the integral operator including the complex number s which resembles to the interest rate i from the real number space or more precisely $s = \ln(1 + i)$.

$$F(s) = \{\mathcal{L}f\}(s) = \int_0^\infty e^{-st} f(t)dt$$

From this follow simplifications known from cybernetics, control theory and system dynamics. Imaginary parts of the complex number *s* describe the oscillating behaviour (compare with the pork cycle, cobweb theorem, and phase shift between commodity price and supply offer) whereas real parts are responsible for representing the effect of compound interest (compare with damping).

Example

A corporation must decide whether to introduce a new product line. The company will have immediate costs of 100,000 at $t = 0$. Recall, a cost is a negative for outgoing cash flow, thus this cash flow is represented as -100,000. The company assumes the product will provide equal benefits of 10,000 for each of 12 years beginning at $t = 1$. For simplicity, assume the company will have no outgoing cash flows after the initial 100,000 cost. This also makes the simplifying assumption that the net cash received or paid is lumped into a single transaction occurring *on the last day* of each year. At the end of the 12 years the product no longer provides any cash flow and is discontinued without any additional costs. Assume that the effective annual discount rate is 10%.

The present value (value at $t = 0$) can be calculated for each year:

Year	Cash flow	Present value
$T = 0$	$\frac{-100,000}{(1+0.10)^0}$	−100,000
$T = 1$	$\frac{10,000}{(1+0.10)^1}$	9,090.91
$T = 2$	$\frac{10,000}{(1+0.10)^2}$	8,264.46
$T = 3$	$\frac{10,000}{(1+0.10)^3}$	7,513.15
$T = 4$	$\frac{10,000}{(1+0.10)^4}$	6,830.13
$T = 5$	$\frac{10,000}{(1+0.10)^5}$	6,209.21
$T = 6$	$\frac{10,000}{(1+0.10)^6}$	5,644.74
$T = 7$	$\frac{10,000}{(1+0.10)^7}$	5,131.58
$T = 8$	$\frac{10,000}{(1+0.10)^8}$	4,665.07
$T = 9$	$\frac{10,000}{(1+0.10)^9}$	4,240.98

T = 10	$\frac{10,000}{(1+0.10)^{10}}$	3,855.43
$T = 11$	$\frac{10,000}{(1+0.10)^{11}}$	3,504.94
T = 12	$\frac{10,000}{(1+0.10)^{12}}$	3,186.31

The total present value of the incoming cash flows is 68,136.91. The total present value of the outgoing cash flows is simply the 100,000 at time $t = 0$. Thus:

$$\text{NPV} = PV(Benefits) - PV(Costs)$$

In this example:

$$\text{NPV} = 68,136.91 - 100,000$$

$$\text{NPV} = -31,863.09$$

Observe that as t increases the present value of each cash flow at t decreases. For example, the final incoming cash flow has a future value of 10,000 at $t = 12$ but has a present value (at $t = 0$) of 3,186.31. The opposite of discounting is compounding. Taking the example in reverse, it is the equivalent of investing 3,186.31 at $t = 0$ (the present value) at an interest rate of 10% compounded for 12 years, which results in a cash flow of 10,000 at $t = 12$ (the future value).

The importance of NPV becomes clear in this instance. Although the incoming cash flows (10,000 x 12 = 120,000) appear to exceed the outgoing cash flow (100,000), the future cash flows are not adjusted using the discount rate. Thus, the project appears misleadingly profitable. When the cash flows are discounted however, it indicates the project would result in a net loss of 31,863.09. Thus, the NPV calculation indicates that this project should be disregarded because investing in this project is the equivalent of a loss of 31,863.09 at $t = 0$. The concept of time value of money indicates that cash flows in different periods of time cannot be accurately compared unless they have been adjusted to reflect their value at the same period of time (in this instance, $t = 0$). It is the present value of each future cash flow that must be determined in order to provide any meaningful comparison between cash flows at different periods of time. There are a few inherent assumptions in this type of analysis:

1. The *investment horizon* of all possible investment projects considered are equally acceptable to the investor (e.g. a 3-year project is not necessarily preferable vs. a 20-year project.)

2. The 10% discount rate is the appropriate (and stable) rate to discount the expected cash flows from each project being considered. Each project is assumed equally speculative.

3. The shareholders cannot get above a 10% return on their money if they were to directly assume an equivalent level of risk. (If the investor could do better elsewhere, no projects should be undertaken by the firm, and the excess capital should be turned over to the shareholder through dividends and stock repurchases.)

More realistic problems would also need to consider other factors, generally including: smaller time buckets, the calculation of taxes (including the cash flow timing), inflation, currency exchange fluctuations, hedged or unhedged commodity costs, risks of technical obsolescence, potential future competitive factors, uneven or unpredictable cash flows, and a more realistic salvage value assumption, as well as many others.

A more simple example of the net present value of incoming cash flow over a set period of time, would be winning a Powerball lottery of $500 million. If one does not select the "CASH" option they will be paid $25,000,000 dollars per year for 20 years, a total of $500,000,000, however, if one does select the "CASH" option, they will receive a one-time lump sum payment of approximately $285 million, the NPV of $500,000,000 paid over time. Consider "other factors" above that could affect the payment amount. Both scenarios are before taxes.

Common Pitfalls

- If, for example, the R_t are generally negative late in the project (*e.g.*, an industrial or mining project might have clean-up and restoration costs), then at that stage the company owes money, so a high discount rate is not cautious but too optimistic. Some people see this as a problem with NPV. A way to avoid this problem is to include explicit provision for financing any losses after the initial investment, that is, explicitly calculate the cost of financing such losses.
- Another common pitfall is to adjust for risk by adding a premium to the discount rate. Whilst a bank might charge a higher rate of interest for a risky project, that does not mean that this is a valid approach to adjusting a net present value for risk, although it can be a reasonable approximation in some specific cases. One reason such an approach may not work well can be seen from the following: if some risk is incurred resulting in some losses, then a discount rate in the NPV will reduce the effect of such losses below their true financial cost. A rigorous approach to risk requires identifying and valuing risks explicitly, *e.g.*, by actuarial or Monte Carlo techniques, and explicitly calculating the cost of financing any losses incurred.
- Yet another issue can result from the compounding of the risk premium. R is a composite of the risk free rate and the risk premium. As a result, future cash flows are discounted by both the risk-free rate as well as the risk premium and this effect is compounded by each subsequent cash flow. This compounding results in a much lower NPV than might be otherwise calculated. The certainty equivalent model can be used to account for the risk premium without compounding its effect on present value.
- Another issue with relying on NPV is that it does not provide an overall picture of the gain or loss of executing a certain project. To see a percentage gain relative to the investments for the project, usually, Internal rate of return or other efficiency measures are used as a complement to NPV.
- Non-specialist users frequently make the error of computing NPV based on cash flows after interest. This is wrong because it double counts the time value of money. Free cash flow should be used as the basis for NPV computations.

History

Net present value as a valuation methodology dates at least to the 19th century. Karl Marx refers to NPV as fictitious capital, and the calculation as "capitalising," writing:

The forming of a fictitious capital is called capitalising. Every periodically repeated income is capitalised by calculating it on the average rate of interest, as an income which would be realised by a capital at this rate of interest.

In mainstream neo-classical economics, NPV was formalized and popularized by Irving Fisher, in his 1907 *The Rate of Interest* and became included in textbooks from the 1950s onwards, starting in finance texts.

Alternative Capital Budgeting Methods

- Adjusted present value (APV): adjusted present value, is the net present value of a project if financed solely by ownership equity plus the present value of all the benefits of financing.
- Accounting rate of return (ARR): a ratio similar to IRR and MIRR
- Cost-benefit analysis: which includes issues other than cash, such as time savings.
- Internal rate of return (IRR): which calculates the rate of return of a project while disregarding the absolute amount of money to be gained.
- Modified internal rate of return (MIRR): similar to IRR, but it makes explicit assumptions about the reinvestment of the cash flows. Sometimes it is called Growth Rate of Return.
- Payback period: which measures the time required for the cash inflows to equal the original outlay. It measures risk, not return.
- Real option: which attempts to value managerial flexibility that is assumed away in NPV.
- Equivalent annual cost (EAC): a capital budgeting technique that is useful in comparing two or more projects with different lifespans.

Internal Rate of Return

The internal rate of return (IRR) is a method of calculating rate of return. The term *internal* refers to the fact that its calculation does not involve external factors, such as inflation or the cost of capital.

It is also called the discounted cash flow rate of return (DCFROR).

In the context of savings and loans, the IRR is also called the effective interest rate.

Definition

The internal rate of return on an investment or project is the "annualized effective compounded return rate" or rate of return that sets the net present value of all cash flows (both positive and negative) from the investment equal to zero. Equivalently, it is the discount rate at which the net present value of future cash flows is equal to the initial investment, and it is also the discount rate at which the total present value of costs (negative cash flows) equals the total present value of the benefits (positive cash flows).

Uses of IRR

Profitability of an Investment

Corporations use IRR in capital budgeting to compare the profitability of capital projects in terms of the rate of return. For example, a corporation will compare an investment in a new plant versus an extension of an existing plant based on the IRR of each project. To maximize returns, the higher a project's IRR, the more desirable it is to undertake the project. If all projects require the same amount of up-front investment, the project with the highest IRR would be considered the best and undertaken first.

Maximizing Net Present Value

The internal rate of return is an indicator of the profitability, efficiency, quality, or yield of an investment. This is in contrast with the net present value, which is an indicator of the net value or magnitude added by making an investment.

Applying the internal rate of return method to maximize the value of the firm, any investment would be accepted, if its profitability, as measured by the internal rate of return, is greater than a minimum acceptable rate of return. The appropriate minimum rate to maximize the value added to the firm is the cost of capital, i.e. the internal rate of return of a new capital project needs to be higher than the company's cost of capital. This is because an investment with an internal rate of return which exceeds the cost of capital has a positive net present value.

However, the selection of investments may be subject to budget constraints, or they may be mutually exclusive competing projects, such as a choice between or the capacity or ability to manage more projects may be practically limited. In the example cited above, of a corporation comparing an investment in a new plant versus an extension of an existing plant, there may be reasons the company would not engage in both projects.

Fixed Income

IRR is also used to calculate yield to maturity and yield to call.

Liabilities

Both the internal rate of return and the net present value can be applied to liabilities as well as investments. For a liability, a lower internal rate of return is preferable to a higher one.

Capital Management

Corporations use internal rate of return to evaluate share issues and stock buyback programs. A share repurchase proceeds if returning capital to shareholders has a higher internal rate of return than candidate capital investment projects or acquisition projects at current market prices. Funding new projects by raising new debt may also involve measuring the cost of the new debt in terms of the yield to maturity (internal rate of return).

Private Equity

IRR is also used for private equity, from the limited partners' perspective, as a measure of the general partner's performance as investment manager. This is because it is the general partner who controls the cash flows, including the limited partners' draw-downs of committed capital.

Calculation

Given a collection of pairs (time, cash flow) involved in a project, the internal rate of return follows from the net present value as a function of the rate of return. A rate of return for which this function being zero is the internal rate of return.

Given the (period, cash flow) pairs (n, C_n) where n is a positive integer, the total number of periods N, and the NPV, (net present value); the IRR is given by r in:

$$\mathrm{NPV} = \sum_{n=0}^{N} \frac{C_n}{(1+r)^n} = 0$$

The period n is usually given in years, but the calculation may be made simpler if r is calculated using the period in which the majority of the problem is defined (e.g., using months if most of the cash flows occur at monthly intervals) and converted to a yearly period thereafter.

Any fixed time can be used in place of the present (e.g., the end of one interval of an annuity); the value obtained is zero if and only if the NPV is zero.

In the case that the cash flows are random variables, such as in the case of a life annuity, the expected values are put into the above formula.

Often, the value of r that satisfies the above equation cannot be found analytically. In this case, numerical methods or graphical methods must be used.

Example

If an investment may be given by the sequence of cash flows

Year (n)	Cash flow (C_n)
0	-123400
1	36200
2	54800
3	48100

then the IRR r is given by

$$\mathrm{NPV} = -123400 + \frac{36200}{(1+r)^1} + \frac{54800}{(1+r)^2} + \frac{48100}{(1+r)^3} = 0.$$

In this case, the answer is 5.96% (in the calculation, that is, r = .0596).

Numerical Solution

Since the above is a manifestation of the general problem of finding the roots of the equation $\text{NPV}(r) = 0$, there are many numerical methods that can be used to estimate r. For example, using the secant method, r is given by

$$r_{n+1} = r_n - \text{NPV}_n \cdot \left(\frac{r_n - r_{n-1}}{\text{NPV}_n - \text{NPV}_{n-1}} \right).$$

where r_n is considered the nth approximation of the IRR.

This r can be found to an arbitrary degree of accuracy. Different accounting packages may provide functions for different accuracy levels.

The convergence behaviour of by the following:

- If the function $\text{NPV}(i)$ has a single real root r, then the sequence converges reproducibly towards r.
- If the function $\text{NPV}(i)$ has n real roots $r_1, r_2, \ldots, r_n$, then the sequence converges to one of the roots, and changing the values of the initial pairs may change the root to which it converges.
- If function $\text{NPV}(i)$ has no real roots, then the sequence tends towards $+\infty$.

Having $r_1 > r_0$ when $\text{NPV}_0 > 0$ or $r_1 < r_0$ when $\text{NPV}_0 < 0$ may speed up convergence of r_n to r.

Numerical Solution for Single Outflow and Multiple Inflows

Of particular interest is the case where the stream of payments consists of a single outflow, followed by multiple inflows occurring at equal periods. In the above notation, this corresponds to:

$$C_0 < 0, \quad C_n \geq 0 \text{ for } n \geq 1.$$

In this case the NPV of the payment stream is a convex, strictly decreasing function of interest rate. There is always a single unique solution for IRR.

Given two estimates r_1 and r_2 for IRR, the secant method equation with $n = 2$ always produces an improved estimate r_3 . This is sometimes referred to as the Hit and Trial (or Trial and Error) method. More accurate interpolation formulas can also be obtained: for instance the secant formula with correction

$$r_{n+1} = r_n - \text{NPV}_n \left(\frac{r_n - r_{n-1}}{\text{NPV}_n - \text{NPV}_{n-1}} \right) \left(1 - 1.4 \frac{\text{NPV}_{n-1}}{\text{NPV}_{n-1} - 3\text{NPV}_n + 2C_0} \right),$$

(which is most accurate when $0 > \text{NPV}_n > \text{NPV}_{n-1}$)) has been shown to be almost 10 times more accurate than the secant formula for a wide range of interest rates and initial guesses. For example, using the stream of payments {−4000, 1200, 1410, 1875, 1050} and initial guesses $r_1 = 0.25$ and $r_2 = 0.2$ the secant formula with correction gives an IRR estimate of 14.2% (0.7% error) as compared to IRR = 13.2% (7% error) from the secant method. Other improved formulas may be found in.

If applied iteratively, either the secant method or the improved formula always converges to the correct solution.

Both the secant method and the improved formula rely on initial guesses for IRR. The following initial guesses may be used:

$$r_1 = \left(A / |C_0|\right)^{2/(N+1)} - 1$$

$$r_2 = (1 + r_1)^p - 1$$

where

$$A = \text{ sum of inflows } = C_1 + \cdots + C_N$$

$$p = \frac{\log(A / |C_0|)}{\log(A / \text{NPV}_{1,in})}.$$

Here, $\text{NPV}_{1,in}$ refers to the NPV of the inflows only (that is, set $C_0 = 0$ and compute NPV).

Exact Dates of Cash Flows

A cash flow C may occur at any time t years after the beginning of the project. t may not be a whole number. The cash flow should still be discounted by a factor $\frac{1}{(1+r)^t}$.

Problems with using Internal Rate of Return

As a tool applied to making an investment decision, to decide whether a project adds value or not, comparing the IRR of a single project with the required rate of return, in isolation from any other projects, is equivalent to the NPV method. If the appropriate IRR (if such can be found correctly) is greater than the required rate of return, then using the required rate of return to discount cash flows to their present value, the NPV of that project will be positive, and vice versa. However, using IRR to sort projects in order of preference does not result in the same order as using NPV.

Maximizing Net Present Value

One possible investment objective is to maximize the total net present value of projects.

When the objective is to maximize total value, the calculated IRR should not be used to choose between mutually exclusive projects.

In cases where one project has a higher initial investment than a second mutually exclusive project, the first project may have a lower IRR (expected return), but a higher NPV (increase in shareholders' wealth) and should thus be accepted over the second project (assuming no capital constraints).

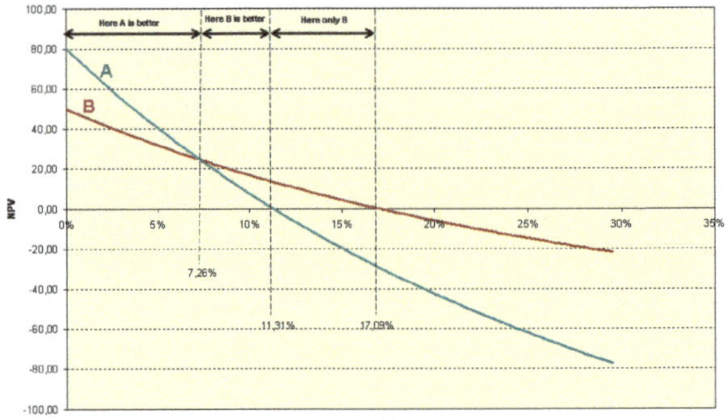

NPV vs discount rate comparison for two mutually exclusive projects. Project 'A' has a higher NPV (for certain discount rates), even though its IRR (= x-axis intercept) is lower than for project 'B' (click to enlarge)

When the objective is to maximize total value, IRR should not be used to compare projects of different duration. For example, the net present value added by a project with longer duration but lower IRR could be greater than that of a project of similar size, in terms of total net cash flows, but with shorter duration and higher IRR.

Practitioner Preference for IRR over NPV

Despite a strong academic preference for NPV, surveys indicate that executives prefer IRR over NPV. Apparently, managers find it easier to compare investments of different sizes in terms of percentage rates of return than by dollars of NPV. However, NPV remains the "more accurate" reflection of value to the business. IRR, as a measure of investment efficiency may give better insights in capital constrained situations. However, when comparing mutually exclusive projects, NPV is the appropriate measure.

Maximizing Long-Term Return

Maximizing total value is not the only conceivable possible investment objective. An alternative objective would for example be to maximize long-term return. Such an objective would rationally lead to accepting first those new projects within the capital budget which have the highest IRR, because adding such projects would tend to maximize overall long-term return.

Example

To see this, consider two investors, Max Value and Max Return. Max Value wishes her net worth to grow as large as possible, and will invest every last cent available to achieve this, whereas Max Return wants to maximize his rate of return over the long term, and would prefer to choose projects with smaller capital outlay but higher returns. Max Value and Max Return can each raise *up to* 100,000 US dollars from their bank at an annual interest rate of 10 percent paid at the end of the year.

Investors Max Value and Max Return are presented with two possible projects to invest in, called Big-Is-Best and Small-Is-Beautiful. Big-Is-Best requires a capital investment of 100,000 US dollars today, and the lucky investor will be repaid 132,000 US dollars in a year's time. Small-Is-Beautiful only requires 10,000 US dollars capital to be invested today, and will repay the investor 13,750 US dollars in a year's time.

Solution

The cost of capital for both investors is 10 percent.

Both Big-Is-Best and Small-Is-Beautiful have positive NPVs:

$$NPV(\text{Big-Is-Best}) = \frac{132,000}{1.1} - 100,000 = 20,000$$

$$NPV(\text{Small-Is-Beautiful}) = \frac{13,750}{1.1} - 10,000 = 2,500$$

and the IRR of each is (of course) greater than the cost of capital:

$$NPV(\text{Big-Is-Best}) = \frac{132,000}{1.32} - 100,000 = 0$$

so the IRR of Big-Is-Best is 32 percent, and

$$NPV(\text{Small-Is-Beautiful}) = \frac{13,750}{1.375} - 10,000 = 0$$

so the IRR of Small-Is-Beautiful is 37.5 percent.

Both investments would be acceptable to both investors, but the twist in the tale is that these are mutually exclusive projects for both investors, because their capital budget is limited to 100,000 US dollars. How will the investors choose rationally between the two?

The happy outcome is that Max Value chooses Big-Is-Best, which has the higher NPV of 20,000 US dollars, over Small-Is-Beautiful, which only has a modest NPV of 2,500, whereas Max Return chooses Small-Is-Beautiful, for its superior 37.5 percent return, over the attractive (but not as attractive) return of 32 percent offered on Big-Is-Best. So there is no squabbling of who gets which project, they are each happy to choose different projects.

How can this be rational for both investors? The answer lies in the fact that the investors do not have to invest the full 100,000 US dollars. Max Return is content to invest only 10,000 US dollars for now. After all, Max Return may rationalize the outcome by thinking that maybe tomorrow there will be new opportunities available to invest the remaining 90,000 US dollars the bank is willing to lend Max Return, at even higher IRRs. Even if only seven more projects come along which are identical to Small-Is-Beautiful, Max Return would be able to match the NPV of Big-Is-Best, on a total investment of only 80,000 US dollars, with 20,000 US dollars left in the budget to spare for truly unmissable opportunities. Max Value is also happy, because she has filled her capital budget straight away, and decides she can take the rest of the year off investing.

Multiple IRRs

In cases where the sign of the cash flows changes more than once, for example where positive cash flows are followed by negative ones and then by positive ones (+ + − − − +) the IRR may have multiple real values. In a series of cash flows like (−10, 21, −11), one initially invests money, so a high rate of return is best, but then receives more than one possesses, so then one owes money, so now a low rate of return is best. In this case it is not even clear whether a high or a low IRR is better.

There may even be multiple real IRRs for a single project, like in the example 0% as well as 10%. Examples of this type of project are strip mines and nuclear power plants, where there is usually a large cash outflow at the end of the project.

The IRR satisfies a polynomial equation. Sturm's theorem can be used to determine if that equation has a unique real solution. In general the IRR equation cannot be solved analytically but only by iteration.

It has been shown that with multiple internal rates of return, the IRR approach can still be interpreted in a way that is consistent with the present value approach provided that the underlying investment stream is correctly identified as net investment or net borrowing.

Modified Internal Rate of Return

Modified Internal Rate of Return (MIRR) considers cost of capital, and is intended to provide a better indication of a project's probable return. Applying a discount rate for borrowing cash, and the IRR calculated for the investment cash flows. This applies in real life for example when a customer makes a deposit before a specific machine is built.

When a project has multiple IRRs it may be more convenient to compute the IRR of the project with the benefits reinvested. Accordingly, MIRR is used, which has an assumed reinvestment rate, usually equal to the project's cost of capital.

Average Internal Rate of Return

Magni (2010) introduced a new approach, named AIRR approach, based on the intuitive notion of mean, that solves the problems of the IRR. However, the above-mentioned difficulties are only some of the many flaws incurred by the IRR. Magni (2013) provided a detailed list of 18 flaws of the IRR and showed how the AIRR approach does not incur the IRR problems.

Mathematics

Mathematically, the value of the investment is assumed to undergo exponential growth or decay according to some rate of return (any value greater than −100%), with discontinuities for cash flows, and the IRR of a series of cash flows is defined as any rate of return that results in a net present value of zero (or equivalently, a rate of return that results in the correct value of zero after the last cash flow).

Thus, internal rate(s) of return follow from the net present value as a function of the rate of return. This function is continuous. Towards a rate of return of −100% the net present value approaches infinity with the sign of the last cash flow, and towards a rate of return of positive infinity the net present value approaches the first cash flow (the one at the present). Therefore, if the first and last cash flow have a different sign there exists an internal rate of return. Examples of time series without an IRR:

- Only negative cash flows — the NPV is negative for every rate of return.

- (−1, 1, −1), rather small positive cash flow between two negative cash flows; the NPV is a quadratic function of $1/(1 + r)$, where r is the rate of return, or put differently, a quadratic function of the discount rate $r/(1 + r)$; the highest NPV is −0.75, for r = 100%.

In the case of a series of exclusively negative cash flows followed by a series of exclusively positive ones, the resulting function of the rate of return is continuous and monotonically decreasing from positive infinity (when the rate of return approaches -100%) to the value of the first cash flow (when the rate of return approaches infinity), so there is a unique rate of return for which it is zero. Hence, the IRR is also unique (and equal). Although the NPV-function itself is not necessarily monotonically decreasing on its whole domain, it *is* at the IRR.

Similarly, in the case of a series of exclusively positive cash flows followed by a series of exclusively negative ones the IRR is also unique.

Finally, by Descartes' rule of signs, the number of internal rates of return can never be more than the number of changes in sign of cash flow.

The Reinvestment Debate

It is often stated that IRR assumes reinvestment of all cash flows until the very end of the project. This assertion has been a matter of debate in the literature.

Sources stating that there is such a hidden assumption include those cited below. Sources arguing that there is no IRR reinvestment assumption include

The IRR method measures return in the presence of external cash flows. The assumptions of users of the method are independent of the IRR method itself. When comparing investments, making a naive implicit assumption that cash flows are reinvested at the same IRR, would tend to lead to false conclusions. If cash flows received are not reinvested at the same rate as the IRR, a project with a relatively short duration and a high IRR does not necessarily add more value over a longer time span than another project with a longer duration and a lower IRR. The Modified Internal Rate of Return (MIRR) addresses this issue by including a second investment at a potentially different rate of return, to calculate a portfolio return without external cash flows over the life of the project. However, for capital budgeting, when the objective is to maximize value, finance theory holds that NPV using the firm's cost of capital is a superior metric.

The Internal Rate of Return in Personal Finance

The IRR can be used to measure the money-weighted performance of financial investments such as an individual investor's brokerage account. For this scenario, an equivalent, more intuitive definition of the IRR is, "The IRR is the annual interest rate of the fixed rate account (like a somewhat idealized savings account) which, when subjected to the same deposits and withdrawals as the actual investment, has the same ending balance as the actual investment." This fixed rate account is also called the *replicating fixed rate account* for the investment. There are examples where the replicating fixed rate account encounters negative balances despite the fact that the actual investment did not. In those cases, the IRR calculation assumes that the same interest rate that is paid on positive balances is charged on negative balances. It has been shown that this way of charging interest is the root cause of the IRR's multiple solutions problem. If the model is modified so that, as is the case in real life, an externally supplied cost of borrowing (possibly varying over time) is charged on negative balances, the multiple solutions issue disappears. The resulting rate is called the *fixed rate equivalent* (*FREQ*).

Unannualized Internal Rate of Return

In the context of investment performance measurement, there is sometimes ambiguity in terminology between the periodic rate of return, such as the internal rate of return as defined above, and a holding period return. The term *internal rate of return* or *IRR* or *Since Inception Internal Rate of Return (SI-IRR)* is in some contexts used to refer to the unannualized return over the period, particularly for periods of less than a year.

Standard Cost

- An estimated or pre-determined cost of performing an operation or producing a good or service, under normal conditions.
- It is used as a basis for cost control through variance analysis.

It is chosen to serve as a benchmark in the standard costing/ budgetary control system. It is a budget for the production of one unit of product or service.

It is a pre-determined cost which is calculated from management's standards of efficient operation and the relevant necessary expenditure.

Standard Costing

It is a cost accounting technique for cost control where standard costs are determined and compared with actual costs, to initiate corrective action.

It is a control method involving the preparation of detailed cost and sales budgets.

A management tool used to facilitate management by exception.

Steps in Standard Costing

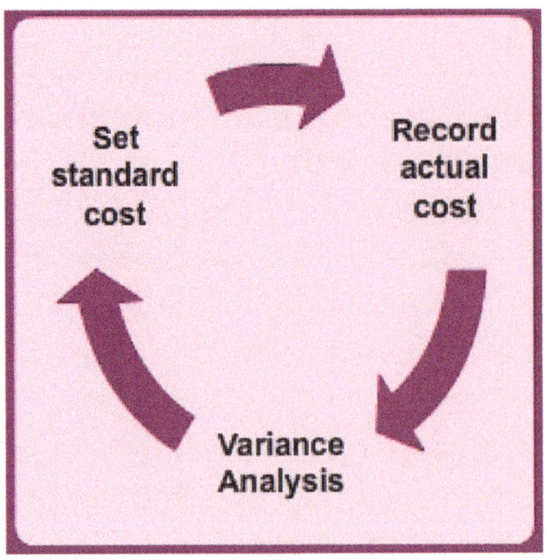

Steps in Standard Costing

- Set the standard cost
  - o A standard quantity is predetermined and standard price per unit is estimated.
  - o Budgeted cost is calculated by using standard cost.
- Record the actual cost
  - o Calculate actual quantity and cost incurred giving full details.
- Variance Analysis
  - o Comparison of the actual cost with the budgeted cost.
  - o The cost variance is used in controlling cost.
  - o Take suitable corrective action.
  - o Fix responsibilities to ensure compliance
  - o Create effective control system.
  - o Resetting the budget, if required.

Types of standards

Ideal Standards

These represents the level of performance attainable when prices for material and labour are most favorable, when the highest output is achieved with the best equipment and layout and when maximum efficiency in utilization of resources results in maximum output with minimum cost.

Normal Standards

These are the standards that may be achieved under normal operating conditions. The normal activity has been defined as number of standard hours which will produce normal efficiency sufficient goods to meet the average sales demand over a term of years.

Basic or Bogey Standards

These standards are use only when they are likely to remain constant or unaltered over long period. According to this standard, a base year is chosen for comparison purposes in the same way as statistician use price indices.

When basic standards are in use, variances are not calculated as the difference between standard and actual cost. Instead, the actual cost is expressed as a percentage of basic cost.

Current Standard

These standards reflect the management's anticipation of what actual cost will be for the current period. These are the costs which the business will incur if the anticipated prices are paid for goods and services and the usage corresponds to that believed to be necessary to produce the planned output.

Standard Cost Accounting

Standard cost accounting is a traditional cost accounting method introduced in the 1920s, as an alternative for the traditional cost accounting method based on historical costs.

Overview

Standard cost accounting uses ratios called efficiencies that compare the labour and materials actually used to produce a good with those that the same goods would have required under "standard" conditions. As long as actual and standard conditions are similar, few problems arise. Unfortunately, standard cost accounting methods developed about 100 years ago, when labor comprised the most important cost in manufactured goods. Standard methods continue to emphasize labor efficiency even though that resource now constitutes a (very) small part of cost in most cases.

Standard cost accounting can hurt managers, workers, and firms in several ways. For example, a policy decision to increase inventory can harm a manufacturing manager's performance evaluation. Increasing inventory requires increased production, which means that processes must operate at higher rates. When (not if) something goes wrong, the process takes longer and uses more than the standard labor time. The manager appears responsible for the excess, even though s/he has no control over the production requirement or the problem.

In adverse economic times, firms use the same efficiencies to downsize, rightsize, or otherwise reduce their labor force. Workers laid off under those circumstances have even less control over excess inventory and cost efficiencies than their managers.

Many financial and cost accountants have agreed for many years on the desirability of replacing standard cost accounting. They have not, however, found a successor.

History

One of the first authors to foresee standard costing was the British accountant George P. Norton in his 1889 *Textile Manufacturers' Bookkeeping*. John Whitmore, a disciple of Alexander Hamilton Church, is credited for actually presenting "the first detailed description of a standard cost system" in 1906/08. The Anglo-American management consultant G. Charter Harrison is credited for designing one of the earliest known complete standard cost systems in the early 1910s.

When cost accounting was developed in the 1890s, labor was the largest fraction of product cost and could be considered a variable cost. Workers often did not know how many hours they would work in a week when they reported on Monday morning because time-keeping systems (based in time book) were rudimentary. Cost accountants, therefore, concentrated on how efficiently managers used labor since it was their most important variable resource. Now however, workers who come to work on Monday morning almost always work 40 hours or more; their cost is fixed rather than variable. However, today, many managers are still evaluated on their labor efficiencies, and many "downsizing," "rightsizing," and other labor reduction campaigns are based on them.

Traditional standard costing (TSC), used in cost accounting, dates back to the 1920s and is a central method in management accounting practiced today because it is used for financial statement reporting for the valuation of income statement and balance sheet line items such as cost of goods sold (COGS) and inventory valuation. Traditional standard costing must comply with generally accepted accounting principles (GAAP US) and actually aligns itself more with answering financial accounting requirements rather than providing solutions for management accountants. Traditional approaches limit themselves by defining cost behavior only in terms of production or sales volume.

Standard Cost Accounting, Topics

Historical Costs

Historical costs are costs whereby materials and labor may be allocated based on past experience. Historical costs are a classification of costs by time. Historical costs are costs incurred in the past. Predetermined costs are computed in advance on basis of factors affecting cost elements. In the 19th century and early 20th century time books were used to register working time, and eventually determine historical costs.

In modern cost account of recording historical costs was taken further, by allocating the company's fixed costs over a given period of time to the items produced during that period, and recording the result as the total cost of production. This allowed the *full cost* of products that were not sold in the period they were produced to be recorded in inventory using a variety of complex accounting methods, which was consistent with the principles of Generally Accepted Accounting Principles (GAAP). It also essentially enabled managers to ignore the fixed costs, and look at the results of each period in relation to the "standard cost" for any given product.

> For example: if the railway coach company normally produced 40 coaches per month, and the fixed costs were still $1000/month, then each coach could be said to incur an Operating Cost/overhead of $25 =($1000 / 40). Adding this to the variable costs of $300 per coach produced a full cost of $325 per coach.

This method tended to slightly distort the resulting unit cost, but in mass-production industries that made one product line, and where the fixed costs were relatively low, the distortion was very minor.

> For example: if the railway coach company made 100 coaches one month, then the unit cost would become $310 per coach ($300 + ($1000 / 100)). If the next month the company made 50 coaches, then the unit cost = $320 per coach ($300 + ($1000 / 50)), a relatively minor difference.

Variance Analysis

An important part of standard cost accounting is a variance analysis, which breaks down the variation between actual cost and standard costs into various components (volume variation, material cost variation, labor cost variation, etc.) so managers can understand *why costs were different from what was planned* and take appropriate action to correct the situation.

Economic Efficiency

Economic efficiency is, roughly speaking, a situation in which nothing can be improved without something else being hurt. Depending on the context, it is usually one of the following two related concepts:

- Allocative or Pareto efficiency: any changes made to assist one person would harm another.
- Productive efficiency: no additional output can be obtained without increasing the amount of inputs, and production proceeds at the lowest possible average total cost.

These definitions are not equivalent: a market or other economic system may be allocatively but not productively efficient, or productively but not allocatively efficient. There are also other definitions and measures. All characterizations of economic efficiency are encompassed by the more general engineering concept that a system is efficient or optimal when it maximizes desired outputs (such as utility) given available inputs.

Strands of Thought

There are two main strains of thought on economic efficiency, which respectively emphasize the distortions created by *governments* (and reduced by *decreasing* government involvement) and the distortions created by *markets* (and reduced by *increasing* government involvement). These are at times competing, at times complementary—either debating the *overall* level of government involvement, or the effects of *specific* government involvement. Broadly speaking, this dialog takes place in the context of economic liberalism or neoliberalism, though these terms are also used more narrowly to refer to particular views, especially advocating laissez faire.

Further, there are differences in views on microeconomic versus macroeconomic efficiency, some advocating a greater role for government in one sphere or the other.

Allocative and Productive Efficiency

A market can be said to have allocative efficiency if the price of a product that the market is supplying is equal to the marginal value consumers place on it, and equals marginal cost. In other words, when every good or service is produced up to the point where one more unit provides a marginal benefit to consumers less than the marginal cost of producing it.

Because productive resources are scarce, the resources must be allocated to various Industries in just the right amounts, otherwise too much or too little output gets produced. When drawing diagrams for firms, allocative efficiency is satisfied if output is produced at the point where marginal cost is equal to average revenue. This is the case for the long-run equilibrium of perfect competition.

Productive efficiency occurs when units of goods are being supplied at the lowest possible average total cost. When drawing diagrams for firms, this condition is satisfied if the equilibrium is at the minimum point of the average total cost curve. This is again the case for the long run equilibrium of perfect competition.

Mainstream Views

The mainstream view is that market economies are generally believed to be closer to efficient than other known alternatives and that government involvement is necessary at the macroeconomic level (via fiscal policy and monetary policy) to counteract the economic cycle – following Keynesian economics. At the microeconomic level there is debate about how to achieve efficiency, with some advocating laissez faire, to remove government distortions, while others advocate regulation, to reduce market failures and imperfections, particularly via internalizing externalities.

The first fundamental welfare theorem provides some basis for the belief in efficiency of market economies, as it states that any perfectly competitive market equilibrium is Pareto efficient. The assumption of perfect competition means that this result is only valid in the absence of market imperfections, which are significant in real markets. Furthermore, Pareto efficiency is a minimal notion of optimality and does not necessarily result in a socially desirable distribution of resources, as it makes no statement about equality or the overall well-being of a society.

Schools of Thought

Advocates of limited government, in the form laissez faire (little or no government role in the economy) follow from the 19th century philosophical tradition classical liberalism, and are particularly associated with the mainstream economic schools of classical economics (through the 1870s) and neoclassical economics (from the 1870s onwards), and with the heterodox Austrian school.

Advocates of an expanded government role follow instead in alternative streams of progressivism; in the Anglosphere (English-speaking countries, notably the United States, United Kingdom, Canada, Australia and New Zealand) this is associated with institutional economics and, at the macroeconomic level, with Keynesian economics. In Germany the guiding philosophy is Ordoliberalism, in the Freiburg School of economics.

Microeconomic Reform

Microeconomic reform is the implementation of policies that aim to reduce economic distortions via deregulation, and move toward economic efficiency. However, there is no clear theoretical basis for the belief that removing a market distortion will always increase economic efficiency. The theory of the second best states that if there is some unavoidable market distortion in one sector, a move toward greater market perfection in another sector may actually decrease efficiency.

Criteria

Economic efficiency can be characterized in many ways:

- Allocative efficiency
- Distributive efficiency
- Dynamic efficiency
- Informational efficiency is used to characterize financial markets

- Kaldor–Hicks efficiency
- Pareto efficiency
- Productive efficiency
- Optimisation of a social welfare function
- Utility maximization
- X-inefficiency

Applications of these principles include:

- Efficient-market hypothesis
- Microeconomic reform
- Production theory basics
- Welfare economics

Productive Efficiency

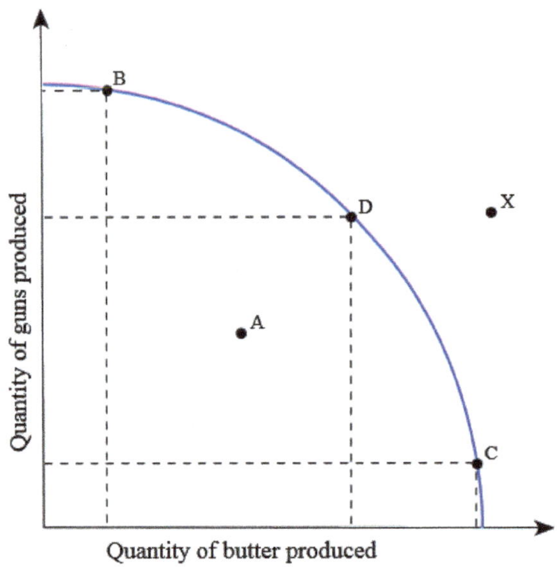

An example PPF: points B, C and D are all productively efficient, but an economy at A would not be, because D involves more production of both goods. Point X cannot be achieved.

Productive efficiency is a situation in which the economy could not produce any more of one good without sacrificing production of another good. In other words, productive efficiency occurs when a good or a service is produced at the lowest possible cost. The concept is illustrated on a production possibility frontier (PPF), where all points on the curve are points of productive efficiency. An equilibrium may be productively efficient without being allocatively efficient— i.e. it may result in a distribution of goods where social welfare is not maximized.

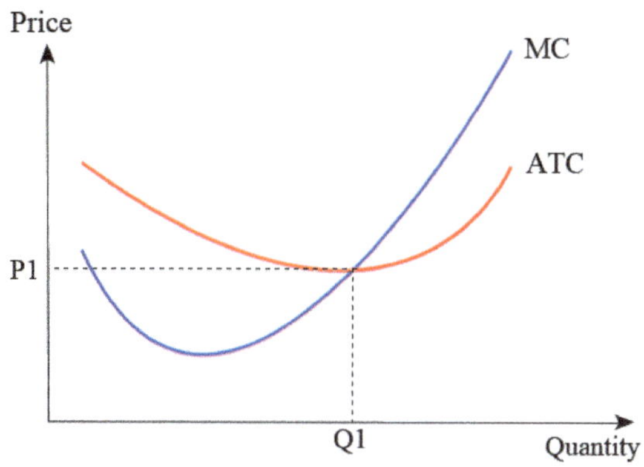

Productive efficiency occurs under competitive equilibrium at the minimum of average total cost for each good, such as the one shown here.

Productive efficiency requires that all firms operate using best-practice technological and managerial processes. By improving these processes, an economy or business can extend its production possibility frontier outward, so that efficient production yields more output than previously.

Productive inefficiency, with the economy operating below its production possibilities frontier, can occur because the productive inputs physical capital and labor are underutilized—that is, some capital or labor is left sitting idle—or because these inputs are allocated in inappropriate combinations to the different industries that use them.

In long-run equilibrium for perfectly competitive markets, productive efficiency occurs at the base of the average total cost curve—i.e. where marginal cost equals average total cost—for each good.

Due to the nature and culture of monopolistic companies, they may not be productively efficient because of X-inefficiency, whereby companies operating in a monopoly have less of an incentive to maximize output due to lack of competition. However, due to economies of scale it can be possible for the profit-maximizing level of output of monopolistic companies to occur with a lower price to the consumer than perfectly competitive companies.

Variance (Accounting)

In budgeting (or management accounting in general), a variance is the difference between a budgeted, planned, or standard cost and the actual amount incurred/sold. Variances can be computed for both costs and revenues.

The concept of variance is intrinsically connected with planned and actual results and effects of the difference between those two on the performance of the entity or company.

Types of Variances

Variances can be divided according to their effect or nature of the underlying amounts.

When effect of variance is concerned, there are two types of variances:

- When actual results are better than expected results given variance is described as favorable variance. In common use favorable variance is denoted by the letter F - usually in parentheses (F).
- When actual results are worse than expected results given variance is described as adverse variance, or unfavourable variance. In common use adverse variance is denoted by the letter U or the letter A - usually in parentheses (A).

The second typology (according to the nature of the underlying amount) is determined by the needs of users of the variance information and may include e.g.:

- Variable cost variances
    - o Direct material variances
    - o Direct labour variances
    - o Variable production overhead variances
- Fixed production overhead variances
- Sales variances

Variance Analysis

Variance analysis, in budgeting (or management accounting in general), is a tool of budgetary control by evaluation of performance by means of variances between budgeted amount, planned amount or standard amount and the actual amount incurred/sold. Variance analysis can be carried out for both costs and revenues.

Variance analysis is usually associated with explaining the difference (or variance) between actual costs and the standard costs allowed for the good output. For example, the difference in materials costs can be divided into a materials price variance and a materials usage variance. The difference between the actual direct labor costs and the standard direct labor costs can be divided into a rate variance and an efficiency variance. The difference in manufacturing overhead can be divided into spending, efficiency, and volume variances. Mix and yield variances can also be calculated.

Variance analysis helps management to understand the present costs and then to control future costs.

Controllable Variance

Controllable variances are those which can be controlled by the departmental heads whereas uncontrollable variances are those which are beyond their control. If uncontrollable variances are of significant nature and are persistent, the standards may need revision.

Variance Analysis

Variance analysis is the dividing of the cost variance into its components to know their causes, so that one can approach for corrective measures.

Variances of Efficiency

Variance arising due to the effectiveness in use of material quantities, labour hours. Here actual quantities are compared with predetermined standards.

Variances of Price Rates

Variances arising due to change in unit material prices, standard labour hour rates and standard allowances for indirect costs. Here actual prices are compared with predetermined ones.

Variances of Due to Volume

Variance due to effect of difference between actual activity and the level of activity estimated when the standard was set.

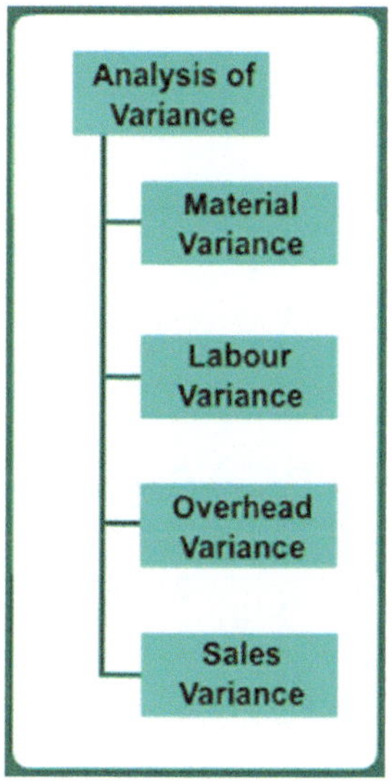

Reasons of Material Variance

- Change in Basic price.
- Fail to purchase anticipated standard quantities at appropriate price.
- Use of sub-standard material.
- Ineffective use of materials.
- Pilferage.

Material Variance

- Material Cost Variance = (Standard Quantity X Standard Price) – (Actual Qty X Act Price)
- Material Price Variance = Actual Quantity (Standard Price - Actual Price)
- Material Usage Variance = Standard Price (Standard Quantity - Actual Quantity)

Reasons of Labour Variance

- Time Related Issues.
- Change in design and quality standard.
- Low Motivation.
- Poor working conditions.
- Improper scheduling/placement of labour.
- Inadequate Training.
- Rate Related Issues.
- Increments / high labour wages.
- Overtime.
- Labour shortage leading to higher rates.
- Union agreement.

Labour Variance

- Labour Cost Variance = (Standard Hrs X Standard Rate Per Hour) –(Actual Hrs X Actual Rate Per Hour)
- Labour Rate Variance = Actual Hrs (Standard Rate - Actual Rate)
- Labour efficiency Variance = Standard Rate (Std Hrs - Actual Hrs worked)
- Idle Time Variance = Idle Hours X Std Rate

Reasons of Overheads Variance

- Under or over absorption of fixed overheads.
- Fall in demand/ Improper planning.
- Breakdowns /Power Failure.
- Labour issues.
- Inflation.
- Lack of planning.
- Lack of cost control.

Variable Overheads (OH) Variance

- Variable OH Cost Variance = (Standard Hrs X Standard Variable OH Rate) – Actual OH Cost

Variable OH Variance

- Variable OH Expenditure Variance = (Actual Hrs X Standard Variable OH Rate) – Actual OH Cost
- Variable OH Efficiency Variance = (Standard Hrs - Actual Hrs) X Standard Variable OH Rate

Fixed Overheads (OH) Variance

- Fixed OH Cost Variance = Absorbed OH – Actual OH
- Absorbed OH = Actual Units * Standard OH Rate per unit

Fixed OH Variance

- Fixed OH Expenditure Variance = Budgeted OH – Actual OH
- Fixed OH Volume Variance = Absorbed OH – Budgeted OH

Reasons of Sales Variance

- Change in price.
- Change in Market size.
- Change in Market share.

Sales Variances

- Sales Value Variance = Budgeted Sales – Actual Sales
- Sales Price Variance = Actual Quantity (Actual Price - Budgeted Price)
- Sales Volume Variance = Budgeted Price (Actual Quantity - Budgeted Quantity)

Advantages of Standard Costing

Advantages

- Basis for sensible cost comparisons.
- Employment of management by exception.
- Means of performance evaluation for employees.
- Result in more stable product cost.

Disadvantages of Standard Costing

Disadvantages

- Too comprehensive hence time-consuming.
- Precise estimation of prices or rates is difficult.

- Requires continuous revision with frequent changes in technology/ market trends.
- Focus on cost minimization rather than quality or innovation.

Material Variance

- Material Cost Variance
- Material Price Variance
- Material Usage Variance
- Can we sub-divide Usage Variance?
- What are its causes, when we have more than one Raw Material?

Material Variance

- Material Cost Variance
- Material Price Variance
- Material Usage Variance
- Material Yield Variance
- Material Mix Variance
- Material Cost Variance = (Standard Quantity X Standard Price) – (Actual Qty X Act Price)
- Material Price Variance = Actual Quantity (Standard Price - Actual Price)
- Material Usage Variance = Standard Price (Standard Quantity - Actual Quantity)
- Material Yield Variance = (Std Input Qty - Actual Input Qty) * Std Price of Std Input
- Material Mix Variance = Standard Price (Revised Standard Quantity - Actual Quantity)

Fixed Overheads (OH) Variance

- Fixed OH Cost Variance = Absorbed OH – Actual OH
- Absorbed OH = Actual Units * Standard OH Rate per unit

Fixed OH Variance

- Fixed OH Expenditure Variance = Budgeted OH – Actual OH
- Fixed OH Volume Variance = Absorbed OH – Budgeted OH

Material Variance

- F OH Cost Variance
- F OH Expenditure Variance
- F OH Volume Variance

- Can we sub-divide Volume Variance?
- What are its causes, why may volume vary?

Fixed OH Variance

- Fixed OH Efficiency Variance = Standard OH Rate per hour (Standard Hrs - Actual Hrs)
- Fixed OH Capacity Variance = Standard OH Rate per hour (Budgeted Hrs - Actual Hrs)

Direct Material Total Variance

In variance analysis (accounting) direct material total variance is the difference between the actual cost of actual number of units produced and its budgeted cost in terms of material. Direct material total variance can be divided into two components:

- the direct material price variance,
- the direct material usage variance.

Example

Let us assume that standard direct material cost of widget is as follows:

2 kg of unobtainium at $ 60 per kg (= $ 120 per unit).

Let us assume further that during the given period, 100 widgets were manufactured, using 212 kg of unobtainium which cost $ 13,144.

Under those assumptions direct material total variance can be calculated as:

100 units should have cost (× $ 120 per unit)	€ 12,000	
but did cost	€ 13,144	
Direct material total variance	€ 1,144	(A)

Direct material total variance can be reconciled to direct material price variance and direct material usage variance by:

Direct material usage variance	€ 720	(A)
Direct material price variance	€ 424	(A)
Direct material total variance	€ 1,144	(A)

Direct Material Price Variance

In variance analysis (accounting) direct material price variance is the difference between the standard cost and the actual cost for the actual quantity of material purchased. It is one of the two components (the other is direct material usage variance) of direct material total variance.

Example

Let us assume that the standard direct material cost of widget is as follows:

2 kg of unobtainium at € 60 per kg (= € 120 per unit).

Let us assume further that during the given period, 100 widgets were manufactured, using 212 kg of unobtainium which cost € 13,144.

Under those assumptions direct material price variance can be calculated as:

212 kg of unobtainium should have cost (× € 60)	€ 12,720	
but did cost	€ 13,144	
Direct material (unobtainium) price variance	€ 424	(A)

Direct material price variance is because Todd pays too much for steel can be reconciled to direct material total variance by way of direct material usage variance:

Direct material usage variance	€ 720	(A)
Direct material price variance	€ 424	(A)
Direct material total variance	€ 1,144	(A)

Direct Material Usage Variance

In variance analysis, direct material usage (efficiency, quantity) variance is the difference between the standard quantity of materials that should have been used for the number of units actually produced, and the actual quantity of materials used, valued at the standard cost per unit of material. It is one of the two components (the other is direct material price variance) of direct material total variance.

Example

Let us assume that standard direct material cost of widget is as follows:

2 kg of unobtainium at € 60 per kg (= € 120 per unit).

Let us assume further that during given period, 100 widgets were manufactured, using 212 kg of unobtainium which cost € 13,144.

Under those assumptions direct material usage variance can be calculated as:

100 units should have used (× 2 kg)	200	kg
but did use	212	kg
Usage variance in kg	12	kg A
× standard cost per kg	× € 60	
Usage variance in €	€ 720	(A)

Direct material usage variance can be reconciled to direct material total variance by way of direct material price variance:

Direct material usage variance	€ 720	(A)
Direct material price variance	€ 424	(A)
Direct material total variance	€ 1,144	(A)

Direct Labour Cost Variance

Direct labour cost variance is the difference between the standard cost for actual production and the actual cost in production.

There are two kinds of labour variances. *Labour Rate Variance* is the difference between the standard cost and the actual cost paid for the actual number of hours. *Labour efficiency variance* is the difference between the standard labour hour that should have been worked for the actual number of units produced and the actual number of hours worked when the labour hours are valued at the standard rate.

Labor Efficiency Variance

Difference between the amount of labor time that should have been used and the labor that was actually used, multiplied by the standard rate. For example, assume that the standard cost of direct labor per unit of product A is 2.5 hours x $14 = $35. Assume further that during the month of March the company recorded 4500 hours of direct labor time. The actual cost of this labor time was $64,800, or an average of $14.40 per hour. The company produced 2000 units of product A during the month. The labor efficiency variance is (4500 - 5000) x $14 = $7000, where 5000 hours = 2.5 hours x 2000 units of output. This variance is favorable since the actual hours used are less than the standard hours allowed. This may be the result of efficient use of labor time due to automation or the use of improved production methods.

Sales Variance

Sales variance is the difference between actual sales and budget sales. It is used to measure the performance of a sales function, and/or analyze business results to better understand market conditions.

There are two reasons actual sales can vary from planned sales: either the volume sold varied from plan (sales volume variance), or sales were at a different price from what was planned (sales price variance). Both scenarios could also simultaneously contribute to the variance.

For example: The plan was to sell 5 widgets at $3 each, for a budgeted sales of: (5*$3)=$15. In reality, 6 widgets were sold at $2 each, for an actual sales of: (6*$2)=$12. The total variance was thus ($12–$15)=$3 (U)nfavourable or minus $3, since total sales was less than planned.

Sales Price Variance

Sales Price Variance: The sales price variance reveals the difference in total revenue caused by charging a different selling price from the planned or standard price. The sales price variance is calculated as: Actual quantity sold * (actual selling price - planned selling price). In the example, the sales price variance was 6*($2–$3)= -$6 (U)nfavourable or minus $6, since the sales price was less than planned.

Sales Volume Variance

Sales Volume Variance is calculated as: budgeted selling price*(actual sales volume-budgeted sales volume)

Sales Volume Variance is further sub-divided into two variances.

1. Sales Mix Variance
2. Sales Quantity Variance

Total Variance

The total variance can thus be seen algebraically to be (minus $6) plus (plus $3), giving (minus $3). Or: -6+3=-3.

This result tells us that the negative effect of selling at a lower price was twice the positive effect of selling at a higher volume than planned. This might have occurred where prices were lowered to increase volume, but actual volume increases did not meet expectations, perhaps due to competitors also cutting their prices, or changes in customer preferences.

References

- Steven Buser: LaPlace Transforms as Present Value Rules: A Note, The Journal of Finance, Vol. 41, No. 1, March, 1986, pp. 243-247
- O'Sullivan, Arthur; Sheffrin, Steven M. (2003). Economics: Principles in Action. Upper Saddle River, New Jersey 07458: Pearson Prentice Hall. p. 502. ISBN 0-13-063085-3
- Moten, J. and Thron, C., Improvements on Secant Method for Estimating Internal Rate of Return, International Journal of Applied Mathematics and Statistics 42:12(2013)
- Kurt, Daniel (2003-11-24). "Net Present Value (NPV) Definition | Investopedia". Investopedia. Retrieved 2016-05-05
- Lin, Grier C. I.; Nagalingam, Sev V. (2000). CIM justification and optimisation. London: Taylor & Francis. p. 36. ISBN 0-7484-0858-4
- Dudley, C.L., "A note on reinvestment assumptions in choosing between net present value and internal rate of return." Journal of Finance 27(4), 1972, 907–15
- Berk, Johnathan; DeMarzo, Peter; Stangeland, David (2015). Corporate Finance (3rd Canadian ed.). Toronto: Pearson Canada. p. 64. ISBN 978-0133552683
- Rich, S.P., and J.T. Rose, "Re-examining an Old Question: Does the IRR Method Implicitly Assume a Reinvestment Rate?" Journal of Financial Education 10(1), 2014, 105-116
- Grubbström, Robert W. (1967). "On the Application of the Laplace Transform to Certain Economic Problems". Management Science. 13: 558–567. doi:10.1287/mnsc.13.7.558
- Khan, M.Y. (1993). Theory & Problems in Financial Management. Boston: McGraw Hill Higher Education. ISBN 978-0-07-463683-1
- Solomons, David. "Costing Pioneers: Some Links with the Past*." The Accounting Historians Journal 21.2 (1994): 136

Permissions

All chapters in this book are published with permission under the Creative Commons Attribution Share Alike License or equivalent. Every chapter published in this book has been scrutinized by our experts. Their significance has been extensively debated. The topics covered herein carry significant information for a comprehensive understanding. They may even be implemented as practical applications or may be referred to as a beginning point for further studies.

We would like to thank the editorial team for lending their expertise to make the book truly unique. They have played a crucial role in the development of this book. Without their invaluable contributions this book wouldn't have been possible. They have made vital efforts to compile up to date information on the varied aspects of this subject to make this book a valuable addition to the collection of many professionals and students.

This book was conceptualized with the vision of imparting up-to-date and integrated information in this field. To ensure the same, a matchless editorial board was set up. Every individual on the board went through rigorous rounds of assessment to prove their worth. After which they invested a large part of their time researching and compiling the most relevant data for our readers.

The editorial board has been involved in producing this book since its inception. They have spent rigorous hours researching and exploring the diverse topics which have resulted in the successful publishing of this book. They have passed on their knowledge of decades through this book. To expedite this challenging task, the publisher supported the team at every step. A small team of assistant editors was also appointed to further simplify the editing procedure and attain best results for the readers.

Apart from the editorial board, the designing team has also invested a significant amount of their time in understanding the subject and creating the most relevant covers. They scrutinized every image to scout for the most suitable representation of the subject and create an appropriate cover for the book.

The publishing team has been an ardent support to the editorial, designing and production team. Their endless efforts to recruit the best for this project, has resulted in the accomplishment of this book. They are a veteran in the field of academics and their pool of knowledge is as vast as their experience in printing. Their expertise and guidance has proved useful at every step. Their uncompromising quality standards have made this book an exceptional effort. Their encouragement from time to time has been an inspiration for everyone.

The publisher and the editorial board hope that this book will prove to be a valuable piece of knowledge for students, practitioners and scholars across the globe.

Index